ROUTLEDGE LIBRARY EDITIONS: URBAN AND REGIONAL ECONOMICS

Volume 8

REGIONAL DEMOGRAPHIC DEVELOPMENT

REGIONAL DEMOGRAPHIC DEVELOPMENT

Edited by
JOHN HOBCRAFT AND PHILIP REES

Routledge
Taylor & Francis Group

LONDON AND NEW YORK

First published in 1979 by Croom Helm

This edition first published in 2018
by Routledge
2 Park Square, Milton Park, Abingdon, Oxon OX14 4RN

and by Routledge
711 Third Avenue, New York, NY 10017

Routledge is an imprint of the Taylor & Francis Group, an informa business

British Library Cataloguing in Publication Data
A catalogue record for this book is available from the British Library

ISBN: 978-1-138-09590-8 (Set)
ISBN: 978-1-315-10306-8 (Set) (ebk)
ISBN: 978-1-138-10192-0 (Volume 8) (hbk)
ISBN: 978-1-138-10238-5 (Volume 8) (pbk)
ISBN: 978-1-315-10323-5 (Volume 8) (ebk)

Publisher's Note
The publisher has gone to great lengths to ensure the quality of this reprint but points out that some imperfections in the original copies may be apparent.

Disclaimer
The publisher has made every effort to trace copyright holders and would welcome correspondence from those they have been unable to trace.

Regional Demographic Development

Edited by John Hobcraft and Philip Rees

CROOM HELM LONDON

© John Hobcraft and Philip Rees
Croom Helm Ltd, 2-10 St John's Road, London SW11

British Library Cataloguing in Publication Data
Regional demographic development
    1. Great Britain — Population — History —
Congresses
    I. Hobcraft, John II. Rees, Philip
    III. British Society of Population Studies.
Conference, Liverpool University, 1977
    IV. Institute of British Geographers.
Population Geography Study Group. Conference,
Liverpool University, 1977
    301. 32'9'41   HB 3583

    ISBN 0-7099-0245-X

Reproduced from copy supplied
printed and bound in Great Britain
by Billing and Sons Limited
Guildford, London, Oxford, Worcester

CONTENTS

Part Four: Projections

TABLES

FIGURES

PREFACE

This volume has its origins in a joint conference of the British Society of Population Studies and the Population Geography Study Group of the Institute of British Geographers, which was held at Liverpool University in September 1977. At the conference fourteen papers were delivered. Owing to pressures of space it has only proved possible to include ten of these in this volume. The papers which are included have been revised subsequent to the conference. As editors, we have adopted a policy of relatively light revision, mainly because we had no wish to destroy the flavour of the papers. This was made possible by the high quality of the original contributions. Our other reason is that when a volume originates in a conference, rather than through explicit commission, authors have already committed themselves to a style and position. There does remain some small overlap between papers, but this is no bad thing, and is never excessive.

Additionally, as a result of its conference origins, there do remain minor gaps in the coverage of the volume. Perhaps the most obvious of these is in the general area of mortality, which with fertility and migration is the third cause of regional population change. The chapter by Lawton does bring out the historical importance of mortality differentials in a broad review, but we have no specific modern contribution. We also have very little on regional planning, with the major exception of the chapter by Eversley, Ermisch and Overton. In an attempt to make the volume (and the original conference) have wide appeal we have also avoided some of the more mathematical work that could have been included. This was quite deliberate.

On the positive side we do have some quite original contributions in those areas covered, and the papers do form a useful and coherent group.

John Hobcraft, Southampton
Philip Rees, Leeds

1 INTRODUCTION

John Hobcraft and Philip Rees

1.1 Four Topics

The main contributions to this volume are divided into four topic areas, namely historical aspects, fertility, migration and projections. The areas are clearly not distinct, with fertility and migration both being important topics in the other two more integrated areas. The organisation is intended to reflect one of the pathways through which useful research on regional aspects of population can proceed. A major concern in any population work is that of *explication*, and the study of historical trends over a long period can often be of assistance in understanding how and why population movements and changes come about. In addition to the relatively broad sweep it is often useful to study more recent trends in depth; the chapters on fertility and migration can be regarded as contributing to this study. Another major concern of population analysis is that of *prediction*. Usually prediction is so imprecise, given our current understanding of population processes and the factors which affect them, that the term projection is used. Nevertheless it is clear that such projections need to be at least forecasts for adequate planning.

1.2 Definition of the Region

Before introducing the main themes of the volume we need to clarify what we mean by *regions*: we have chosen a fairly flexible approach to the definition for this volume. There has not been a fixed definition of region in the sense of the Registrar-General's Standard Regions for the long period being considered here. For earlier periods different regional definitions are often adopted, although Lawton does give figures for the 1971 Standard Regions over the entire census period of 1801-1971. On the other hand, Brass adopts a different regional structure, which is deliberately chosen to give greater homogeneity of fertility trends; owing to the non-availability of early data Wall is forced to work with just five sub-areas of the country. For more recent periods some problems still remain: most of the chapter by Simons considers recent national fertility trends, as regional changes are largely homogeneous and the main changes are at a national level; at the other extreme Hobcraft is forced to work with individual-level data so as to retain an

17

adequate sample size, although Kiernan's work on inter-regional
movement with the same data set suggests that similar effects hold for
inter-regional migrants and may well be stronger; the final deviant is
Kennett, who works with metropolitan labour areas and sub-areas
within these. For his purposes this choice is necessary and is also very
useful in identifying one of the major migratory movements which is
vital for regional planners, namely the flight from inner cities outward.
Thus it will be seen that we have allowed a wide range of approaches
to the definition of region here. We deliberately excluded studies of
single small areas. These tensions over definition of regions are
common enough: too rigid a definition would preclude useful work
which sensibly uses a different definition; however, such variability
does often make it difficult to compare and integrate differing pieces
of work.

1.3 Why Consider Regional Populations?

Why is it useful or necessary to look at British population at the
regional level? The prime question here is whether there is variation at
the regional level, however defined, which is not explainable as a
national phenomenon. For example, both Brass and Simons can be
interpreted as arguing that the major determinants of fertility change
are national, and that explanation has, as a consequence, to be sought
at this level rather than a regional one. Even if this is true, there have
been substantial variations in fertility between regions in the past, and
these have had consequential effects on the evolution of the population
in the areas. There are still quite substantial variations, especially within
regions. The consequences of regional fertility differentials over time
are discussed by Lawton. Although it might be possible to argue that
national economic, social and cultural trends were the major
determinants of overall migration levels, this case has not been made
at all clearly as yet. Of course even for fertility the regional trends have
not been entirely homogeneous and explanations for the shifts in
relative status are still required. Thus regional variability relative to
national trends requires explanation and, even more importantly,
regional variability of any kind has consequences for the evolution of
regional population size and structure. For many planning purposes
broad regions are inadequate, and data and forecasts are required for
very small areas, often down to ward or constituency level: although
this work is very important we have decided to confine this book
(as a result of so defining the original conference) to a broader
framework. Even highly localised planning requires as a background

county or metropolitan area and regional figures. Without such information it is not really possible to plan adequately, even for a small area. It is quite possible without such a background that every small local authority area will predict a growing population when the regional or national population is declining. Indeed it is still possible with the background information that local authorities will not co-ordinate their forecasts to agree with regional or national areas, however absurd this might be. The important factor is that all sub-areas interact, one area's in-migrant having to come from another, and that it makes sense for these interactions to be inbuilt into the planning and forecasting process. Of course there are problems in taking an extreme position here; not only are current forecasts even at the national level very imprecise, but even at a county level the volume of data required for integrated projections or forecasts can be enormous (see Hobcraft, p. 234, for examples). Thus a case can be made for working at the regional or perhaps county level for many population purposes. The problems of allocation of population within regions or counties are very different from those considered here.

1.4 Population Change and Redistribution Themes

Turning now to the contributions this volume makes to those areas, we shall try to identify major themes running through the contributions, as well as highlighting some of the important results. The chapter by Lawton lays the foundations of the book. He reviews and brings together the overall pattern of trends in regional migration, fertility and mortality and their conjoint impact on population change and structure from the eighteenth century to the present day. This chapter traces the changes in population from a relatively rural one, through industrialisation and consequent urbanisation to the trends towards suburbanisation in more recent times. The trend towards suburbanisation is a major theme of the chapter by Kennett using post-war data, and some of the policy implications of this and other recent trends are taken up by Eversley, Ermisch and Overton. Both Lawton and Wall identify a rise in fertility and probable decline in mortality starting around the 1780s. This led to substantial population growth with a doubling over the following fifty years. Internal migration helped to reduce surplus growth in the rural areas which had lower mortality. Lawton and others mention the interactions that occur between migration and fertility. Without entering the controversy over whether migrants have higher or lower fertility than either the sending or receiving areas, or, as often argued, intermediate fertility, there is a clear tendency for high in-migration rates to generate higher numbers of births, owing to migrants typically being young adults. In addition, the sending areas have lost young adults and thus have fewer births, independently of age-specific or migration-status-specific variations in fertility. Thus high out-migration areas not only lose their young and often more dynamic adults, but also lose children and subsequent births of these migrants. This has the effect of somewhat depressing the sending area. It should be noted that, over a period of such out-migration, the age structure of the sending area is not as badly distorted as is often supposed, as the older cohorts are depleted by earlier migration. Naturally the reverse effects hold for receiving areas. These aspects of migration selectivity are covered especially well by Kiernan, and also by Gleave and Palmer. Such selection can seriously affect the potential strength of a region. In further work, reported during the discussion at the conference, Kiernan has found that, of those people in her study who were living in the Northern region at age 16 and obtained 'A' levels or above, every one left the Northern region to study and/or work elsewhere. This is for a relatively small sample, but demonstrates some of the effects migration selectivity can have, denuding areas of qualified manpower. For other examples one need look no further than several mining villages or the rural west of Ireland, where whole villages are dying as a result of emigration of almost all the young people. As Kennett also shows, a similar effect has occurred in the core areas of large cities. For example, in Inner London the problems have become so severe that the teaching hospitals 'imported' suburban mothers to provide enough patients for doctor training. And over a period when national cohort sizes had dropped by some 25 per cent at school entry ages, the school entry in Inner London was reduced by some 50 per cent, with the excess being due mainly to migration. London is only an example of similar problems occurring in many inner-city areas.

1.5 Fertility Themes

Turning now to fertility, there are the descriptive aspects of what has happened, although no one confines attention solely to this. Lawton and Wall both identify a rise around the 1780s, probably largely due to a declining age at marriage. Brass and Lawton identify the long-term fertility decline as starting somewhere very close to 1876. This is easily the most popular date. Among other advantages it was the year of the Bradlaugh-Besant trial for the circulation of pamphlets on birth control. More importantly, several authors have identified it as the year when most regions and even sub-regions began to experience decline. Perhaps the most notable is Elderton (1914) in her careful study of fertility by local authority area for the whole of Northern England, which was also notable for the introduction of an indirect standardisation procedure pre-dating, but very like the one used in the Princeton Studies of European fertility (see Coale, 1967). More interestingly, Brass shows a remarkable homogeneity of proportional fertility declines by region over the period 1876 to 1928, which raises some serious doubts about trying to 'explain' fertility decline by regional factors, at least for Britain. Given the huge investment of time and money in the Princeton European Fertility Project, which has been looking precisely at regional patterns of decline, this finding of Brass poses a severe challenge. In addition we know that since 1928 this regional homogeneity in trend has not persisted. Both Simons and Eversley, Ermisch and Overton show that current regional fertility levels differ by about 10 per cent between the highest and lowest, whereas the differences were about 40 to 45 per cent during the period Brass examined. The period of change since 1928 does need more careful regional analysis to study the ways in which regional differentials have largely disappeared. There are still some substantial variations; for example, Northern Ireland still has considerably higher fertility than the rest of the UK (Eversley, Ermisch and Overton) and Lawton cites the case of Liverpool, with inner areas 75 per cent above the national average and outer areas 25 per cent above. So there is still some diversity, especially within regions.

By now everyone knows of the dramatic fertility declines which occurred throughout the Western world between the mid-1960s and late 1970s. The chapter by Simons examines possible explanations for these changes at the national rather than regional level, which is legitimated by the fact that all regions have responded to fertility decline. There do remain interesting variations around the declines in general fertility rate, being relatively large in Scotland and the South-West and relatively small in Northern Ireland, Wales and East Anglia (a curiosity is that Brass identified East Anglia as being slow to decline in the late nineteenth century as well). Both Brass and Eversley, Ermisch and Overton base their analysis on relatively unsophisticated measures of fertility which do not take account of the structure by age or marital status within the childbearing age range (except for Brass's marital fertility index). More careful analysis of these areas is needed before really firm conclusions can be reached. Eversley, Ermisch and Overton look at the very important topic of the consequences of recent fertility declines and their possible continuance on planning and housing. These effects are potentially great, especially if the proportion of couples never bearing children rises substantially again (we have recently experienced very low proportions of childnessness in comparison with thirty years or so ago). The major effects of out-migration from inner cities, combined with declining fertility, are shown to be of vital importance in determining regional policies. Many of these planning problems have been exacerbated by projections which failed to predict correctly either the high out-migration or the reduced fertility, leading to a planning strategy to remove jobs and people from the inner cities at a time when they were already under severe stress through depopulation.

1.6 Migration Themes

Our contributions to the study of migration are varied and interesting. First, at a macro-level, Kennett reports on part of a larger project working with Metropolitan Labour Areas, rather than with regions in the more usual sense. Many economists argue that only migration between Metropolitan Labour Areas or functional equivalents should be treated as genuine migration – this usually means labour migration. Thankfully, Kennett's study looks at intra-area movement as well, which he shows to have been a very important phenomenon in the period studied. Such study of intra-area movement is especially important in the context of the major cities, which cover a very large hinterland. In addition to his overall study, he gives special attention to the 'million cities' (under the Metropolitan Economic Labour Area definition), and emphasises the massive movements away from the core areas. He is also able to aggregate the urban zones into their relevant planning regions, which highlights the recent intra-regional patterns of movement. At this stage his work has been mainly descriptive, but in areas of the unknown description is both valuable and necessary.

The chapter by Gleave and Palmer also treats migration at the macro-level, but is even more explicitly directed towards problems of labour migration. In particular, they are concerned with the important relationships between occupational and geographical mobility. This partly poses the question of 'who moves?' Is the growth through migration mainly due to particular occupations being highly mobile? Are areas being denuded of particular occupational skills? Are some occupational groups highly immobile? Identification of such differentials implies enormous consequences for the growth and structure of the population. Additionally Gleave and Palmer search for explanations for these differences. In general, their analyses experience substantial methodological problems, as there are no published tables directly relating geographical and occupational mobility. Their analyses are thus indirect, with inherent possibilities of problems of ecological correlation. As this is an important topic it is indeed unfortunate that no use has ever been made of the tabulation possibilities of the 1971 Census. Questions were asked on both residence and occupation one year before, but to the best of our knowledge no cross-tabulations of geographical and occupational mobility by age from these questions have been carried out. Given the value of such studies this is a regrettable waste of a potentially useful data source.

The other work on migration in the volume is at the other extreme in several respects, being based on micro-level data, and not having an economic bias. The longitudinal survey data organised and analysed by Kiernan constitutes one of the richest data sources on migration in the world. As the cohort born in 1946 have been followed throughout their lives without too high a loss rate, she has prospective information on changes of address at frequent intervals in addition to an overwhelming amount of detailed data on the characteristics of the respondents (and their families). A major problem with such a rich data source is screening the possible variables; the very richness makes analysis more problematic but much more rewarding, too. Kiernan identifies many dimensions of migration selectivity, almost all of which have consequences for population structure and many of which are themselves interrelated. The differences in the propensities to migrate are astonishingly large for several of the control variables. Perhaps her most interesting findings are that terminal age of education and even more so, qualification level, show the highest dispersion of migration propensities. This finding may have important consequences for those who insist on labour migration as being the important dimension in studying the determinants of migration. Additionally, educational or qualification level is a much more fixed attribute in later life, making projection by this characteristic far easier than by much more changeable variables such as occupation (see Hobcraft's chapter). Of course, further work is needed to confirm these findings as the cohort were still fairly young at their most recent interview (aged 26), and occupational mobility may become a better discriminator in later life. As the cohort are followed through later life, the relative importance of these factors should become clearer, although further fragmentary data could be obtained either from careful use of the General Household Survey or preferably from a Public Use sample from census data, which would give a much larger sample.

Another important area in the study of migration has been more projection-oriented. This is the question of whether the non-Markovian nature of aggregated projections is due to population heterogeneity or to a duration of residence or frequency of past movement phenomenon. Almost certainly there is some mixture of the two. Hobcraft follows up Kiernan's analysis of frequency of movement by a more detailed analysis based on her data. Although he does find relationships between frequency of previous movement and propensity to migrate and equivalently duration of residence and propensity to migrate, the relationships are nowhere near as strong as those found by other authors. He suggests that this is due to a much closer control on age in combination with a control on qualification level (which Kiernan's work suggests as the factor causing most heterogeneity) and on social class of parents. Thus the suggestion is that most of the observed relationships found in other studies are due to heterogeneity of migration propensities or uncontrolled or inadequately controlled factors. Some residual frequency effects were found, but there is some indication that these are brought about by other heterogeneities. Again it is necessary to caution on the tentative nature of these findings.

1.7 Projection Themes

Our final topic in the volume is that of population projections for regions. There are two contributions here, with the contributions dwelling on the problems of making adequate regional projections. At a practical level Rees takes several projections for regions that have been made in recent years and subjects the results to scrutiny. His analysis is hampered by the differing base dates for the various projections, which leads in particular to widely differing inputs on projected fertility. This illustrates one of the major problems with projections even at the regional level. Both at regional and even more at national level the lack of adequate methods for predicting fertility is one of the most crucial factors in making projections unreliable. This is one reason why fertility has dominated demographic research for the past fifteen or twenty years. For several reasons it is more difficult to assess how important are errors or changes in the projected inter-regional migration rates in determining the variability between sets of regional projections. First, and most importantly, as we lack a population register, we do not have adequate long-run series of inter-regional (or any other kind of) migration rates even by simple characteristics such as age and sex to permit assessment of the degree of volatility of inter-regional migration. Secondly, many comparisons, such as those by Rees, are clouded by variations in the other inputs of mortality and especially fertility. Some progress can be made by exploratory calculations. Problems of predicting mortality are usually regarded as minor, mainly due to the general lack of major volatility of death rates over time: mortality is far less subject to volitional change than migration or fertility, as virtually everyone agrees that it is a bad idea to die. The final element in variability between projections is the model used for the projection. As this is to some extent a residual element, it is even harder to study empirical forecasts controlling for variability in the inputs. Given the enormous increase in complexity brought about by using a truly multi-regional model for projections, we need to demonstrate improved efficiency fairly convincingly. We need to know whether it is adequate for projections for the South-East (say) to work with the South-East ignoring interactions (but allowing migration), with just the South-East and the rest of Britain, with the South-East plus one or two key neighbouring regions and the rest of Britain, or with all the regions of Britain. In addition, for any of these frameworks we need to take decisions about whether or not to include the rest of the world as another region. These are important questions, which Rees is unable to answer fully owing to the confounding of the other elements in the projections he considers. Hobcraft raises many of the aforementioned issues on a more theoretical level, pointing out that the decisions about the regional level of disaggregation cannot be made in isolation from the other inputs of fertility, migration and mortality. For all of these too, there are problems about the level of disaggregation required for efficient projection, which are in effect competing with regional disaggregation, in the sense that the projection calculations have to be possible and must not require too many sub-categories. It should be noted that these theoretical issues are not intended to override the needs of the user of projections, who will require disaggregation by characteristics which are useful for planning. There is undoubtedly a very great need for further careful, empirical research into these areas, but no one potential field for disaggregation can be considered entirely in isolation from another. The road to efficient, relatively simple regional or country projections stretches a long way ahead, and may require work at extremely high levels of disaggregation, before the aggregation process can be carried out.

The search for efficient sub-classification of mortality or fertility or migration at a regional level has much to offer towards improving the projection process. Those who argue that the only way we shall get good population predictions is by modelling all the interrelations which cause change in the population model variables have still to prove their case. Further careful research along the lines of Rogers (1976) is needed.

1.8 Conclusion

The general tenor of this work is then to consider in some detail the regional aspects of British population. The contributions raise at least as many questions as they are able to answer, which is a sign of a field well worth further enquiry. Given the appallingly inadequate attention, funding and training given to population in Britain, we hope to provide a stimulus to such further work.

References

Coale, A.J. 1967. Factors associated with the development of low fertility: an historic summary. *Proceedings of the World Population Conference, 1965*, vol. II, pp. 205-9. New York: United Nations.

Elderton, E. 1914. *Report on the English Birth Rate, Part I: England North of the Humber*. London: Dulau and Co.

Rogers, A. 1976. Shrinking large-scale population projection models by aggregation and decomposition. *Environment and Planning A*, 8, 515-54.

PART ONE: POPULATION HISTORY

2 REGIONAL POPULATION TRENDS IN ENGLAND AND WALES, 1750-1971

Richard Lawton

The essential characteristics of the distribution of population in Britain were shaped in the period from the mid-eighteenth century to the First World War. The demographic transition was accompanied by major changes in the regional distribution of population which reflect changes in the structure and distribution of economic activity and are reflected in social changes, both of which have been profoundly influenced by, and in turn have influenced, the course of demographic change. The course of these changes in time and space in England and Wales during the period from the late eighteenth century to the present is the theme of this chapter.

2.1 The General Context

At the national level this period has been conventionally classified into three distinct phases: first, an early industrial period from around 1740 to 1830, during which the onset of the demographic transition, probably due largely to a substantial reduction in death rate,[1] led to greatly accelerated rates of growth averaging 1.6 per cent per annum and reaching a peak of 1.8 per cent per annum in the census decade 1811-1821; secondly, a period of steady, consistent growth of between 1.6 and 1.1 per cent per annum from 1831 to the First World War during which reduction in the birth rate from the 1880s was offset by a second phase of substantially declining mortality — especially infant mortality — and in which temporal fluctuations in rates of population growth owed much to fluctuations in net migration in which variations in the rate of emigration played the more important role; thirdly, a 'modern' post-1918 era in which the achievement of a low controlled birth rate and death rate have kept natural increase at around 0.5 per cent per annum.

While these national trends show all the features associated with the classic model of the demographic transition, it has been suggested that in England and Wales the passage to Phase III from a lengthy Phase II in which reduced mortality substantially increased the rate of natural increase was prolonged — in contrast to France — by the demand for labour in towns and areas of rapid industrial growth to which rural

1881 (2)	25,974	1.74	11,332	1.63	32,362	4.66	21,030	3.03	+ 745	+ 0.11
1921 (2)	37,887	1.15	14,188	1.37	35,440	3.41	21,252	2.05	−2,275	− 0.22
1951 (3)	43,815	0.52	5,732	0.50	20,445	1.80	14,713	1.29	+ 196	+ 0.02
1971 (3)	48,841	0.57	4,701	0.54	15,456	1.76	10,762	1.23	+ 352	+ 0.04

Sources: (1) Deane and Cole, 1969; (2) Mitchell and Deane, 1962; (3) Lawton, 1977, and Registrar-General, *Annual Statistical Review* (various).

surpluses moved. Hence it is important to consider regional differentials and, in particular, the role of rural-urban migration in assessing the transition from a high to a low demographic balance (i.e. from Phase I to Phase IV) in England and Wales. Dov Friedlander (1969) has argued that there are different demographic models, particularly 'in the *emphasis* and the *timing* in the different responses' to modernisation, and that in the English model the decline in rural birth rates in particular was late and modest because of the early urban and industrial development which, together with modest emigration, successfully absorbed the rural surpluses. In such a model differentials in regional rates of natural increase are offset by even wider contrasts in levels of internal migration. The early movement into the second phase of Zelinsky's mobility transition (Zelinsky, 1971)[2] is an essential complementary component in this broad, macro-model of modern population trends in England.

There have been very different regional responses to general features of declining mortality, of reduced fertility from the late nineteenth century and considerable inter- and intra-regional mobility. Regional population growth diverges from the national experience in the timing of vital trends and in the relationship between natural and migrational components of population growth. There is need for a comparison of the actual regional experience with the national model of the transition. Nevertheless, despite contrasts in the regional response, there is more continuity in regional trends of population between the nineteenth and twentieth centuries than is commonly believed.[3]

Two themes have dominated the changing distribution of population in England since the late eighteenth century. First, there has been a relative and then, from the mid-nineteenth century, absolute movement of population from rural to urban and industrial areas which, Friedlander (1969, pp. 372-7) has argued, allowed rates of natural increase due largely to a relatively high birth rate to persist in most rural areas until late in the nineteenth century. Moreover, out-migration from the rural reservoirs of very large numbers of young adults — both men and women — provided the stock from which, in the eighteenth century, the large towns, in particular London, were able to sustain relatively rapid growth despite high mortality. During the nineteenth century in-migrants gave momentum over short periods of very rapid growth to individual areas from which, subsequently, high rates of growth could be sustained largely by natural increase. In the twentieth century, rural migrants have been relatively less significant as a source of population for urban growth: indeed, there has been much overspill into the rural-urban fringe, especially in the last thirty years, giving an illusion of population growth in many administratively 'rural' districts. Nevertheless, there is a continuing loss of young people from the 'hard core' areas of rural depopulation (Willatts and Newson, 1953) towards the urban-industrial areas.

The second persistent trend, most marked in the context of the British Isles as a whole rather than of England and Wales, has been a continuing redistribution of population by migration from the periphery to the core. The extent of this core of maximum population growth and economic concentration and the relative importance of the several sub-regions within it has varied, but essentially it consists of the highly urbanised and industrialised area from South Lancashire and West Yorkshire, through the industrial Midlands to Greater London. Outside this major area of growth other nodes of attraction and rapid population increase existed, particularly during the nineteenth century, including Central Scotland, North-East England and South Wales. But since the First World War these have been essentially areas of net migrational loss and have joined other peripheral areas in contributing to the growth of the Midlands and South-East to which the Barlow Report drew urgent attention[4] and which has continued to be a major feature of post-1945 population trends and a preoccupation of post-war regional planning.

2.2 Phases and Spatial Patterns of Regional Population Development, 1780-1976

The very generalised view of trends and changing distribution outlined above must be qualified in relation to both temporal and regional fluctuations in population development since the late eighteenth century. In this section, first, major phases of development are outlined in terms of major economic and demographic features and, secondly, general changes in the regional distribution of population are briefly described.

During the later eighteenth century there was a dual upsurge of population in England and Wales. The years 1740-60 saw the beginnings of sustained increase in demographic as well as economic terms, and from 1780 a substantial reduction of death rate and some increases in births, due partly to earlier marriage and increased nuptiality, produced unprecedented rates of natural increase which have not since been equalled: Deane and Cole (1969) estimate a population increase of 38 per cent during 1781-1811 in England and Wales, and of 100 per cent during 1781-1831.[5] The shift in the balance between agriculture and industry during that half-century was reflected in increased levels of urbanisation[6] in which the draw of London and the big provincial cities was reflected in considerable in-migration. But natural increases were often higher in rural areas, due mainly to a lower death rate, and both extension of the cultivated area and intensification of farming, together with rurally based industry, retained much of the movement in the countryside. The main pull of migrants up to the early nineteenth century was to London and the Metropolitan counties and Deane and Cole believe that 'not until 1800 [was there] a general movement of population. . .to new industrial centres' (Deane and Cole, 1969, p. 113). These grew mainly by natural increase fed also by short-range movement from adjacent areas.

Between 1831 and 1881 the rural increment of population was slackening and migration from the countryside accelerating. Over these fifty years, though rural fertility and natural increments remained relatively high, they were progressively directed towards rapidly growing industrial areas, to the coalfields of the Midlands and North and to the rapidly growing towns (Law, 1967), among which London dominated. Much of the transfer of population was short-range, though major cities always had a strong pull which reached out to more distant regions. Moreover, fed by young adults, the towns and industrial regions provided much of their population increment from their own natural growth.

Although during the years from the 1880s to the First World War there was continuing rural depopulation and further concentration on the towns and industrial regions, there were some new features which affected regional trends in population. As the rural reservoirs were drained of their younger people natural increases declined, especially due to falling births. In complementary fashion the towns and especially the coalfield areas provided most of their increment from natural increase in which a big factor was the rapid fall in death rate (due mainly to falling infant mortality) from the late nineteenth century (Table 2.2). The changing patterns of many older staple industries, and the areas of early industrialisation associated with them, shifted the balance of attraction towards the South-East and, to some extent, the West and East Midlands. Moreover, as the rural reservoir drained, the emphasis shifted from mainly short-range rural-urban movements, though rural emigration and out-migration did persist, to inter-regional movements of population, much of it urban-urban in character and including longer-distance migrations.

Between the wars longer-distance, inter-regional migration was

Table 2.2: Vital Trends, England and Wales, 1841-1976

Average annual (1)	Birth rate	General fertility rate	Death rate	Infant mortality rate
1841-50	32.6	136.9	22.4	154
1851-60	34.2	145.1	22.2	153
1861-70	35.2	151.3	22.5	154
1871-80	35.4	153.9	21.4	149
1881-90	32.5	139.3	19.1	142
1891-1900	29.9	123.1	18.2	153
1901-10	27.2	109.3	15.4	127
1911-20	23.8	104.1	14.4	101
1921-30	18.3	74.0	10.9	72
1931-38	15.0	62.3	12.0	52
Year (2)				
1951	15.5	71.6	12.5	30
1961	17.6	89.1	11.9	21
1964	18.5	92.5	11.3	20
1971	16.0	84.0	11.6	18
1976	11.9	60.9	12.2	14

Notes: Birth rate: live births per 1,000 population; General fertility rate: live births per 1,000 women aged 15-44; Death rate: deaths per 1,000 population; Infant mortality rate: deaths of infants under 1 year of age per 1,000 live births.

Sources: (1) Mitchell and Deane, 1962; (2) Lawton, 1977, and Registrar-General's *Annual Statistical Review* (various).

accelerated by acute industrial depression and high unemployment in many older industrial areas, particularly on the coalfields. While rural losses from marginal agricultural regions, especially those remote from urban services, remained a problem, the greatest migrational losses were from the peripheral industrial areas and the main gains made by the Midlands and South-East. These trends were accentuated in many of these declining regions by the persistence of higher rates of natural increase arising from above-average birth rates.

Despite the efforts to arrest 'the drift South-East' through regional planning, post-1945 population trends have continued to show many of the basic features which have characterised regional population development since the turn of the century. There have been continuing losses of younger people from the remoter rural areas and the peripheral regions as migration continues to draw them to the Midlands and South-East. Moreover, the decanting of population from the inner metropolitan areas has spread these gains into the adjacent parts of the South-West and East Anglian regions, extending the areas of gain over most areas of England south of the Mersey-Humber line. While to some extent this may represent a shedding of surplus population from the poorer regions, arising from their higher birth rates, the continuing tendency of fertility to even out suggests that the real factor in such losses is continuing imbalance of economic and social resources between the regions. Perhaps a more significant feature of the post-war years has been the increasing disparity between inner and outer city areas, reflected in severe losses of population from the inner residential areas of all cities, and contrasts in intra-regional population trends which are more marked than the predominantly urban-urban inter-regional redistribution by migration.

This broad review of the major features of changing regional population trends in England over the last two hundred years has drawn attention to the population response both to fluctuating levels of prosperity, reflected in particular in changing levels and directions of inter-regional migration, and also to persistent tendencies such as the change in the rural-urban balance. The implications of these for the components of population change and their effects on the structure of population are examined in the next section, but it will first be convenient to summarise their principal results in terms of the broad regional features of total numbers and relative change.

Table 2.3 sets out the changing share of Great Britain's population in the Standard Regions of England and Wales as defined in 1971, together with the percentage increase over four time periods and the relative growth rate, as compared with Britain as a whole, during those periods. The time intervals adopted differ from those previously suggested as having significance in both economic and demographic terms, but they show very clearly several distinctive regional patterns of population development over the period for which census figures are available.

South-East England alone has consistently grown faster than the national rate of population increase in every period from 1801-1971. As a result it has markedly increased its share of the population of Great Britain. In the early nineteenth century the region's growth was largely focused on London and, overall, was only marginally above the national figure, reflecting also the greater relative growth at that time of the early industrial areas of the Midlands and North-West England.

South-East	52	104	106	44	14	114	106	136	137	128
West Midlands	56	100	74	48	16	126	102	96	150	149
East Midlands	47	80	75	43	17	104	81	96	136	162
East Anglia	30	68	8	22	22	68	69	10	69	204
South-West	26	67	15	26	17	57	68	19	80	160
Yorks./Humberside	82	121	94	29	7	182	123	121	90	64
North-West	110	186	109	22	5	242	190	140	69	49
North	33	83	115	26	5	72	85	148	80	50
Wales	35	98	73	29	5	77	100	94	91	49

The regions are the revised standard regions of 1971.

Sources: Deane and Cole, 1969, Table 24; Department of the Environment, 1971, Tables 1.4, 1.5, 1.6 and 1.12; Lawton, 1977, Table 2.4.

But, from 1851 until recently, its rate of population increase has been much above the national level. Since 1945 out-movement from Greater London and adjacent parts of the region has accelerated and is reflected in the much-reduced population growth of the 1960s and 1970s, and in the transfer of a large part of the area's increment to adjacent parts of the South-West and East Anglia.

In the nineteenth century the West Midlands retained a level of population growth close to the national average, though the relative decline of the Black Country after 1870 is reflected in a very slight fall in the region's share of the national population by 1901. The revival of industry and, in particular, the twentieth-century boom in the engineering and consumer durables industries is reflected in its relatively high growth rates and increasing share of the nation's population between 1901 and 1971, a trend which has slowed down only with the recession of the 1970s.

The other regions of England south of the Mersey-Humber have all experienced an acceleration of population growth in the twentieth century after a relative decline in the nineteenth. Indeed in East Anglia and the South-West persistent out-migration from their predominantly rural areas and relatively slower urban development saw a marked reduction in their share of the national population, especially in the second half of the nineteenth century. The slowing down of out-migration between 1901-51 due to urban development and, especially in the South-West, retirement migration, pointed the way to a very rapid increase in the rate of population growth in the post-war period, some of which has resulted from the outward spread of London's influence and migration field.

In the East Midlands the relative decline in population in the nineteenth century was modest and its growth rates were never far behind the national average. Indeed in the later nineteenth century the towns and diversified industries of the region attracted population from adjacent and northern areas leading to an acceleration in population growth which is reflected in the twentieth century in increases in the proportion of the national population living in the region. The post-war growth of population has been — and continues — at a relatively high level.

The remaining regions of England and Wales have declined in relative importance and in rates of population growth from the late nineteenth or early twentieth centuries. The profiles of the North-West and Yorkshire are very similar. Rapid nineteenth-century growth — pronounced in the North-West in the early part of the century, and

reflecting the emergence of the Lancashire textile area as one of the
first specialist industrial regions of modern times — was followed by a
fall of rates of increase from the late nineteenth century in many areas
of the regions, with a sharp decline in relative importance, especially in
the North-West. Outside the larger cities there has been persistent out-
migration since the First World War — indeed in many of the textile
districts from the late nineteenth century — accompanied by natural
increase, reduced birth rates and an ageing population.

Similar trends have been experienced in Wales and Northern England
where rapid development in coal-mining and heavy industry in the mid-
and late nineteenth century are reflected in high rates of population
growth. The sharp decline in these industries after 1918 led to a sharp
fall in rates of growth and a declining share of the national population.
The upsurge of population in the South Wales coalfield in the later
nineteenth century is concealed in Table 2.3 by massive rural losses to
England from the rest of the region. But since the First World War most
of the rural and older industrial areas of both Wales and Northern
England have been among the areas of heaviest migrational loss, as
reflected in their very slow growth and continuing decline in relative
importance.

2.3 The Components of Regional Population Change, 1780-1971: General Remarks

It is not easy to make a detailed, exact and directly comparable analysis
of vital and migrational components of population change in England
and Wales over this period. Prior to the development of civil registration
of vital statistics with the creation of the Office of Registrar-General in
1837, vital trends must be assessed from baptismal and burial registers,
both of which, especially the former, are deficient in a number of ways.
Moreover, the earlier censuses of 1801-31 are little more than
enumerations and data on age and sex were limited. Even after the
adoption of civil registration, vital data, especially on births, were
defective,[7] but this is not a major difficulty in the study of the broader
regional features of population change, though it often poses problems
in more detailed demographic analyses. Moreover, despite the much
increased details of age and sex composition and of occupations
contained in the censuses from 1841, and more particularly from 1851,
it is difficult to calculate standardised measures of fertility and
mortality. Hence, in this review more attention will be given to a crude
and rather simplistic approach — the contribution these make to the
rate of change in various areas.

Direct information on migration was not gathered in this country until the 1961 census when a 10 per cent sample answered questions on change of residence in the year preceding the census. Population registers, like those of Sweden, for example, in which movements of individuals are recorded, have never been kept, though wartime registration enabled analyses of mobility between 1939 and 1952 to be made (Newton and Jeffrey, 1951). Hence migration may only be calculated indirectly: first, by estimating net migration from a comparison of natural with total population change in an area, usually measured over an inter-censal period; and, secondly, by using census information on birth place, available in varying detail from the 1841 census onwards, either directly to give a crude index of lifetime migration into a particular area[8] or, indirectly, by estimating true inter-censal migration between areas from birth places as recorded in successive censuses.[9]

A further major difficulty in comparing regional trends over such a long time-span lies in the changing areal units in official statistics. In general, no attempt has been made in this chapter, other than in section 2.2 and Table 2.3, to use a set of standard areas as the basis of regional comparisons over the whole period. Essentially section 2.4 of the following discussion uses the geographical county; section 2.5 is based on registration districts, and combinations of regions and types of area based on those; while in section 2.6 local authority areas and, for the post-1951 period, Standard Regions and planning sub-regions provide the essential framework of discussion. This mixed approach is based on the units used for vital registration and census tabulation: these were, prior to 1841, the traditional units of parish and county; from 1841 to 1911 registration districts, counties and divisions were used for the tabulation of vital data but local authority administrative areas for other data; and from 1921 local authority and, since the 1950s, planning regions have been used.[10]

2.4 The Components of Regional Population Change: 1780-1830

Population trends in the eighteenth century were a cause of contemporary controversy and remain an active subject of academic debate.[11] However, relatively little attention has been given to the analysis of regional population change, though current work on parish registers by the Cambridge Group for the History of Population and Social Structure is providing the essential techniques and detailed statistics at parish level on which more accurate regional studies may eventually be based. One of the fullest analyses, given by Deane and

Cole (1969), is the basis for the following discussion.[12] Their exhaustive study is based on counties which they combined into four regions for certain aspects of this analysis (see Table 2.4) and uses the Brownlee estimates of births and deaths based on the Parish Register abstracts of the 1801-41 censuses. These are analysed cartographically in figures 2.1 and 2.2.

During the later eighteenth and early nineteenth centuries population increases were general in all regions of England and Wales, whether they were rural, industrial or urban. Much of the direct impact of the early Industrial Revolution was on an industrialised countryside in which handicraft and water-powered industry created an accelerating level of population growth which was as marked in many rural counties as in the industrial ones.[13] From the 1780s, however, the pull to London – always strong – and the major provincial cities was increasing and the newer industrial countries, particularly in the North-West, West Yorkshire and the West Midlands together with parts of the South Wales and the North-East coalfields, were growing rapidly. In very broad terms, the North-West (including in Deane and Cole's definition the textile areas of Lancashire-Yorkshire and the whole of Staffordshire) showed the most marked relative increase between 1781 and 1830 (Table 2.4), rather ahead of London, the other area of relatively high growth. Much of these increases was due to migrational gain. In the case of the London area this was less pronounced in the later eighteenth and early nineteenth centuries than in the early eighteenth. But the pull of the North-West and the Northern and Welsh coalfield areas increased in this period, accounting for a substantial element of total growth in Lancashire, Monmouth and Durham. Nevertheless, in general, Deane and Cole believe that 'it is not until 1800 that the statistics reveal a general movement to these new industrial counties' (Deane and Cole, 1969, p. 113). This view must be qualified for – as they admit – the growth counties of the late eighteenth and early nineteenth centuries did attract a good deal of short-range movement, a feature which Redford (1964) stressed in his study of early nineteenth-century migration.

While high migration, often from considerable distances, was required to sustain the rapid growth of London and the major provincial cities, the major element and key factor in regional contrasts in population growth lay in varying rates of natural increase. The fall in death rate from the 1740s was uneven in incidence, especially as between towns and industrial areas and the rural counties. In London deaths remained above births until the 1780s, and indeed there and in

Table 2.4a: Migration and Natural Increase by Regions, 1701-1831 (thousands)

	North-West	North	North and North-West	London	South	London and South
Per cent population, 1701	20.3	23.2	43.5	17.8	38.7	56.5
Population increase, 1701-51	138	75	213	35	66	101
Estimated natural increase, 1701-51	350	284	634	-568	250	-318
Net migration, 1701-51	-212	-209	-421	602	-184	418
Per cent population, 1751	21.5	23.2	44.7	17.5	37.8	55.3
Population increase, 1751-81	500	302	801	234	356	590
Estimated natural increase, 1751-81	604	387	991	-171	570	399
Net migration, 1751-81	-104	-85	-190	405	-214	191
Per cent population, 1781	24.2	22.9	47.1	17.4	35.6	52.9
Population increase, 1781-1801	569	309	877	366	381	748
Estimated natural increase, 1781-1801	535	367	902	81	640	721
Net migration, 1781-1801	33	-58	-25	285	-258	27
Per cent population, 1801	26.1	22.2	48.3	18.3	33.4	51.7
Population increase, 1801-31	1,589	1,002	2,591	998	1,307	2,305
Estimated natural increase, 1801-31	1,476	1,077	2,553	525	1,821	2,346
Net migration, 1801-31	113	-75	38	473	-515	-41
Per cent population, 1831	28.3	21.6	49.9	19.0	31.1	50.1

The regions are comprised of geographical counties as follows:

North-West: Cumberland, Westmorland, Lancashire, Cheshire, North Yorkshire, West Yorkshire, Derbyshire, Staffordshire.
North: Northumberland, Durham, East Yorkshire, Lincolnshire, Nottinghamshire, Leicestershire, Rutland, Warwickshire, Worcestershire, Shropshire, Herefordshire, Wales and Monmouth.
South: Norfolk, Suffolk, Cambridge, Huntingdon, Bedford, Northampton, Buckingham, Hertfordshire, Berkshire, Oxfordshire, Wiltshire, Hampshire, Dorset, Gloucestershire, Somerset, Devon, Cornwall.
London: Essex, Middlesex, Surrey, Kent, Sussex.

Source: Deane and Cole, 1969, Table 2.4A from p. 118 and Table 2.4B from p. 126.

Figure 2.1: Population Trends in England and Wales, 1781-1800

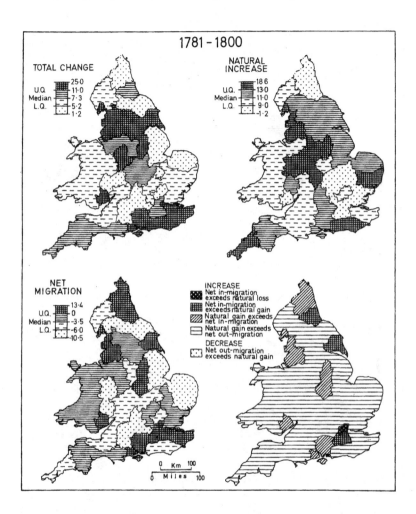

Average annual rates of change per 1,000 population are shown by quartile group
for English counties and for Wales and Monmouth.
Source: Deane and Cole, 1969, Table 26, p. 115.

Figure 2.2: Population Trends in England and Wales, 1801-1830

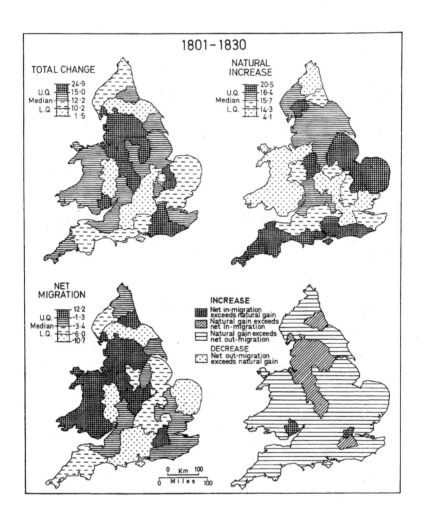

Average annual rates of change per 1,000 population by quartiles
   (as in Figure 2.1).
Source: Deane and Cole, 1969.

the provincial cities this was intermittently so until the mid-Victorian period. Though sharing the general fall in death rate, the 'industrial counties', especially of the North-West and Midlands, had generally higher mortality than the rural counties.

Indeed it was lower mortality which contributed to above-average rates of increase in the rural areas, especially before the early nineteenth century. Generally birth rates in such areas were moderate, apart from somewhat higher rates in regions with a continuing tradition of craft industry, such as the South-West and the East Midlands. The position in the Midlands and North was more variable but did include a considerable number of counties of relatively high fertility, sometimes within the emerging industrial areas but often in their periphery, which acted as a supplier of labour. In such cases industrialisation may well have promoted more general and younger ages of marriage, and led to increased births.[14] Birth rates in the centres of towns were generally relatively low: they grew rapidly essentially through in-migration. But the surrounding areas often had very high fertility, a notable feature of Kent and Surrey, for example, and of parts of South Lancashire and the West Midlands.

Much detailed work remains to be done before a satisfactory account can be given of regional contrasts and fluctuations in the components of population change, not least at an intra-regional level. But the conclusion of Deane and Cole is that while the London area depended on high in-migration for its growth, the industrial areas and towns of the Midlands, North and North-West depended more on high rates of natural increase, to which increased births as well as a falling death rate contributed. Much of the increment was redistributed within these regions by short-distance migration. There is evidence to support the view that different levels of natural increase contributed more to regional differentials in population growth, though migration was undoubtedly significant in the big cities.[15]

2.5 The Components of Regional Population Change: 1831-1911

The regional analysis of both natural and migrational components of population change becomes more secure, especially from the 1840s, with the more detailed census base from 1841 and the beginnings of civil registration in 1837. Nevertheless births in particular continued to suffer from under-registration at least until mid-Victorian times, although at the regional level the errors are not likely to be significant and are probably consistent from one region to another.[16] While figures of actual migration are lacking, estimates of net migration can be made by comparing vital changes, given in the Registrar-General's Annual Report for Registration Districts and Sub-Districts, with total change recorded in the censuses from 1851 for the same areas. It is also possible to analyse both regional and intra-regional population change in some detail for inter-censal decades from 1841. The first analysis of this type was carried out by Welton (1911) on a basis which was used for a review of population trends between 1841 and 1911 by Cairncross (1949, 1953, pp. 65-83), while the author has analysed these data cartographically for registration districts in England and Wales (Lawton, 1968) and for sub-districts in a number of regions (Lawton, 1962; Lawton and Pooley, 1976).

Structural changes in the economy, with a marked fall in employment in agriculture in relative terms up to 1851 and, thereafter, absolutely to a mere 6 per cent of the work-force in 1911, and a shift in manufacturing to larger units and greater regional and urban concentration saw a continuing shift in the mid- and later nineteenth century in the centre of gravity of population towards the North and West and, in particular, rapid urbanisation accompanied by large-scale out-migration from the countryside (Figure 2.3). Whereas the rural areas lost over 4.5 million people by net migration between 1841 and 1911, absorbing 85 per cent of their natural increment, the towns and 'colliery districts' gained 3.3 million, about one-sixth of their total increase (Table 2.5). The wide fluctuations in migration differentials, over time and from region to region, account largely for temporal and spatial variations in population trends in the period since 1831. Though regional variations in birth and death rates persisted, and still persist, they seem to have been less significant in differential growth than in the eighteenth and early nineteenth centuries, suggesting that population became more responsive to economic forces through increased mobility.[17] In turn, progressive concentration of population, especially in London and the major provincial conurbations, has undoubtedly been, in part, a causative factor in regional economic growth, especially in an economy in which, from the mid-nineteenth century, building, transport and services were growing more rapidly than manufacturing industry.

The differential patterns of growth may be looked at from two points of view: first, as between different types of area, an exercise first attempted by Welton (1911) and, more recently, by Cairncross (1949); secondly, on a regional basis in which vital and migrational components of change for Registration Districts can be analysed reasonably accurately from the census decade 1841-51 (Figures 2.4-2.6).

Figure 2.3: Total Population Change in England and Wales, 1801-51 and 1851-1911

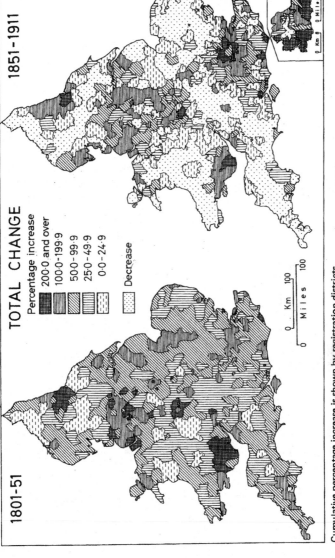

TOTAL CHANGE

Percentage increase
- 200·0 and over
- 100·0-199·9
- 50·0-99·9
- 25·0-49·9
- 0·0-24·9
- Decrease

1851-1911

1801-51

0   Km   100
0   Miles   100

Cumulative percentage increase is shown by registration districts.
Source: Census of Great Britain, 1851; Censuses of England and Wales,
1861-1911.

16 Southern	470,821	1,212,413	616,644	+ 124,948	+ 20.3	157.5

Northern Towns	4,037,726	11,394,161	6,369,985	+ 986,450	+ 15.5	182.2
Southern Towns	4,385,222	12,381,525	6,331,165	+ 1,665,138	+ 26.3	182.3
All Towns	8,669,167	23,775,686	12,701,150	+ 2,651,588	+ 20.9	174.3
2. Colliery Districts 9 Northern	1,320,342	5,334,002	3,363,112	+ 650,548	+ 19.3	304.0
3. Rural Residues 12 Northern	2,425,614	2,875,113	2,093,257	−1,643,770	−78.6	18.5
12 Southern	3,740,228	4,085,691	3,208,729	−2,863,266	−89.2	9.2
Total	6,165,842	6,960,804	5,301,986	−4,507,036	−85.0	12.9
North of England	7,783,682	19,602,876	11,825,942	− 7,648	− 0.1	151.8
South of England	8,125,450	16,467,616	9,540,294	−1,198,128	−12.6	102.7
Total	15,914,148	36,070,492	21,366,236	−1,209,892	− 5.7	126.6

Figure 2.4: Migrational Trends in England and Wales, 1851-1911

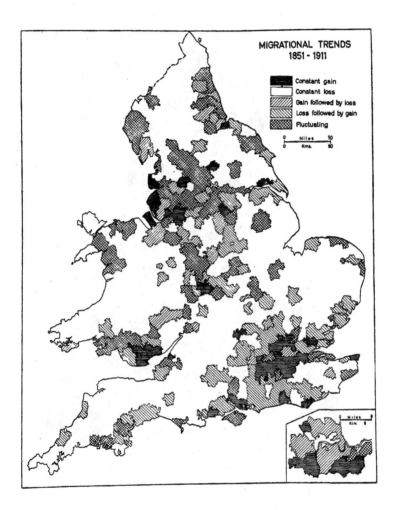

Types of net migrational decadal change over the period are shown by
    registration districts.
Source: Censuses of England and Wales, 1861-1911.

Figure 2.5: Natural Change in England and Wales, 1851-1911

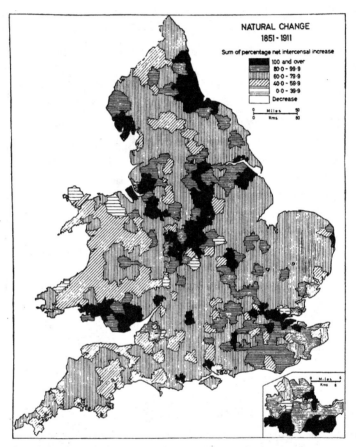

Cumulative percentage change is shown by registration districts.
Source: Censuses of England and Wales, 1861-1911.

Figure 2.6: Population Trends in England and Wales, 1851-1911

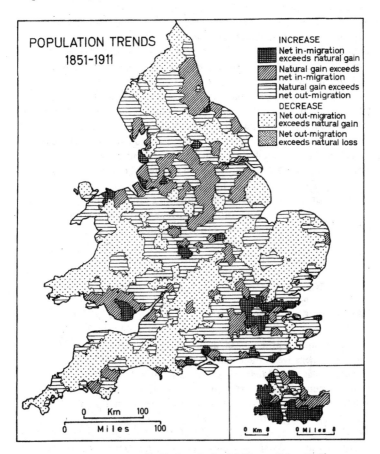

Types of trend are shown by registration district (cf. Figures 2.1 and 2.2).
Source: Censuses of England and Wales, 1861-1911.

Cairncross's summary of the overall changes in nine types of area (with further subdivisions) shown in Table 2.5 underlines the extent of the slackening of the rate of increase and the considerable scale of net out-migration from the rural areas. Such movements were large and sustained, though they fluctuated from decade to decade, depending largely on the power of urban labour markets to absorb this mainly unskilled labour.

Although, in general, London and the larger towns made large gains by migration throughout the nineteenth century, equal to about one-third of the growth due to net migration, they too fluctuated in their demand for labour. Again the 1880s seem to have been a time of change in which the pull of the cities weakened and, in particular, there was a marked swing from the attraction of internal migration by the northern industrial towns to a loss. While many of those people emigrated others moved, often over quite long distances, to the Midlands and southern parts of the country, a feature which was to persist into the inter-war years of the twentieth century.

Clearly there are considerable contrasts in the level and pattern of mobility in various regions of England from the railway age. But the concentration of population surplus into a relatively few areas is very marked (Figure 2.4). Moreover, the relative contribution of migration to total population growth made over the period 1841-1911 differs considerably from one type of area to another: it was considerable in London and the larger towns; very marked in the residential towns; persistent, but not pronounced, in the colliery districts; and limited and, after 1881, negative in the industrial towns. Thomas (1954; 1972, Chapter 2) has argued that migration is a sensitive index of British economic conditions, in particular as measured by building fluctuations, which are in turn inversely related to those of the United States, so that when growth is strong in Britain, levels of internal migration are high (as in the decades 1861-70, 1871-80 and 1890-1901), but when growth and the building cycle are weak in Britain, external migration increases to absorb surplus population which is particularly directed towards North America, as in the decades 1881-90 and 1901-10. Certainly this seems to be borne out by migrational behaviour in British towns and industrial areas of the later nineteenth century.

While migration differentials largely account for regional and temporal fluctuations in population growth in this period, the distinctive regional contrasts in natural growth rates persisted, though the vital rates which underlie such contrasts have yet to be fully analysed (Figure 2.5). Despite the high mortality in the cities, which did not begin to fall nearer the national average until the 1880s, urban and industrial areas generally had above-average rates of natural growth. Much of this they owed to their population structure, with migration adding large numbers of young adults, thereby contributing to a relatively high crude birth rate and lowering the crude mortality rates. Thus the high migration gains of the large towns and textile regions in the early and mid-nineteenth century later gave a built-in predisposition to high natural growth, while heavy in-migration to the coalfields, as from the mid-nineteenth century, provided the basis of the large families and high natural growth of the end of the century.

As already noted, the level of births remained relatively high in rural areas well into the nineteenth century. Nevertheless, a prolonged outflow of young men and women, the potential parents of the next generation, reduced the potential for growth, despite relatively low mortality, and there was a sharp downturn in natural increase in rural areas after 1891. Rural births peaked in the south of the country in the 1860s and in northern areas in the 1870s. By the early twentieth century rural birth rates were 30 per cent below their nineteenth-century peak and an ageing rural population had little potential for natural growth;[18] the draining of the rural reservoir was reflected in reduced levels of out-migration.

The vital experience in the urban and industrial areas varied considerably, not least within individual regions. The major cities were areas of relatively high natural growth, though an above-average birth rate was offset by relatively high mortality until after 1900. London, however, had below-average birth rates until the period 1901-10, again with slightly above-average mortality. Moreover, within the cities there were marked contrasts: in the inner areas, because of high mortality, often relatively low fertility and persistent out-migration, population declined rapidly after the mid-century; the suburbs, on the other hand, gained by in-movement of young people, birth rates were relatively high and mortality moderate to low. Similar contrasts exist between 'residential' districts and poorer-class areas of the industrial regions but require analysis at the level of the registration sub-district or in even more detail to bring out the contrasts.[19] At this level of analysis the contrasts in the components of population change vary much more widely than in the aggregated analysis of Table 2.5 (Figure 2.6). Many textile areas showed considerable evidence of demographic decline by the late nineteenth century. Not only did they generally lose population by migration, but birth rates declined from the 1880s to a figure well below the national average. In contrast, despite relatively high mortality rates, colliery districts sustained their late-nineteenth-century growth largely from a high natural increase, in turn the product of high fertility, relatively early marriage and large families.[20]

Temporal and spatial variations in fertility and mortality deserve fuller analysis than is possible here and in the present state of knowledge. One important aspect is the influence on population structure and vital trends of differential mobility. There is little direct information on this, other than the classification of birth-place data in the censuses from 1851 to 1871 under two broad age groups, under and over 20, and more particularly the detailed breakdown by age of persons born and enumerated in a selected number of counties in 1911. By comparison of projected age distribution with lifetime migrants born in these selected counties and enumerated elsewhere, Friedlander and Roshier (1966) have calculated the correction to be applied to the age-group survivorship ratio in order to estimate the inter-censal levels of migration in a series of age groups under 20, 20-24, 25-34, 35-44, 45-54, 55-64 and 65 and over. From these ratios it is apparent that recorded lifetime migrants in 1911 generally exceeded the number projected from age structure in the under-35 age groups, though in certain areas — as in the movements from London to adjacent areas — the 'surpluses' were often found in the under-25 and over-45 age groups, suggesting the suburbanward movement of older households and, perhaps, retirement migration which has become such a marked feature of the mid-twentieth century.

Contemporary observers were in no doubt that migration was to a considerable degree age- and, sometimes, sex-selective. Ravenstein (1885) noted that 'females are more migratory than males'. Welton (1911, Appendix B) made an early analysis of the estimated net migration gain or loss by age groups, calculating changes not attributable to mortality for the various groups of areas listed in Table 2.5. Between 1881 and 1900 large towns showed considerable gains in the 15-34 age groups and, perhaps surprisingly, the over-65 groups; in the 'old towns' the gains were mainly of young females (no doubt for domestic service) and older ages of both sexes; in the colliery and heavy industrial districts the largest 'gains' were of men under 35 and women between 25 and 39, in residential towns the age-migration gain among men was in the over-35 groups but among women in most age groups with a bi-modal emphasis on ages 15-24 and over 40; rural areas showed a deficiency in nearly all age groups except the 70-74, but there were massive estimated net migrational losses of men and women aged 15-29, though losses among women were also quite large in the middle age groups.

Age and sex structures have not been sufficiently studied to enable any detailed statement on the regional impact of mobility differentials. However, Thomas's analysis of natural increase and migration for population aged 20-44 in a number of urban areas from 1871 to 1910 has revealed interesting fluctuations within the period, for example the declining power of attraction of North-Western England after 1876, leading to actual losses in the early 1900s.[21] Such fluctuations are even more pronounced within regions, especially the rapidly expanding urban regions of the mid- and late nineteenth century. The migrants to inner areas of the city tend to be weighted towards single persons among the younger age groups. Family migration towards the suburbs often occurs after marriage and at distinctive stages in the family cycle, creating different demographic structures within the urban region[22] which were made more distinctive by the later nineteenth century as longer journeys to work developed.

The impact of differential migration on the countryside has been more fully studied, particularly by Saville (1957). In a detailed discussion of migration differentials he has shown considerable differences between the age structure of rural districts and the rest of England and Wales with deficits in the 20-44 age groups (20-39 for females) and markedly ageing populations, both the products of long-standing out-movement of young people, a feature which continues into the twentieth century.

2.6 The Components of Regional Population Change: 1921-1971

By the eve of the First World War nearly four-fifths of the population of England and Wales were town-dwellers. Three generations of migration from the countryside had left many parishes with fewer people than they had at their mid-nineteenth-century peak. Yet further urbanisation, with continuing rural losses, has persisted, albeit in rather different ways. By the end of the nineteenth century, accelerating physical expansion of large towns and improving public transport were extending urban influence into adjacent rural areas. Continuing decanting of population from inner areas and progressive sifting into marked social areas, a process to which public housing policies have contributed, have led to the massive intra-regional residential mobility which has underlain the tremendous spread of urbanisation that is one of the most noticeable features of modern population trends.[23]

The second major feature of twentieth-century population trends, also presaged in the late nineteenth century, was the declining rates of increase and loss of population by migration from some of the older industrial areas. The major growth regions of the twentieth century, principally in the Midlands and South-East, have also been the main beneficiaries of migration from the inter-war depressed areas, the economic weakness of which, despite post-1945 regional planning, have persisted into the 1970s. The resulting urban/urban migration accounts for much of the inter-regional variation in population change in England and Wales, though regional differences in fertility are an important contributory factor.

The essential continuity in both the distribution and pattern of regional change throughout the last sixty years has led to a partial reversal of the relative redistribution of population of the eighteenth and early nineteenth centuries, with inter-regional migration contributing largely to the increased emphasis on the South-East and Midlands and adjacent areas. The rapid fall in fertility of the inter-war years (Table 2.2) affected all sections of society in all regions, though regional differences in birth rates persisted and were a further factor behind the need to shed population from the depressed areas. Despite higher mortality in the northern cities and industrial regions, the North-West—South-East regional gradient of natural change created a demographic differential between northern and southern England.

2.6.1 The Components of Regional Population Change: 1921-1950

During the inter-war years the major part of population growth was concentrated into three of the present standard regions – the South-East and the West and East Midlands, particularly in the former. The higher birth rates of the older industrial regions were offset by higher mortality, but the regional gradient of natural change was quite marked, between Northern England (with rates of 0.5 per cent per annum) and Southern England (0.2-0.3 per cent per annum). There was still massive out-migration from the North and Wales, and the drift South-East loomed large in the evidence to the Royal Commission on the Distribution of the Industrial Population.

During the depression of the 1930s unemployment rates in the Midlands and South-East were in general only half of the national average. Between 1921 and 1951 the South-East gained 1.2 millions by migration, the Midlands over 300,000 and the South-West rather less than 300,000: in contrast Northern England lost 912,000, Wales 434,000 and Scotland 675,000. While the greatest numbers of movers came from the towns and industrial areas, losses continued from the hard-core, purely rural areas which Willatts and Newson (1953, pp. 432-5, Figure 1) identified in much of rural Wales, parts of the northern Pennines and smaller areas in north Devon, east and north Yorkshire, and south Suffolk. These areas had experienced heavy losses during the nineteenth century, and continuing selective out-migration of younger people had produced an ageing population with little growth potential.

In contrast, many rural districts around London and the major provincial towns showed persistent increases in population between 1921 and 1939 and those areas of increase were extended during and especially after the war. Most of this was due to the extension of commuting and associated residential mobility around all major cities. Even in 1921, of the 2.73 millions occupied population living in rural districts, 14.2 per cent travelled to work in urban areas, though in most rural districts, apart from those close to the towns, less than 10 per cent of residents were involved in such movements. By 1951, however, there had been a marked increase in commuting virtually throughout the axial belt of maximum population and around industrial areas in South Wales and North-East England (Lawton, 1963). This reflects the growth during the inter-war years of adventitious population, resident in rural areas but dependent on the town for employment (Vince, 1952).

Many of the persistent and large-scale features of population change 1921-51 were the result of inter-regional migration. The patterns of net movement identified by Willatts and Newson (1953) underline the heavy and persistent losses from North-East England, South Wales, much of east Lancashire and West Yorkshire and parts of the North Midlands. Much of the persistent increase in South-East England, excluding inner London, parts of the Midlands and on Severnside was associated with inter-regional movement, much of it of a long-distance character.[24] Such movements underlie the considerable increase in average distance of migration between non-adjacent counties in 1911-51 noted by Friedlander and Roshier (1966, Table 4, pp. 265-8; and Figure, p. 262), which they have linked with outward migration from the north to the eastern, south-eastern and southern counties, and from South Wales to the Midlands and South-East and North Wales. Indeed over the period 1881-1951 they calculate that Essex, Surrey, Sussex and Hampshire were the only counties to gain consistently, while almost the whole of England south and east of the Humber to the Severn, at least from 1911 following nineteenth-century losses, gained in longer-distance movement. In contrast, Northern England and South Wales lost, often heavily, after migration gains up to the late nineteenth century.

Webb (1963) believes that between 1921 and 1931 net migration had 'become the most important factor' in regional population change; and showed that the migrational component was the dominant element in population change in nearly two-thirds (756) of urban areas and over three-quarters (497) of rural areas (Figure 2.7). The regional significance of migration in regional growth is apparent. Gains in the outer areas of the London region and similar though more limited attraction to the periphery of other conurbations were mainly due to in-migration, while out-migration accounted largely for losses from the inner areas of large cities, from the older industrial regions and from the newer rural areas.

2.6.2 The Components of Regional Population Change: 1951-1971

The discussion which follows is only a brief summary based on the author's recent account (Lawton, 1977), together with detailed parallel analyses by Champion (1976) and Eversley (1971). The trends discussed must be updated in the light of the continuing decline in natural growth as outlined by Eversley, Ermisch and Overton in Chapter 6 of this volume.

One of the major features has been the continuing loss of population from the inner areas of all large towns, particularly from the conurbations which lost a total of 725,000 people in 1961-71, a fall of 5 per cent (to 33 per cent) in their share of the country's population. Moreover, the growth of towns of over 100,000 slowed to only one-third of the national average in 1961-71. These trends date back to before the First World War when many large cities reached their peak population and have since maintained growth by expanding into successively more distant suburban satellites. As large-scale intra-urban mobility continues, the population gradient between city centre and periphery has been reduced and large-scale overspill into peripheral 'rural districts' has extended the real city regions. The corollary may be seen in the extension of labour areas which reflect an increasing range and complexity of journeys to work (Hall *et al.*, 1973), though with decentralisation of industry and, to some extent, service activities, the level of commuting to many city centres is, in fact, declining.

Secondly, rural population has continued to decline. Following a century and a half of outward migration, the population of many of the more thinly peopled areas is declining, demographically as well as in economic and social terms, with an excess of deaths over births and continuing outward migration (H.M. Treasury, 1976). The reversal of

Figure 2.7: Population Trends in England and Wales, 1921-1931

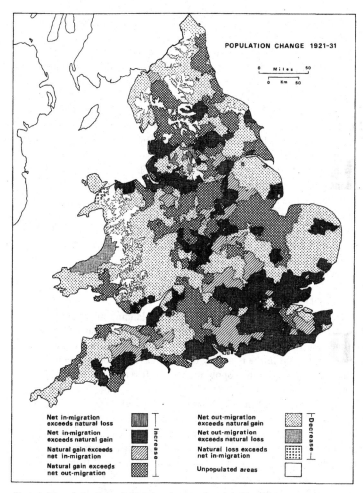

Types of trend are shown by local authority areas (cf. Figures 2.1, 2.2 and 2.6).
Source: Webb, 1963, Figure 12.

the fall in aggregate population in the rural districts in 1961-71 has been largely due to the dispersal of town-dwellers or, as in certain areas, particularly of Southern and South-Western England and in seaside areas of North Wales and the North-West, to retirement migration.

Thirdly, at the regional level, the essential features of inter-war population change have persisted, despite the attempts of post-war planning to diminish the continuing drain from the inter-war depressed areas and the hard-core rural areas. Between 1951 and 1961 the South-East region gained 438,000 by migration (nearly two-fifths of its total increase), while there was considerable migration gain in the West and East Midlands. All other regions lost by migration in that decade, the losses being marked from the North-West (Table 2.6). Despite vigorous attempts in the 1960s to provide a sufficient supply of new jobs in the development areas and to control the increase in jobs in the growth regions, these trends have persisted. The South-East has lost population by migration due largely to a fall of 536,000 in Greater London's population in 1961-71, though these went mainly to the Outer South-East and adjacent areas of East Anglia and the South-West. Nevertheless, the slowing down in population growth in the Midlands and the reduction of outward movement from Wales and Yorkshire and Humberside indicate a degree of success for regional policies: in Eversley's words, 'without government policies the situation would be far worse' (Eversley, 1971, p. 227).

The components of population change in planning sub-regions (Department of the Environment, 1971) underline the major features outlined above (Figure 2.8). In Southern England migration is the major component in the relatively large increases of population in most of the inner and outer metropolitan areas, as it is also over much of the South-West and East Anglia and in the outer areas of the West Midlands. But, apart from the commuter areas of north Cheshire and mid-Yorkshire, there are no other such areas in England and Wales. However, heavy selective retirement migration has led to population increases in coastal areas of the North-West, North Wales and Sussex, offsetting natural losses or very slow growth which result from extreme imbalance in the age structure (Law and Warnes, 1976). In contrast, the relatively rapid growth of population in the East Midlands, many parts of the West Midlands and parts of the Outer Metropolitan Area is due mainly to natural increase, resulting particularly from relatively high birth rates.

Areas of relative decline are of two types: first, those in which natural increase exceeded migrational loss, which includes most of the

Table 2.6: Regional Population Trends, England and Wales, 1951-1971

Region	1951 Population	1951-61 Average annual change		1961 Population	1961-71 Average annual change		1971 Population	1971 Total		1951-71 Total change			
		Natural	Migration		Natural	Migration				Natural		Migration	
								No.	Per cent	No.	Per cent	No.	Per cent
North	3,127	19.3	− 7.4	3,246	17.4	−12.7	3,293	166	5.3	367	11.7	−201	− 6.4
Yorkshire and Humberside	4,509	19.5	− 7.3	4,631	26.5	− 8.5	4,811	302	6.7	460	10.2	−158	− 3.5
North-West	6,417	23.5	−10.7	6,545	34.0	−13.8	6,474	330	5.1	575	2.0	−245	− 3.8
East Midlands	2,896	15.8	+ 5.4	3,108	22.4	+ 5.8	3,390	494	17.1	382	13.2	+ 112	+ 3.9
West Midlands	4,426	27.6	+ 5.9	4,761	39.5	− 3.5	5,121	695	15.7	671	15.2	+ 25	+ 0.6
South-East	15,216	66.4	+46.6	16,346	99.6	− 5.3	17,289	2,073	13.6	1,660	10.9	+413	+ 2.7
Greater London	8,206	33.3	−56.2	7,977	45.6	−99.2	7,441	−765	−9.3	789	9.6	−1,554	−18.9
Outer Metropolitan	3,509	24.2	+77.0	4,521	41.2	+41.2	5,345	1,836	52.3	654	18.6	+1,182	+33.7
Outer South-East	3,502	8.9	+25.7	3,848	13.3	+52.1	4,502	1,000	28.6	222	6.3	+778	+22.3
East Anglia	1,388	6.5	+ 3.6	1,489	8.4	+11.3	1,686	298	21.5	149	10.7	+149	+10.7
South-West	3,247	10.5	+ 8.4	3,436	15.0	+20.6	3,792	545	16.8	255	7.9	+290	+ 8.9
Wales	2,589	8.4	− 3.8	2,635	9.7	− 0.9	2,723	134	5.2	181	7.0	− 47	− 1.8

Sources: Lawton, 1977, based on figures from the Registrar-General's mid-year estimates. Figures are in thousands.

conurbations and older industrial areas, together with the less remote rural districts of South Wales and Northern England; secondly, hard-core regions – both rural and industrial – of long-standing economic decline in which low rates of natural growth, due mainly to low birth rates in an ageing population, have resulted from prolonged out-migration.

Variations in natural change reflect long-standing differences in economic and social conditions but are also the outcome of population structures, the differences in which are largely determined by differential migration (Figure 2.8). While all parts of the country have been affected by the fluctuation in birth rates since 1945, significant variations in fertility remain, both between social classes and in different parts of the country. Geographical patterns of birth rate vary at two levels. First, they reflect the social zoning within city regions: for example, Merseyside – traditionally an area of high fertility – shows a clear zonation from high rates, 75 per cent above the national average, in the inner areas to low values, only 20-25 per cent higher, in the outer areas. Secondly, despite the general narrowing in fertility rates during the 1960s and 1970s, crude regional birth rates range widely; within England and Wales the higher rates are found in the residential suburbs of industrial areas of south Lancashire, south Yorkshire and of the Midlands and parts of the South-East where higher proportions of manual workers and relatively youthful population structures may both account for higher rates. The recent fall in birth rates, which seems to have affected such areas proportionally more, may in future be reflected in lower natural increase. If so, there may be less need for such areas to shed surplus population by migration.

However, in the twentieth as much as in the nineteenth century, birth rates have helped to compensate for relatively high mortality in the urban and industrial areas of the North, and especially in the inner city. General mortality still has a regional gradient from North-West to South-East; the average risk of death in Salford, one of the areas of highest mortality, is one-third higher than in Bournemouth, one of the lowest. On Merseyside there is an even sharper gradient within cities, as between an inner area such as Bootle, with an adjusted death rate of 16.2 per 1,000 (in 1969) and middle-class suburbs such as Wirral (10.7) or Formby (7.2). The continuing gap in social conditions between the 'privileged' and 'less privileged' regions has been emphasised by many writers (for example, by Coates and Rawstron, 1971). Howe's maps of mortality and morbidity have shown the striking concentration of high mortality in Northern and Western Britain: of 53

Figure 2.8: Population Trends in England and Wales, 1951-1969

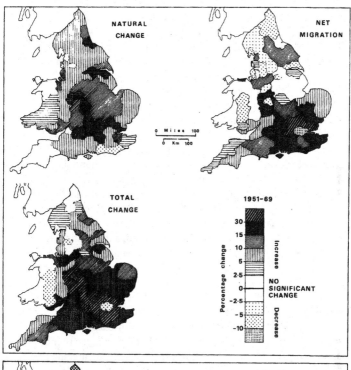

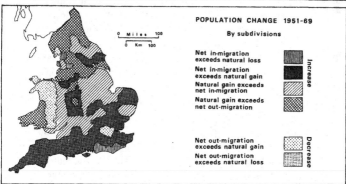

Total, natural and net migrational trends, together with components of
population change, are shown by planning sub-regions.
Source: Department of the Environment, 1971.

areas with very high male mortality, only 4 were in the London area, while south Lancashire had a very considerable concentration (Howe, 1970). Significantly, there are similar regional variations in infant mortality, despite the sharp fall in general rates since 1945.

Post-war migration has increased in volume, and will no doubt continue to increase. Much of it is due to short-range, intra-regional or even intra-city residential mobility (see Chapter 7 of this volume): as such it is reflected in the growing volume and distance of commuting. Nevertheless, inter-regional migration continues to play a significant role in differential population growth between regions and, though the net balance of migration, as revealed by the residential mobility questions in the census from 1961, is often relatively small, the considerable in- and out-movements involved have substantial effects on population structure and future potential for growth.

The greatest mobility rates in 1960-1 were in East Anglia and the South-West, followed by the East and West Midlands, though the greatest number of moves were to and from the South-East. By 1965-6 the position of the West Midlands had weakened, and the slight inward flow to Wales suggested that development area policies were beginning to make an impact on population trends. But the interaction between regions is very complex. Rather than direct transfers from 'exporting' to 'importing' regions, there is a 'shunting' movement culminating in the transfer of considerable numbers to only four regions in the period 1961-6: East Anglia, the East Midlands, the South-West and the Outer South-East. Champion (1976, pp. 404-10) has shown a persistence of these tendencies to 1971, though there has been an encouraging reversal of the flow from Wales, and a considerable reduction of net loss from the Northern region. However, losses from the rest of the industrial North and the West Midlands increased in the later 1960s.

The effects of migration on both sending and receiving areas are greater than are apparent from the total of those involved. Migration is selective in both demographic and socio-economic terms. The census information on residential mobility permits some analysis of the effects of differential inter-regional movement in the 1960s.

Population migration is highly age-selective. The category 15-24 is by far the most mobile age group, with migration rates 35 per cent above the next most mobile group (25-34 years) in 1970-1. Many younger people flock to the inner urban areas, especially Greater London, which despite its considerable *total* migration losses, still has a large gain of 15-24-year-olds from all regions of the UK (see Chapter 9 of this volume). In contrast, the three northern regions of England experienced migrational loss almost throughout the 1960s. The West Midlands, which still had modest gains in the younger age groups in 1960-1, lost in all ages after the mid-1960s, reflecting perhaps relatively high birth rate and declining prosperity. The regions of migrational gain also show contrasts. East Anglia and the East Midlands made their greatest gains among the under-45s. In the South-West, however, over one-third of the net migration gain in 1965-6 was in the over-60 group. Much of the key to this selective redistribution lies in the South-East which contributes much family migration to East Anglia, as reflected in the large net gains in the 25-44 and 0-14 age groups, and provides many of the over-45s who predominate in movement to the South-West.

One aspect of socio-economic differentiation in migration, overseas immigration, which became a significant factor in 1958-62, must be dealt with very briefly. Although immigration, more particularly of coloured Commonwealth immigrants, is not large in relation to the total population of the UK, it tends to concentrate both regionally and within the inner areas of cities. Young adults of 25-44 predominated among the immigrants of the early 1960s, and this has been followed by a high rate of natural increase. With the decline in further immigration of the 1970s, such features are unlikely to persist, at least in such a marked form, but they illustrate some of the problems of absorbing a migrant group into the population.

A second socio-economic differential is more complex in its impact. It has long been observed that rural depopulation takes not only the younger but more ambitious, so that country areas tend to be 'denuded of people of superior abilities' (Musgrove, 1963). In a perhaps less obvious way, varying social and economic opportunities are important in both inter- and intra-regional migration (see Chapter 8 of this volume). The consequences for the inner city of outward movement of professional, managerial and skilled manual workers and their families and their replacement by less skilled, often single, people are considerable. The concentration of the higher occupational (and better educated) groups into the outer city is paralleled in the over-concentration of higher services on relatively few areas, which has led to a pronounced mobility among such groups and their concentration into the South-East in particular (Waugh, 1969). The evidence of the General Household Survey of 1972 is that these trends continue: in the five years prior to the survey 50 per cent of households of professional and non-manual workers had moved, whereas only 30 per cent of manual workers had done so.

2.7 Conclusion

In conclusion, what light may this very broad and incomplete review shed on present and future regional trends of population in Britain? First, that regional populations have responded to changing economic circumstances mainly in terms of migration. The rise and decline of the older Northern and Welsh industrial regions and the recent recession in the West Midlands, for example, are reflected in the changing pattern of migration. Underlying these fluctuations, however, there are persistent features which have operated over a very long period: rural-urban movement; increasing metropolitanisation; and the pull to London and the South-East region. These reflect long-standing socio-economic differentials which repel and pull population in a selective fashion, often ensuring further divergence in population trends. Secondly, regional contrasts in natural changes have tended to show greater long-term stability. Thus much of the early growth in the North and parts of the Midlands seems to have been due to higher birth rates which continued to provide much of the population for nineteenth-century industrial expansion, during which the growth potential was increased by selective in-migration. Indeed many of the areas of higher natural growth were exporting surplus population before the post-First World War decline in their economy. Moreover, a north-south gradient in fertility and mortality has continued to persist, though those regional differences are often less than intra-regional contrasts between town and country, and between the inner city and the suburbs.

However, much work is still needed at both the broader regional and more detailed intra-regional scale on the characteristics of regional population development in Britain, including the ways in which these affect population structure and, in turn, influence regional development.

Notes

1. McKeown, 1976. For an alternative view on the significance of fluctuation of birth rates for late-eighteenth and early-nineteenth-century population growth see Krause, 1958. The question is reviewed carefully and objectively by Deane and Cole, 1969.

2. Zelinsky (1971) has outlined five phases in such a transition.

3. For example, Osborne (1964) discusses population change in Britain in three main phases, up to 1801, 1801-1921 and 1921-61. He has tabulated regional change (by county groups) for 1801-61, 1861-1921 and 1921-61 (Osborne, 1964, pp. 340-1).

The Barlow Commission (1940, p. 17), in reviewing 'changes in the distribution of industry and the industrial population since the beginning of the nineteenth century', thought it convenient to divide the period into two parts, separated by the war of 1914-18.

The more recent study by Department of the Environment (1971) reviews trends from 1801-1969 in 4 phases: 1801-51, 1851-1901, 1901-51 and 1951-69 (see Tables 1.4-1.7, and 1.12-1.15 and Figure 1.7).

4. See the Barlow Commission (1940, paragraphs 48-59, pp. 20-5) for a concise statement of the essential features of this tendency in the period 1801-1937.

5. See Deane and Cole (1969, Chapter 3) for a concise and balanced view of population change in the eighteenth and early nineteenth centuries.

6. In the mid-eighteenth century some 15-16 per cent of the population lived in towns of over 5,000, in 1801 25 per cent, and in 1831 44 per cent. A full review of eighteenth-century local censuses — many for towns — is given by Law, 1969.

7. For a review of the development of census-taking and vital registration in England and Wales, see Glass, 1973.

8. This provides the basis for the classic study by Ravenstein, 1885.

9. There have been a number of such attempts, most notably by Friedlander and Roshier, 1966. Such methods as applied to the nineteenth century are reviewed by Baines, 1972.

10. This complex issue cannot be analysed, even cursorily, here: for the nineteenth century there is a full discussion of the problem in general and as related to various categories of census data in Lawton, 1978.

11. The literature is voluminous: useful summaries are given by Flinn, 1970; Habakkuk, 1971; and Glass and Eversley, 1969, Part II, 'Great Britain'.

12. See 'Industrialization and population change in the eighteenth and early nineteenth centuries', Chapter III of Deane and Cole, 1969, which also discusses the pioneering work of John Rickman, on whose estimates of births and deaths from parish registers much subsequent work has been based, and analyses the major contributions to this debate.

13. See Deane and Cole, 1969, and Lawton, 1964.

14. This has been argued in the case of Nottinghamshire by Chambers, 1957. The point is discussed in a more general context in Chambers, 1972.

15. Deane and Cole (1969, p. 117) quote Cairncross (1953, p. 79): 'the north of England triumphed over the south mainly by superior fertility (and not as we used to be taught by attracting migrants)', as applying to the period of early industrialisation as well as after 1840.

16. See Glass, 1951-2. For a regional analysis see Teitelbaum, 1974.

17. Deane and Cole (1969, p. 289) state categorically that 'for most of the nineteenth century the changes in the rate of natural increase are of less significance in relation to economic growth than the changes in the rate of migration'.

18. Cairncross, 1949, p.80. For a discussion of the effect of rural losses on the age structure see Saville, 1957. For a discussion of components of rural population change see Lawton, 1967.

19. These are analysed for Merseyside in Lawton and Pooley, 1976, pp. 38-40 and Figures 5-15.

20. This has been noted by Glass, 1938, and fully analysed by Friedlander, 1973.

21. Thomas, 1972, Chapter 2, Appendix B.

22. Illustrating certain facets of this aspect of mobility, there are an increasing number of studies based on micro-scale analysis using census enumerators' books: for some effects of migration on the age structure of migrant population in

mid-Victorian Liverpool see Lawton and Pooley, 1976, pp. 78-94, and on age and life-cycle migration within Huddersfield, see Dennis, 1977.

23. In an analysis based on counties, Friedlander (1970) has shown that one of the fastest decades of increase was 1901-11.

24. See Newton and Jeffrey, 1951, for a study of internal mobility based on the wartime National Register.

References

Baines, D.E. 1972. The use of published census data in migration studies. In *Nineteenth Century Society*, ed. E.A. Wrigley. Cambridge: Cambridge University Press.

Barlow Commission. 1940. *The Report of the Royal Commission on the Distribution of the Industrial Population*, Cmnd. 6153. London: HMSO

Cairncross, A.K. 1949. Internal migration in Victorian England. *The Manchester School*, 17, 67-87

Cairncross, A.K. 1953. *Home and Foreign Investment, 1870-1913*. Cambridge: Cambridge University Press

Chambers, J.D. 1957. *The Vale of Trent, 1670-1800*, Supplement 3 to *Economic History Review*. Cambridge: Cambridge University Press

Chambers, J.D. 1972. *Population, Economy and Society in Pre-industrial England.* London: Oxford University Press

Champion, A.G. 1976. Evolving patterns of population distribution in England and Wales. *Transactions, Institute of British Geographers*, new series, 1, 401-20

Coates, B.E. and Rawstron, E.M. 1971. *Regional Variations in Britain.* London: Batsford

Deane, Phyllis and Cole, W.A. 1969. *British Economic Growth, 1688-1959*, 2nd edn. Cambridge: Cambridge University Press

Dennis, R.J. 1977. Intercensal mobility in a Victorian city. *Transactions, Institute of British Geographers*, new series, 2, 349-63

Department of the Environment. 1971. *Long Term Population Distribution in Great Britain – a Study.* London: HMSO

Eversley, D.E.C. 1971. Population change and regional policies since the war. *Regional Studies*, 5, 211-28

Flinn, M.W. 1970. *British Population Growth 1700-1850.* London: Macmillan

Friedlander, D. 1969. Demographic responses and population change. *Demography*, 6, 359-81

Friedlander, D. 1970. The spread of urbanization in England and Wales, 1851-1951. *Population Studies*, 24, 423-43

Friedlander, D. 1973. Demographic patterns and socio-economic characteristics of the coal mining population of England and Wales in the nineteenth century. *Economic Development and Cultural Change*, 22, 39-51

Friedlander, D. and Roshier, R.J. 1966. A study of internal migration in England and Wales, Part I. *Population Studies*, 19, 239-79

Glass, D.V. 1938. Changes in fertility in England and Wales. In *Political Arithmetic*, ed. L. Hogben. London: Allen and Unwin

Glass, D.V. 1951-2. A note on under-registration of births in Britain in the nineteenth century. *Population Studies*, 5, 70-88

Glass, D.V. 1973. *Numbering the People.* Farnborough: Saxon House

Glass, D.V. and Eversley, D.E.C. (eds.) 1969. *Population in History: Essays in Historical Demography.* London: Edward Arnold

Habbakuk, H.J. 1971. *Population Growth and Economic Development since 1750*. Leicester: Leicester University Press

Hall, P. *et al.* 1973. *The Containment of Urban England*, 2 vols. London: Allen and Unwin

H.M. Treasury. 1976. *Rural Population. Report by an Inter-departmental Group*. London: HMSO

Howe, G.M. 1970. *National Atlas of Disease Mortality in the United Kingdom*, 2nd edn. London: Nelson

Krause, J.T. 1958. Changes in English fertility and mortality, 1781-1850. *Economic History Review*, second series, 11, 52-70

Law, C.M. 1967. The growth of urban population in England and Wales. *Transactions, Institute of British Geographers*, no. 41, 125-43

Law, C.M. 1969. Local censuses in the eighteenth century. *Population Studies*, 23, 87-100

Law, C.M. and Warnes, A.M. 1976. The changing geography of the elderly in England and Wales. *Transactions, Institute of British Geographers*, new series, 1, 453-71

Lawton, R. 1962. Population trends in Lancashire and Cheshire from 1801. *Transactions of the Historical Society of Lancashire and Cheshire*, 114, 189-213

Lawton, R. 1963. The journey to work in England and Wales: forty years of change. *Tijdschrift Voor Economische en Sociale Geographie*, 54, 61-9

Lawton, R. 1964. Historical geography: the industrial revolution. In *The British Isles: a Systematic Geography*, eds. J.W. Watson and J.B. Sissons, Ch. 12. London: Nelson

Lawton, R. 1967. Rural depopulation in nineteenth-century England. In *Liverpool Essays in Geography*, eds. R.W. Steel and R. Lawton, pp. 227-55. London: Longmans

Lawton, R. 1968. Population changes in England and Wales in the later nineteenth century. *Transactions, Institute of British Geographers*, no. 44, 55-74

Lawton, R. 1977. People and work. In *The U.K. Space: Resources, Environment and the Future*, ed. J.W. House, 2nd edn. London: Weidenfeld and Nicolson

Lawton, R. (ed.) 1978. *The Census and Social Structure: an Interpretative Guide to Nineteenth-Century Censuses for England and Wales*. London: Cass

Lawton, R. and Pooley, C.G. 1976. The social geography of Merseyside in the nineteenth century. Final report to the SSRC, Department of Geography, University of Liverpool. Available through the British Library, Lending Division

McKeown, T. 1976. *The Modern Rise of Population*. London: Edward Arnold

Mitchell, B.R. and Deane, Phyllis. 1962. *Abstract of British Historical Statistics*. Cambridge: Cambridge University Press

Musgrove, F. 1963. *The Migratory Elite*. London: Heinemann

Newton, M.R. and Jeffrey, J.R. 1951. *Internal Migration*. General Register Office, Studies in Medical and Population Subjects, no. 5. London: HMSO

Osborne, R.H. 1964. Population. In *The British Isles: a Systematic Geography*, eds. J.W. Watson and J.B. Sissons. London: Nelson

Ravenstein, E.G. 1885. The laws of migration. *Journal of the Statistical Society*, 48, 167-235

Redford, A. 1964. *Labour Migration in England, 1800-1850*, 2nd edn. Manchester: University of Manchester Press

Saville, J. 1957. *Rural Depopulation in England and Wales, 1851-1951*. London: Routledge and Kegan Paul

Teitelbaum, M.S. 1974. Birth under-registration in the constituent counties of England and Wales: 1841-1910. *Population Studies*, 28, 329-43

Thomas, B. 1954. *Migration and Economic Growth: a Study of Great Britain and the Atlantic Economy.* Cambridge: Cambridge University Press

Thomas, B. 1972. *Migration and Urban Development.* London: Methuen

Vince, S.W. 1952. Reflections on the structure and distribution of rural population in England and Wales, 1921-31. *Transactions, Institute of British Geographers,* no. 18, 224-33

Waugh, M. 1969. The changing distribution of professional and managerial manpower in England and Wales between 1961 and 1969. *Regional Studies,* 3, 157-69

Webb, J.W. 1963. Natural and migrational components of population change in England and Wales, 1921-31. *Economic Geography,* 39, 130-48

Welton, T.A. 1911. *England's Recent Progress. . .in the Twenty Years from 1881 to 1901.* London: Chapman and Hall

Willatts, E.C. and Newson, Marion G.C. 1953. The geographical pattern of population changes in England and Wales, 1921-1951. *Geographical Journal,* 119, 432-50

Zelinsky, W. 1971. The hypothesis of the mobility transition. *Geographical Review,* 61, 219-49

3 REGIONAL VARIATIONS IN FERTILITY AND CHILD MORTALITY DURING THE DEMOGRAPHIC TRANSITION IN ENGLAND AND WALES

William Brass and Mohammad Kabir

3.1 Introduction

The objective of this chapter is to report the main results of an extensive study of the trends in fertility and child mortality in the regions and counties of England and Wales. The period covered by the study is from the establishment of vital registration, effectively in the fifth decade of the nineteenth century, to the present. The full examination and presentation of the data are contained in Mohammad Kabir's doctoral thesis. Here attention will be concentrated on the earlier stages of the demographic transition (say from around 1875 to 1915), although some use will be made of measures outside this range for comparisons. With this limitation of the period it can be assumed that the basic records of census and vital registration from which the measures are derived were of high accuracy, certainly relative to the purposes for which they are used.

In planned experiments nuisance influences can be eliminated to decrease heterogeneity and the factors of variation controlled and reduced to a few. In observational studies where this is not possible some of these benefits can be partially achieved by comparative analysis of groups in a similar overall environment but with local variations. This is the context of regional examination of demographic trends such as the one reported. By this means plausible conclusions about the determinants of change may be reached or, more realistically, certain hypotheses may be shown to be unlikely. In fact, the more specific aim of the study is the evaluation of the evidence of the effects of falling child mortality on fertility. There is an extensive literature, much of it from the medical profession, which claims that the reduction of child mortality has a major impact in the establishment of fertility falls. For a general review see CICRED (1975).

The strategy of the research was as follows. In the first instance England and Wales were divided into a reasonably small number of geographical regions, chosen as ten. Their size was fixed by the desire to reduce the effect of extraneous variability in the measures. Such variability obviously arises through random fluctuations from year to year but also from problems of migration and of where the event was registered (births and child deaths) in relation to the population at risk. The resulting measures were still too erratic and a smoothing procedure was introduced by taking five-year moving averages over each set of values. By this approach several yearly series of indices for regions were constructed with the properties desired, that is the trends were sufficiently 'noise' free and regular for their main characteristics, both internally and in relation to each other, to be perceived. It thus became possible to discern consistency properties. For the further examination of the validity of these properties it was necessary to turn to the corresponding sixty series of measures for counties where the populations in each group were substantially smaller and the random nuisance effects larger.

3.2 Measurements

One index of child mortality, the death rate under five years, was the focus of the analysis, although the incidences at under one and one to four years were also studied. The trends in these components have been substantially different and separate investigation is needed for a comprehensive description. However, since the features of the fertility-mortality interrelations which are the specific basis of the study were not notably different for the death rates under one and at one to four years, the aggregate index results are presented.

The simplest fertility measure calculated was the births in a year divided by the number of women aged 15-44 years, usually called the General Fertility (GF). Following Coale (1967), standardised indices of overall fertility, marital fertility and nuptiality, OF, MF and N were derived from:

$$OF = \frac{Births}{\Sigma w_i F_i}, \qquad MF = \frac{Births}{\Sigma m_i F_i}, \qquad N = \frac{\Sigma m_i F_i}{\Sigma w_i F_i}$$

Here w_i and m_i are the numbers of all women and currently married women in the ith five-year age group and F_i is a standard marital fertility rate for women of this age. Summation is over the reproductive period. The indices thus allow for the effects of varying age and nuptiality distributions over the reproductive period, weighted by the potential contribution to births per woman in a group, F_i. The identity $OF = N \times MF$ expresses overall fertility as the product of the nuptiality and marital fertility indices.

In the calculations of the unstandardised measures of mortality and fertility, populations at risk for inter-censal years were found by simple linear interpolation. The corrections for age and marital distributions were computed for census years and again linearly interpolated for the intermediate points. More elaborate and accurate methods could be used, but are not likely to be productive because of the other sources of erratic variation; and the concentration is on the broad sweep of change rather than the precise movement at any particular time.

In this outline mainly the cruder indices of mortality and fertility will be utilised with some reference to marital fertility and nuptiality. This is all that is required for the general findings, although a detailed examination of the standardised indices helps to refine and strengthen the picture. Only a small sample of the basic measures for selected years are presented for regions; none is shown for counties but the significant secondary analyses are discussed. The regions adopted are defined in Table 3.1. They were based on the classification of the 1851 census with some small modification to preserve consistency over the whole time range. Clearly, the identification of the population of a region by the same label over a century or so implies a conceptualisation with many implications which will not be fully considered here. The individuals in the population will change with births, deaths and migration. For the label to be useful, it must be assumed that there are cultural, economic and environmental factors in operation which determine the demographic trends and are differentiated by region in a consistent way over long periods. At present, it is sufficient to say that there is much evidence, particularly from the programme of study of the European Fertility Transition, centred on the Office of Population Research, Princeton University, that such assumptions are valid (Coale, 1973; Knodel, 1974; Livi-Bacci, 1971).

3.3 Fertility Trends

The outstanding features of fertility change by region have a simple structure sufficiently indicated by Table 3.2. Note that the years given are the central ones of averages over five years, as explained above. Prior to 1876 there were fluctuations but no consistent trends (certainly not downwards). This is clearly shown by the comparison of the peak levels with those of 1876. The maximum difference for any region is less than 3 per cent and the average around 1 per cent. In the decade following 1876 there were considerable falls in the General Fertility, averaging about 1 per cent per year, except in the Eastern region, where there was a slight postponement. Marital fertility behaved

Table 3.1: Definition of Regions

No.	Region	Counties
1	London and South-Eastern	London, Kent, Middlesex, Surrey, Sussex.
2	Eastern	Bedford, Cambridge, Isle of Ely, Essex, Hertford, Huntingdon, Norfolk, Suffolk.
3	Midland	Hereford, Shropshire, Staffordshire, Warwickshire, Worcestershire.
4	North-Western	Cheshire, Derbyshire, Lancashire.
5	North Midland	Leicester, Lincoln, Northampton, Nottingham, Peterborough, Rutland.
6	Northern	Cumberland, Durham, Northumberland, Westmoreland, North Riding, Yorkshire.
7	South-Western	Cornwall, Devonshire, Gloucester, Somerset, Wiltshire.
8	East and West Riding	East and West Riding, Yorkshire.
9	Southern	Berkshire, Buckinghamshire, Dorset, Hampshire, Oxford, Isle of Wight.
10	Wales	(13 counties)

similarly with a slightly lower rate of reduction and an additional sluggishness in the Southern region. There are, then, convincing reasons for locating the start of the fall in fertility in the quinquennium around 1876, effectively for all regions of the country in broad terms.

From around that time the fall was rapid and regular until the 1930s. The striking consistency of change is illustrated by the ratios of the 1928 levels to the 1876 ones. For the country as a whole general fertility in 1928 was 43 per cent of its 1876 value, with the regions ranging only from 41 to 47 per cent. Reductions in marital fertility were even more similar with ratios varying between 43 and 46 per cent. These characteristics can be brought out further by comparing the range of variation in levels in 1876 and 1928 and also by ranking the regions by the measures in these years as illustrated in Table 3.3.

In 1876 the highest general fertility level was 40 per cent greater than the mean for the lowest two; in 1928 for exactly the same regions in the same relative positions the excess was 33 per cent. Similar results held for marital fertility, with a lower range in 1876 but increasing to near equivalence with the general fertility value in 1928. For both indices the rank correlation of the measures at the two dates was 0.82. Thus the huge fall in fertility level over the fifty-year period hardly altered the regional hierarchy of values.

Table 3.2a: General Fertility per Thousand Women

	Region	Peak Year	Peak Level	1876	1885	Years 1898	1914	1928	Per Cent 1928/1876
1	London and South-East	1867	143	139	130	107	85	59	42
2	Eastern	1870	154	152	150	121	90	66	43
3	Midland	1876	174	174	153	134	100	74	43
4	North-Western	1876	163	163	144	119	91	67	41
5	North Midland	1878	165	165	155	129	94	70	42
6	Northern	1873	195	193	166	141	115	85	44
7	South-Western	1864	141	137	128	105	76	63	46
8	East/West Riding	1876	170	170	140	122	96	68	40
9	Southern	1865	148	144	136	107	83	67	47
10	Wales	1876	170	170	151	140	116	77	45
	England and Wales	1876	157	157	142	119	93	68	43

Table 3.2b: Marital Fertility Indices

	Region	1876	1885	Years 1898	1914	1928	Per Cent 1928/1876
1	London and South-East	700	674	575	454	311	44
2	Eastern	723	722	592	459	323	45
3	Midland	800	727	661	503	356	44
4	North-Western	770	697	602	461	335	44
5	North Midland	760	723	634	451	331	44
6	Northern	854	752	666	543	396	46
7	South-Western	729	699	580	418	321	44
8	East/West Riding	767	656	583	458	326	43
9	Southern	710	699	568	427	325	46
10	Wales	823	733	679	537	362	44
	England and Wales	754	700	602	470	341	45

The consistency in fertility falls by region from 1876 to 1928 does not mean that the changes were clearly parallel over all shorter time intervals. Apart from the slow starters from 1876 already mentioned, the Northern region, for example, experienced a fast decrease in the first ten years, slower than average over the next twenty and a modal decline subsequently. An inspection of measures at five-year intervals

Table 3.3: Rank Order of Fertility Levels

Region	General		Marital	
	1876	1928	1876	1928
1	9	10	10	10
2	7	8	8	8
3	2	3	3	3
4	6	6	4	4
5	5	4	6	5
6	1	1	1	1
7	10	9	7	9
8	4	5	5	6
9	8	7	9	7
10	3	2	2	2
Rank correlation	0.82		0.82	
Max./Min.	1.40[a]	1.33[a]	1.22	1.27

a. Regions 1 and 7 were treated as jointly lowest for general fertility because
   of their reversal of order from 1876 to 1928

reveals considerable variations in rates of change among regions but, as shown, these largely cancel out over the longer term. Thus the impact of the factors operating differed with the conditions of the particular period but the differences were in the timing and not the overall size of the fertility decline during the half-century.

3.4 Mortality Trends

The national and regional trends in child mortality were more complicated, as is illustrated in Table 3.4. Peak mortalities were recorded around the 1860s but some at least of the earlier rise was probably due to improving registration of deaths. In the period of interest there were quite substantial falls in death rates up to about 1885 (a 17 per cent decrease for England and Wales as a whole). Between then and 1898 there was little change. The turn of the century coincided with the initiation of the extremely rapid decreases in the child death rate which continued to the end of the time span considered. The general pattern of change was broadly similar in the regions but with more heterogeneity than for fertility. For example, although no region experienced reductions in mortality in 1885-98 which were other than modest relative to trends before and after, the Eastern and South-Western areas did show some fall as contrasted with

Table 3.4: Death Rate under Five Years per 10,000

Region	Peak Year	Peak Level	1876	1885	Year 1898	1913	1938	Per Cent 1913/1898	Per Cent 1938/1898
1 London and South-East	1865	729	629	603	582	340	116	58	20
2 Eastern	1863	579	472	475	442	200	82	45	19
3 Midland	1864	726	663	567	633	172	62	27	10
4 North-Western	1867	864	783	690	681	172	63	25	9
5 North Midland	1861	636	591	539	560	206	81	37	14
6 Northern	1873	745	694	580	599	298	93	50	16
7 South-Western	1864	571	510	469	423	169	74	40	17
8 East/West Riding	1870	798	752	618	641	199	61	31	10
9 Southern	1857	536	448	420	398	153	71	38	18
10 Wales	1857	594	592	537	582	316	148	54	25
England and Wales	1865	696	625	578	573	230	90	40	16

appreciable increases in several others, most notably the Midlands and Wales. Although, throughout, 1898 can be taken as the start of the dramatic decline, there were notable variations in the rates of fall among regions as can be seen from the percentages in the last two columns of Table 3.4.

The fact that the Midlands, North-Western and Yorkshire East and West Ridings did particularly well from high starting levels might suggest a consistent tendency towards equalisation, but inspection shows no regular relation between the 1898 mortality level and the percentage reductions by 1913 or 1938. This has been confirmed more rigorously from the measures for counties. The size of the mortality decline is not significantly correlated with the initial 1898 death rate. Nor was there an 'evening up' of levels among the regions. In fact the range of values, relative to the average, almost doubled between 1898 and 1938.

A further aspect of the same theme can be seen from the rankings of the regions by the child mortaility rates shown in Table 3.5. The small positive rank correlation between the values in 1898 and 1913 had become negative for 1898 to 1938, but neither is statistically significant. The 1913 to 1938 correlation is higher but does not suggest more than a modest relationship. In contrast to fertility, the trends for child mortality show that, although the factors determining the movements were broadly operating in the same way over all, there were diversities due to particular conditions. The specific features in the regions had a substantial influence on what was happening.

Table 3.5: Rank Order of Mortality Levels

Region	1898	1913	1938
1	6	1	2
2	8	5	4
3	3	8	9
4	1	7	8
5	7	4	5
6	4	3	3
7	9	9	6
8	2	6	10
9	10	10	7
10	5	2	1
Rank correlation	.16	.56	
		− .11	

3.5 Relations between Fertility and Mortality Trends

The investigation of relations among time series with sufficient rigour is a demanding task which will be attempted here by a number of simple approaches. Obviously the trends in fertility and mortality have common features, notably the steady declines from around 1900 onwards, but these by themselves give little if any help in the determination of the nature of the interactions. However, the ten regions form a sample for which the associations of level and change measures at points of time can be analysed. This is done here by rank correlation methods to avoid distributional problems which might arise from small numbers and outlying values. Ten measures are too few to lead to very firm conclusions, but the exploration suggests the further analyses of county indices which should be made. Kendall's τ coefficient is used with plus one and minus one showing perfect direct or inverse associations between the two rankings. Zero indicates a random relationship and (for ten measures) a numerical value greater than 0.5 would occur by chance, if there was no true association in fewer than 5 per cent of totals. Table 3.6 shows the rank correlations between the levels of child mortality and fertility for the five-year periods around census dates. Although correlations tend to be positive the direct association is clearly at most a weak one.

The relevant issue, however, is not the association between levels but between trends. The percentage changes over five-yearly intervals were calculated (these are from non-overlapping moving averages) and correlated between mortality and fertility. The question being asked, therefore, is whether movements over short intervals in the two indices tend to be related. The overall trend is eliminated by the procedure; in effect it is deviations from this trend which are being associated. The

Table 3.6: Rank Correlations between Fertility and Under-Five Death Rate in Regions

Year	General fertility	Marital fertility
1861	0.33	−0.11
1871	0.29	0.20
1881	0.16	−0.07
1891	0.20	0.07
1901	0.38	0.42
1911	0.38	0.47
1921	0.33	0.24

Table 3.7: Rank Correlations between Changes in General Fertility
and Child Mortality in Regions

Period of mortality change	Time advance of fertility in years				
	0	+5	+10	+15	+20
1863-8	0.24	0.29	−0.24	−0.42	−0.51[a]
1868-73	0.73[a]	−0.51[a]	−0.33	−0.20	0.73[a]
1873-8	0.24	0.64[a]	0.42	−0.51[a]	−0.51[a]
1878-83	0.51[a]	0.24	−0.24	−0.24	0.29
1883-8	0.11	0.47	0.20	−0.16	0.02
1888-93	0.73[a]	0.51[a]	0.33	0.38	0.29
1893-8	0.38	0.20	0.07	−0.16	0.02
1898-1903	0.51[a]	0.29	0.16	−0.47	−0.07
1903-8	0.42	−0.11	−0.47	0.07	−0.29
1908-13	−0.02	−0.16	−0.16	−0.16	0.07
1913-18	0.24	0.16	0.07	0.20	
1918-23	0.20	−0.33	−0.56[a]		
1923-38	0.56[a]	0.42			

a = significant at 5 per cent level.

analysis was carried out both for simultaneous measures and with time
lags. Thus '+5' signifies that the changes in mortality were correlated
with the fertility changes five years later. Since the nature and
implications of the results are similar for general and marital fertility
(although the individual values differ erratically) only the former are
displayed in Table 3.7.

The sample errors of the correlation coefficients are, of course, high
and a value over 0.5 is required for significance. Nevertheless, the
indications are clear enough. For the simultaneous occurrence of the
mortality and fertility changes, the correlations are (with a marginal
exception) positive and five of the thirteen are significant. The mean of
the thirteen values is 0.37 with a negligible probability of occurring by
chance if there is no true association. With a five-year time lag there is
still some tendency towards a positive association but one of the three
significant values is negative and the mean is only 0.16. With longer lags
no relation can be claimed. There are no signs of pattern differences by
periods within the time range. The tentative conclusions must be that
the factors determining changes in childhood mortality are operating
in some way to affect fertility at the same time. This does not of course
preclude complex and even spurious interactions between the

Table 3.8: Average Rank Correlations between Changes in General
Fertility and Child Mortality: Regions

Time displacement[a] (years)	Average correlation
−5	−0.02
−4	0.04
−3	0.12
−2	0.27
−1	0.32
0	0.34
+ 1	0.35
+ 2	0.32
+ 3	0.28
+ 4	0.23
+ 5	0.17

a. Plus is for fertility change later than mortality.
(Note: The small differences for 0 and +5 from the averages of the values in
Table 3.7 arise because they are here calculated on all single-year lags,
instead of only quinquennial observations.)

influential factors.

A further step is to examine time lags shorter than five years. The
results are summarised in Table 3.8. To reduce the sampling
fluctuations and display the patterns more clearly, the correlations
have been averaged. Since there are overlaps between the intervals of
change due to the moving average process, the measures are not
independent of each other. For example, a typical zero lag correlation
is for movement between 1861-5 and 1866-70 in both measures
whereas a +1 lag relates the child mortality rate of change between
1861-5 and 1866-70 with the fertility rate of change between 1862-6
and 1867-71. This smoothing is, in fact, convenient for tracing the
shape of the correlation curve with displacement of the timing of the
change measures.

As was to be expected from the previous evidence on longer lags,
the correlations are at their highest near to the point of zero
displacement, with a steady reduction with moves further away. It
would appear, in fact, that the central maximum is at about +1 rather
than zero. It is of interest to note that this would coincide closely with
a zero displacement if births were allocated to the date of conception
rather than parturition. Too much should not be made of this, however,

in view of the possible size of random errors.

The sixty county units provide a much larger sample, although the benefits in terms of the smaller sample errors of the correlation coefficients might be reduced by the more erratic fluctuations of the basic measures. The same procedures were applied to the county units as to the regional ones and the main results are summarised in Tables 3.9 and 3.10.

The simultaneous correlations average 0.36, which is a little lower than the corresponding value for regions over the same time range (0.45). But the 5 per cent significance level is now 0.18, which is exceeded by all the period correlations except one. The measures for the longer time lags are not shown since they display no features that alter the indications from the regional evidence. The pattern with short time displacement of Table 3.10 is again consistent with a maximum relationship around the zero point with some suggestion of a marginal shift in the peak towards a lag of fertility relative to mortality.

Although the mortality-fertility correlations are highest for simultaneous occurrence they are still considerable with time lags. To investigate more incisively the relative contributions partial rank correlation analyses were carried out. In these the measure for the relationship between a change in child mortality and a lagged change in fertility is adjusted to allow for the 'no displacement' association and vice versa. This eliminates the indirect effect of the correlation between changes in fertility in a county in near time periods. The key results are given in Table 3.11.

A shows the partial correlations with zero displacement when adjustment is made for the relation of mortality change to fertility change five years later and the corresponding values for the lagged association when the simultaneous relation is allowed for. B gives the same measures for ten-year displacements. The results accord well with expectation. The simultaneous correlations are little changed. For the ten-year displacements the residual correlation, once the simultaneous association is removed, is small and unsystematic; with a lag of plus five years there is still some residual, although the zero displacement relation is strongly dominant. The indications are, therefore, that the correlation between the mortality and fertility time series is determined by factors operating close to the period of change.

3.6 Nuptiality Relations

Comparison of correlations between childhood mortality and general fertility with those between childhood mortality and marital fertility

Table 3.9: Rank Correlations between Changes in General Fertility and Child Mortality in Counties (no time displacement)

Period of change	Correlation
1868-73	0.44
1873-8	0.09
1878-83	0.42
1883-8	0.22
1888-93	0.50
1893-8	0.51
1898-1903	0.45
1903-8	0.23

Table 3.10: Average Rank Correlations between Changes in General Fertility and Child Mortality: Counties

Time displacement	Average correlation
−5	0.10
−4	−0.05
−3	0.12
−2	0.20
−1	0.22
0	0.36
+ 1	0.30
+ 2	0.22
+ 3	0.24
+ 4	0.18
+ 5	0.16

Table 3.11: Partial Rank Correlations between Changes in Fertility and Child Mortality in Counties

Fertility change period	A No displacement	+5	B No displacement	+10
1873-8	0.10	0.02	—	—
1878-83	0.44	0.21	0.43	−0.28
1883-8	0.24	0.07	0.24	0.14
1888-93	0.52	0.16	0.50	0.03
1893-8	0.51	0.18	0.51	−0.04
1898-1903	0.43	0.15	0.45	0.04
1903-8	0.23	0.08	0.23	0.10

shows that the latter are, in general, rather the lower. It is not clear why this should be so and the effect may be a chance one. However, a closer inspection of the nuptiality component of the general fertility measures is justified. Table 3.12 gives the rank order correlations between marital fertility (MF) and the nuptiality index N for the regions in census years. The index N is calculated from the proportions of women currently married in each five-year age group as shown at the census. The correlations for the inter-censal changes are also shown.

There is a strong association between the levels of marital fertility and of nuptiality in the regions. Since the latter index is designed to measure exposure to risk, independently of rates of childbearing of those exposed, the analysis brings out the separate contributions of the two factors to the regional variations in general fertility. Thus the regions which have a high-risk exposure also tend to have high marital fertility, a family-favouring syndrome as it were. More specific to the present purpose, ther are also indications that changes in risk exposure as measured by the nuptiality index are related to changes in marital fertility.

Changes in nuptiality are correlated directly with movements in child mortality in Table 3.13. Although, not surprisingly, the correlations are erratic, two are individually significant at the 5 per cent level. The suggestion then is that decreases in childhood mortality are, to some extent, associated with simultaneous reductions in the proportions currently married as well as falls in marital fertility. When the two latter factors are combined in general fertility, the correlation is stronger, as noted at the beginning of this section.

Table 3.12: Rank Correlations between Marital Fertility and Nuptiality in Regions

Year	Levels	Period of change	Changes
1871	0.38	1871-81	−0.24
1881	0.42	1881-91	0.42
1891	0.47	1891-1901	−0.24
1901	0.60	1901-11	0.20
1911	0.60	1911-21	0.20
1921	0.60	1921-31	0.33
1931	0.47		

Table 3.13: Rank Correlations between Changes in Child Mortality
and in the Nuptiality Index in Regions

Period of change	Correlation
1861-71	0.56[a]
1871-81	0.24
1881-91	0.16
1891-1901	−0.24
1901-11	0.24
1911-21	−0.11
1921-31	0.51[a]

a. Significant at 5 per cent level.

3.7 Discussion

Although the study reported is essentially descriptive, the particular
configuration of the results has an important bearing on explanation.
It constrains the types of determinants, primarily of fertility fall, which
can plausibly be postulated. The examination of the evidence is most
conveniently organised by a consideration first of the narrower
objective of the research, that is the assessment of the impact of
changes in child mortality on fertility. It has been demonstrated that
there is a sizeable correlation between the short-term changes in child
mortality and fertility in areas but that this operates without an
appreciable time lag. There are some 'spill-over' relations when there
is displacement of the measures but the partial correlation analysis
reveals that these are small and only extend over a short time period.
It seems impossible to define any sensible mechanism by which changes
in childhood mortality can directly influence fertility occurring
simultaneously. As a minimum there would be a two- or three-year
delay from the death of a child to any effect on the next birth. More
plausibly the lag would be considerably longer if it depends, as has
been suggested, on the realisation by parents that with reduced child
deaths fewer births are required to meet their needs for surviving
offspring. There are other features which cast doubt on the hypothesis
that child mortality falls are a significant factor. The correlation
between the changes exist when consistent falls are not taking place.
In particular, between 1885 and 1898 fertility declined, but child
mortality rose in some areas and fell in others with little average change.
Thus the high correlations in this period reflect a relation of the smaller

decreases in fertility with rises in mortality. It is not easy to see how any causal effect could be postulated in such circumstances. The indications of an association between falls in child mortality and risk exposure within marriage further increases the plausibility of an explanation in terms of external factors modifying the demographic rates simultaneously.

Of course, the conclusion that a direct influence of child mortality on fertility cannot be detected does not rigorously rule out the possibility of diffuse effects operating with long lags and different timing in the regions. The fertility reductions after 1876 could have been prompted by the earlier falls in child mortality and continued from momentum to the end of the century, to be reinforced by the further rapid lowering of the death rates. The congruence of this explanation with the trends is, however, far from impressive. Here the barrier is the remarkable consistency in the timing and size of fertility declines in regions despite considerable diversity in child mortality, in initial levels and patterns of change, both in the earlier and later phases. All that is left is a tenuous concept in which child mortality falls contribute to the modification of attitudes, which are diffused over the whole country and form part of a web of determinants.

The possibility that the results can be interpreted in terms of direct effects of fertility on child mortality, through bio-social factors such as the nutrition and care of children in larger as compared with smaller families, can be dealt with more briefly. Again, time lags would be anticipated but on this hypothesis in the other direction with the mortality changes following the fertility movements. The comparatively low association between absolute levels of the two measures in areas is also a contra-indication. Perhaps the weightiest argument is the difficulty of formulating a quantitative description of how the relatively small changes in fertility in an interval could have such strong impacts on the child deaths.

The discussion of the specific issue leads to the broader one of the determinants of demographic and, in particular, fertility change. The strong, time-localised correlations of trends in areas are entirely consistent with the view that the causative factors were largely the same for fertility as for child mortality. The slight but very limited extension of the relationship outside the simultaneous occurrence of change indicates that the factors had some persistence but were, nevertheless, operating quite sharply within short periods. These findings fit in with views that economic and social development is the driving force with emphasis perhaps on the former as more likely to provide the pattern of time variation by areas which would suit the correlation structure. The configuration of trends in child mortality by regions seems entirely sensible in this scheme. It displays the temporal and spatial diversity which would follow logically from the variations in the type and pace of socio-economic change. There is, of course, a mass of evidence in favour of such an explanation. The fact that between 1875 and 1900 child mortality in, for example, South Wales, Nottingham and the East Riding of Yorkshire showed no decline, while it fell by some 30 per cent in Kent, Bedford and Oxford is no occasion for surprise.

But the fertility evidence is more complex. There is the striking paradox that despite the high correlations with child mortality trends, the regional diversity of the latter is not reflected in the former. The single most notable finding is the astonishing consistency of the falls in fertility by regions and the almost total preservation of the relative differentials of 1876, fifty years later. Although the uniformity is extreme, however, the continuation of historical differentials during the European fertility transition has been well established, particularly in the monographs on Italy by Livi-Bacci and Russia by Coale, which are in the course of publication. The only conclusion is that direct economic cum social factors have controlled the time-localised characteristics of fertility falls but that other determinants have dominated the long-term trends. These determinants have acted in a remarkably uniform way over the whole country without, however, destroying family-building behaviour which is particular to regions. An explanation in terms of changing social attitudes communicated rapidly throughout all areas seems the most likely. Of course this is an answer to one problem by changing it to another, namely the determinants of the social attitudes, and through this there is a return to the same socio-economic developments. But the record of failure in the attempts to explain the fertility transition in valid quantitative terms demonstrates that the wrong questions have been asked in relation to the data available. The problem needs redefinition. The lack of variation in the response of regions to the factors causing fertility decline (whatever these are) suggests that explanations are not to be found in sub-aggregate comparative studies, whether these be of regions, counties or even families. The close inspection of the details of differentiation will not reveal the influences which are common to all, and these appear to dominate. Adequate variation may only be obtainable from aggregates at national or near-national level. Cross-population studies have formidable difficulties but they may nevertheless provide the most promising research strategy for a better understanding of fertility determinants.

References

CICRED. 1975. *Seminar on Infant Mortality in Relation to the Level of Fertility.* Paris: Committee for International Co-ordination of National Research in Demography

Coale, A.J. 1967. Factors associated with the development of low fertility: an historic summary. In *Proceedings of the World Population Conference, 1965,* vol. II, pp. 205-9. New York: United Nations

Coale, A.J. 1973. The demographic transition reconsidered. In *Proceedings of the International Population Conference, Liege,* vol. 1, pp. 53-72. Liege: International Union for the Scientific Study of Population

Knodel, J. 1974. *The Decline of Fertility in Germany.* Princeton: Princeton University Press

Livi-Bacci, M. 1971. *A Century of Portuguese Fertility.* Princeton: Princeton University Press

4 REGIONAL AND TEMPORAL VARIATIONS IN ENGLISH HOUSEHOLD STRUCTURE FROM 1650

Richard Wall

4.1 Introduction[1]

One possible approach to any new research is to concentrate on the national picture, however roughly it has to be delineated. Without repeating all of the initial work by Peter Laslett into the structure of the English household, it is appropriate to reaffirm that the English household of pre-industrial times was typically small (mean household size 4.75), its structure simple (few kin), that there were large numbers of servants (30 per cent of households contained them), but surprisingly few children (the mean size of offspring group was 2.7). Some years have elapsed since this comprehensive account of the English pre-industrial household was first published (Laslett, 1969) during which time it has advanced into something approaching a stereotype, more particularly in regard to mean household size, to be applied to all manner of English communities regardless of location or time period. The purpose of the present paper is to attempt a correction by charting variations in household size and structure between the seventeenth and nineteenth centuries and between one part of the country and another. The problem is that the lists of inhabitants which provided Mr Laslett with the information on households with kin and the number of resident children are strung out in date (the earliest 1574 and the latest 1821), and only at rare moments is it possible to find a number of neighbouring settlements surveyed together. One such opportunity occurs at the end of the seventeenth century where the operation of the Marriage Duty Act has left a number of lists which divide the population into households. Some quirk of the administration has resulted in more of these documents surviving for urban areas than is warranted by their actual contribution to the total population of the country at this date. Nevertheless there are sufficient rural survivals to permit urban-rural comparisons and allow an estimate of whether variations in household structure between different parts of the country are likely. First, however, I want to consider the question of a shift in household composition during the period in which, along with many other changes, England moved from a position of population stagnation to one of population growth.

4.2 The Structure of the Household over Time

It has come to be generally recognised that the second half of the
seventeenth century saw little if any growth in the population and that
the late eighteenth century saw sustained growth. At the level of the
individual parish it can be demonstrated that the change involved a
move from late age at first marriage, low fertility and high mortality
to a regime with a much lower age at marriage, higher fertility and
lower mortality. In the case of Colyton, for example, age-specific
marital fertility for women aged 30-34 rose from 272 to 347 births
per 1,000 woman years lived between the late seventeenth and late
eighteenth centuries. At the same time mean age at first marriage for
women fell from 28.8 to 26.4 and mortality for the age group 1-4 fell
from 113 to 75 per 1,000. There is some uncertainty about the course
of adult mortality but this was probably also in decline (Wrigley, 1966,
1968). The results from other, so far unpublished, reconstitutions and
more approximate measures derived from tabulations of baptisms,
marriages and burials of 404 English parishes provide general
confirmation. Between the late seventeenth and late eighteenth
centuries there would appear to have been an increase in the number
of children born per marraige of approximately a third, while child
mortality fell, as did adult mortality, though more modestly
(information, R.S. Schofield). These developments are critical because
of the powerful impact they must have exerted on both the marital
and age composition of the population.

As far as age structure is concerned, very little can be said directly
given the lack of information on ages in the lists of inhabitants (only
half a dozen lists give complete information on this prior to 1800).
We have therefore to concentrate on marital status with such rough
indications as it affords of changes in age structure, for example in the
proportion of the population celibate. If the demographic framework
that was sketched in above is no more than approximately correct one
would anticipate, comparing the late eighteenth century in relation to
the late seventeenth, an expansion of the proportion celibate and a
concomitant decline in the proportion widowed and married. It might
further be posited that the fall in the proportion widowed would
exceed the fall in the proportion married, since fewer marriages would
be broken by early death. There are, however, complicating factors.
The lowering of the age at first marriage will have reduced the
proportion celibate, countering in part the consequences of the

increase in fertility. Secondly, the lengthening of the period of marriage may conceivably have promoted an alteration in the position in society of the widowed who would, in the late eighteenth century, be represented by a considerably older population than had been the case earlier and may therefore have found it less easy to remarry.

If we now look at the first of the tables with these points in mind it will be seen that the changes between pre- and post-1750[2] accord with the original expectation, revealing a rise in the proportion single, and with the fall in the proportion widowed exceeding that of the married. What we were not able to predict was that the fall in the proportion who were married would be steeper for males than it was for females (Table 4.2). This implies a rise in the sex ratio (number of males per 100 females) in the widowed and single population. In fact other figures, not reproduced here, show a rise in the sex ratio of the child population; one of the main, though not the only components (because of servants and a few celibate adults) of the single population. For this there is a simple enough explanation. Masculinity is highest at birth and declines with age. Other things being equal, a rise in the birth rate as occurred in the late eighteenth century will increase the proportion of younger age groups and consequently the proportion of males in the population. This applies both to the child population on its own as well as to the population as a whole.[3]

It is important, however, to add a rider to these results and others to be presented later in this section of the paper. To make these comparisons it is necessary to group such lists as have survived into two broad categories according to whether the enumeration was before or after 1750. The division is an extremely simple one and makes it impossible to observe when these changes occurred but in practice it is very doubtful whether sufficient lists exist for this purpose. Secondly, it has to be emphasised that most of the measurements are in the form of a mean. For example, the percentage married or the mean size of the household has been calculated for each settlement and an average taken of these figures and no claim is being advanced here for a universal seventeenth- or eighteenth-century pattern or even for a uniform move from one to the other. The third qualification that has to be made stems from the fact that the settlements examined in the two periods are not identical.[4] In theory it is conceivable that the two groups always differed, that there is no change over time, and that supposing all the enumerations had taken place in 1750 the differences would stand exactly as they appear in the tables. Yet in practice it is extremely unlikely that the lists would

Table 4.1: Marital Status of the Population (per cent)

Population	Period I 1650-1749 30 settlements Period II 1750-1821 29 settlements		
	Period I	Period II	Per Cent Change
Single	58.4	62.4	+6.8
Married	34.8	32.4	−6.9
Widowed	6.9	5.2	−24.7

All figures are for means of the percentages for individual settlements.

Table 4.2: Percentage of Each Sex Married

	Period I 30 settlements Period II 29 settlements		
	Period I (1650-1749)	Period II (1750-1821)	Per Cent Change
Male	36.4	32.9	−9.7
Female	33.5	32.1	−4.2

All figures are for means of the percentages for individual settlements.

divide in such a way and although the difficulty remains of like not being compared with like there is some comfort to be gained from the fact that most changes which one is seeking to identify ought to be of sufficient magnitude and frequency to be observable in distinct communities.

All these points have had to be borne in mind as we pass from considerations of shifts in the age and marital composition of the population to the structure of the household and family. The two are, of course, closely connected. For example, the fall in the percentage of widowed in the population could result in a reduction in the percentage of small households, if to live on one's own was the norm for the widowed. Alternatively, if the norm was incorporation into the households of kin then a reduction in the number of complex households could be expected. From the rise in fertility one might predict, all things remaining equal, a rise in the mean size of the offspring group, that is in the number of children of whatever age who live with their parents. Of course, customs may have changed in response to different demographic circumstances. For example, a rise in the size of the child group might encourage children to leave home at a somewhat younger age than had previously been the case, reinforcing the trend towards earlier marriage. Nor should one exclude the possibility of norms undergoing change without any demographic push. The household might therefore have been modified in a number of different ways during this period. Table 4.3 sets out what actually occurred.

The selection of the household and population characteristics was deliberately catholic within the general constraint of information being available for a reasonable number of settlements from each of the time periods (1650-1749 and 1750-1821).[5] In the table the characteristics are ranked according to the variation that occurred between the two periods and divided into three completely arbitrary groups according to whether the rate of change was in excess of 20 per cent, fell between 10 and 19 per cent, or was under 10 per cent. The most dramatic modifications concerned the presence in the household of kin and servants and the number of households headed by women. In Laslett and Wall (1972) it was established that kin were more prevalent in mid-nineteenth-century households than they were in pre-industrial ones. The figures in Tables 4.3 would suggest that the trend was established before the end of the eighteenth century but it would be difficult to argue in favour of the change being 'significant', given that only a small minority of households contained kin (still under 13 per cent even in the second period). More remarkable in my opinion is the fall in the percentage of households with a female head. Since four out of five women heading households were widows, the fall is best seen in the context of the decline in the percentage widowed in the population. It is, however, the consequences of this change that need careful consideration. One possible interpretation of the fact that women were less often in charge of a household after 1750 might be that they now played a less important role in society. Such an argument, however, is fraught with difficulties given that so little is known about the rigidity of sex roles and, in particular, whether there were any tasks of economic consequence which a woman was able to pursue relatively unhindered when her husband was head of the household. This objection would also apply if one were to adopt the opposite position and argue that the help or direction the widow may have received from others when widowed rendered her only nominally independent.

The third substantial change comparing 1650-1749 with 1750-1821 concerns servants, but the fall in proportions over time is to some extent simply an artifact of the inclusion of some London parishes in

Table 4.3: Changes in Household Size and Composition, 1650-1821

Characteristic	Period I (1650-1749) N		Period II (1750-1821) N		Per Cent Increase	Per Cent Decrease
Percentage households of 3+ generations	28	4.9	29	7.0	42.8	—
Percentage servants in population	29	18.4	31	10.6	—	42.4
Percentage households with servants	30	39.3	32	26.6	—	32.3
Percentage resident kin in population	24	3.2	18	4.2	31.2	—
Percentage households with resident kin	23	10.3	18	12.9	25.2	—
Percentage households headed by women	34	18.3	32	13.9	—	24.0
Percentage children in population	30	37.6	29	45.6	21.2	—
Mean size of sibling group	32	2.49	31	2.97	19.3	—
Percentage households headed by single, widowed men and men of unknown marital status	34	11.5	32	13.4	16.5	—
Percentage persons in households of size 1-3	43	18.7	50	16.6	—	11.2
Percentage households of 1 generation	28	26.7	29	23.9	—	10.5
Percentage households 6+ persons	43	32.5	50	35.1	8.0	—
Percentage households with children	32	71.1	31	76.7	7.9	—
Percentage households 1-3 persons	43	36.5	50	34.0	—	6.9
Percentage persons in households size 6+	43	51.3	50	53.9	5.1	—
Percentage persons in households size 4-5	43	29.7	50	28.9	—	2.7
Mean household size	45	4.75	50	4.86	2.3	—
Percentage children + servants in population	26	55.3	28	56.3	1.8	—
Percentage households of 2 generations	28	68.4	29	69.2	1.2	—
Percentage households 4-5 persons	43	30.9	50	30.8	—	0.3

All figures are for means of the figures for individual settlements. The number of settlements used in each calculation is indicated in the appropriate N column.

the first time period but not the second. Remembering that most servants were young (most were between 15 and 25 according to Laslett, 1977) there should be little surprise that the lower the percentage of servants in the population, the higher the percentage of children and the mean size of the sibling group. The real surprise, bearing in mind that there was a rise in the proportion of the population single, must be that the proportion which servants and children together constitute of the total population should vary so little between the two periods. The 'surplus' single persons are therefore not offspring or servants but heads of their own households and, though probably to a lesser extent, kin (see the reference below, p. 99, to the increase in the number of children appearing in the lists as grandchildren).

At the same time, however, it would be wrong to gloss over other less obvious changes. The increase in the size of the sibling group may seem unremarkable but further analysis (not reproduced in Table 4.3) reveals it involved a fall in the proportion of 'only' children of 35 per cent and a rise of children living in groups of five of 30 per cent and in groups of 7 or more of 200 per cent. Secondly, concerning servants, it is worth pointing out that their proportion in the population fell faster than did the proportion of households with servants. It follows, therefore, that in the second period households were managing with fewer servants.[6]

Leaving the question of servants, I want to consider briefly those characteristics where, if one adopts the arbitrary grouping of Table 4.3, the amount of change was minimal. Included in this category are the percentage of households headed by married couples, the percentage of households that consist of two generations, and almost all the mean measures of household size. The changes that have been identified occurred, therefore, without any overall shift in the size of the household. It would be misleading, however, to rely entirely on percentage change as in Table 4.3, since these percentages are themselves based on two further percentages, one for each period, whose values also have to be taken into consideration. What seems an important development, such as the growth in the number of households composed of three or more generations, in fact concerns only a small minority of the population. Conversely, an apparently less significant change as the rise of 7 per cent in households with children affects a much larger number of households.

Another reason for some uncertainty about the amount and type of change to the household between the late seventeenth and late eighteenth centuries arises from the range of variation between

individual settlements. Take, for example, the question of kin. Even in
the post-1750 period it is possible to find settlements with almost no
kin at all,[7] whereas in others kin accounted for more than 10 per cent
of the population. The range in the percentage of households with
servants is even greater. In a quarter of settlements enumerated between
1750 and 1821 there were fewer than 18 per cent of households with
servants, while in another quarter more than a third of the households
had servants. These distributions with others as set out in Table 4.4
suggest a rather greater amount of change than was evident from the
mean figures alone. In fact, not only is the increase in the numbers of
kin and in the size of the offspring group confirmed but in the case of
household size, for example, it emerges that in the post-1750 period
there were fewer settlements with low mean household sizes .
(particularly under 4) but that upward movement in the distribution
was countered by a decline in the number of settlements with large
mean household sizes. It also follows that the distribution of
settlements by mean household size was much narrower than it had
been earlier. The tendency for the communities to be more diverse
before 1750 is also noticeable in regard to the size of the sibling group,
the percentage of households with servants and proportions married.
On the other hand, with kin and with the proportion of servants who
were male, the greater differences between settlements were registered
after 1750. It is pertinent also to enquire whether, in comparing
1650-1749 with 1750-1821, changes at the lower end of the
distribution were more important than those at the higher end. In the
case of the size of the sibling group, it is clearly the former, while with
servants it is the latter, the absence of the London parishes in the
second period being no doubt the critical factor.

Whether it is possible to identify areas of the country with a
distinctive household structure is something that is considered further
below. First I want to make a quick comparison with the mid-
nineteenth century using the data provided by Hall (1974) and Ebery
and Preston (1976) as well as the analysis of household structure
contained in the Report on the Census of Great Britain (1851). It is
worth pointing out that the two latter included a selection of widely
dispersed settlements (though not a true random sample) and that we
may have some confidence in the typicality of the findings. In Table 4.5
mean figures for various attributes of the household in the mid-
nineteenth century are set alongside those of the seventeenth and
eighteenth centuries, revealing the very considerable changes that had
occurred even by 1851, affecting not only kin, but servants and

Table 4.4: Distribution of Settlements by Household Size and Composition

	Period I (1650-1749) Percentage of Settlements					Period II (1750-1821) Percentage of Settlements				
	10	25	50	75	90	10	25	50	75	90
Children										
Mean size of sibling group	2.02	2.17	2.52	2.73	3.05	2.54	2.66	2.92	3.23	3.38
Servants										
Percentage households with servants	18	25	30	48	74	14	17	22	33	44
Percentage servants male	41	45	51	63	65	35	40	53	58	64
Kin										
Percentage kin in population	2	2	3	3	4	1	3	4	6	7
Percentage households 3+ generations	0	1	3	5	13	0	3	6	10	14
Marital status										
Percentage males married	27	32	33	39	43	26	31	33	35	40
Percentage females married	27	30	31	34	41	25	30	32	35	37
Percentage widowed	4	5	7	8	9	3	4	5	7	8
Household size										
Percentage households size 4-5	25	28	31	33	37	20	27	30	34	38
Percentage households over 5	19	25	32	38	47	26	30	35	40	44
Mean household size	3.92	4.22	4.68	5.06	5.71	4.27	4.49	4.75	5.21	5.41

Table 4.5: Servants, Kin and Children 1650-1871

	Period I (1650-1749)	Period II (1750-1821)	1851	1861	1871
Servants					
Percentage in population	18.4	10.6	—	8.1	—
Percentage of households with servants	39.3	26.6	19.8	—	15.5
Percentage servants male	52.7	49.7	—	—	7.4
Percentage sole servant in household	21.0	35.3	—	—	63.5
Kin					
Percentage in population	3.2	4.2	—	9.3	—
Percentage households with kin	10.3	12.9	20.8	—	19.0
Children					
Percentage in population	37.6	45.6	—	38.8	—
Mean size of sibling group	2.49	2.97	2.63	—	—
Mean household size	4.75	4.86	—	4.81	4.56

All figures are means of the figures for individual settlements unless otherwise indicated.

Sources: Period I: Table 4.3, apart from the percentage of servants male (N = 29) and sole servants in household (N = 28). Period II: Table 4.3, apart from the percentage of servants male (N = 31) and sole servants in household (N = 31). 1851: Ebery and Preston, 1976. N = 17 (servants) N = 20 (kin). Mean size of sibling group is overall mean calculated from Census of Great Britain (1851) N = 14. 1861: Hall, 1974. N = 15. 1871: Ebery and Preston, 1976. N = 20.

children as well. Reduction in the percentage of households with servants reflects the increasing tendency for service to represent domestic service and, characteristically, feminine employment, whereas in the pre-industrial times it had encompassed agricultural and other workers who lived with, and worked for, a master. It is important to recognise, however, that this is not just a change in nomenclature and that farm workers were not present in the households of their Victorian masters under another name. Turning to kin, it can be emphasised again that the rise in the percentage of households with kin is also dramatic, dwarfing earlier changes. It is something which transcends economic boundaries, rural communities such as Elmdon in Essex (Robin, 1973), and urban ones such as Ashford, Kent, and Preston, Lancashire (Pearce, and Anderson, 1972), producing percentages of households with kin considerably up on pre-industrial levels.

However, not all the characteristics of the household in the mid-nineteenth century were so novel. Mean household size followed no consistent trend, whereas it has been argued for Austria that the transference of the unit of production from family to factory ushered in a dramatic decline in mean household size (Mitterauer, 1977). The evidence also suggests that by 1851 the percentage of children in the population had fallen below that experienced during the period 1750-1821. Even though we are dealing only with children resident with their parents (or parent) and not for instance with children ever born, this seems somewhat surprising given the notions that prevail about the large size of some Victorian families. There is need for caution, however, in that the figure for 1851 is available only as an overall mean and may be unduly representative of a few major towns where smaller groups of children were more common (compare below). In addition, the second set of data on children in the nineteenth century relates only to Derbyshire. There is no reason to think of this area as being exceptional, but it could have been so.

To progress further it would be necessary to take into consideration more information than is currently available. The lack of an occupational dimension is much to be regretted and will be difficult to fill for the pre-industrial period. More information is needed too on the ages of the children at home, the percentage of households headed by widows and the 'new kin'. In the case of the last of these, the available evidence points in a number of contradictory directions. In the first place it can be demonstrated (as in Table 4.3 above) that households spanning three generations, that is households composed of grandparent and grandchild with or without the presence of the intervening generation, were more prevalent after 1750 than they had been before. Yet if one looks at the few nineteenth-century communities where the kin group has been analysed in depth (Anderson, 1972; Armstrong, 1974; and Lees, forthcoming) and, anticipating a little, compares the shape of the kin group in the seventeenth century, it is clear that grandchildren do not predominate to any greater extent than they did earlier. Indeed one might go further and claim that the composition of the entire kin group had not changed between the seventeenth and nineteenth centuries. One problem, however, is the large size of the 'other kin' (exact relationship unknown) for the pre-industrial period. Depending on how these were distributed amongst the various categories of kin, there might have been some change to one or more of these. Some of the unknowns might have been nephews and nieces of the household head who feature prominently in the more detailed nineteenth-century censuses and who constitute at first sight the one clear new element in the composition of the kin group. Otherwise, despite its expansion, the kin group of the nineteenth century seems in its essential elements identical to the much smaller group of the late seventeenth century with even the balance between the various categories of kin largely unchanged over time. The only qualification to be made is that as more censuses in the nineteenth century are investigated, it will be possible to look more closely at the kin group, suggesting perhaps certain adjustments to the picture presented here.

4.3 Variations in Household Composition across Five Areas in 1700

In 1695 enumerations were made of the inhabitants of the parish of Bury St Edmunds St James, and Barbon, Westmoreland. Ringmore in Devon was listed in 1698; Ash-next-Sandwich, Kent, in 1705. In all, 108 lists of inhabitants are known to survive for the period 1695-1705 outside the two cities of London and Bristol which are comprehensively covered. Yet this is not a large number in relation to the total number of ancient parishes (about 10,000) and some of the lists are for settlements within parishes rather than whole parishes. In addition, the quality of the lists varies. Some fail to distinguish between one household and another or include a number of people of unspecified relationship to the head of the household. Other lists are complete except for the fact that bachelors and widowers above the age of 25, and subject to a special tax, were listed separately. It is true, of course, that a list without information on kin might still contain valuable information on children, if the descriptions are adequate, but it is impossible to take account of them here as the household needs to be seen in its entirety.

A further important consideration arises from the fact that many of the places for which lists survive are very small. Only when a number of neighbouring communities are listed at the same time can one hope to distinguish the chance patterns of a parish from those which typify an area. In practice this means that it is possible to examine household structure in just two rural areas, East Kent and East Wiltshire, and three urban ones, the city of London, Shrewsbury and Southampton. An analysis of regional variation in household structure is therefore a non-starter, and it is the differences between these areas that have to be our concern. In particular we shall attempt to discover whether urban and rural areas are associated with a distinctive household structure. It is appropriate also to ask whether, within the urban element,

Shrewsbury can be distinguished from London or from Southampton, or, taking the rural element, whether the household in Kent differs from the household in Wiltshire. Descending a further level, one might also look for variations in household structure between one part of a town and another. There can be little doubt that these were considerable, reflecting some of the differences between social classes (for a demonstration of the importance of the latter nationally, see Laslett and Wall, 1972). However, the difference in the sizes of the respective towns and the lack of occupational detail, except in the case of Shrewsbury, make it a difficult matter to pursue, but it is one that we should keep in mind as we make the comparisons between areas. First, however, it is necessary to describe these in more detail.

The coverage of London being so much fuller (the City only, it should be noted, since there are no surviving lists for Middlesex parishes), a selection of parishes was made using random number tables. This was a particularly important process since we have reason to believe that the original sample of London parishes (Laslett and Wall, 1972) was biased in favour of central and wealthier parishes. On this occasion, therefore, the parishes were first grouped according to the proportion of 'substantial' households, that is, those liable for the higher rates of marriage tax (Glass, 1966). This ensured a representative selection of poor as well as rich parishes. It would, however, not be appropriate to claim that all levels of society are accurately represented in our London population, since the distribution of the various social classes in London is much less easily obtained than that of parishes of various types. There is also the further complication that the two poorest parishes, St Ann, Blackfriars, and St Botolph, Bishopsgate, were so large that a second sample had to be taken based this time on the number of pages in each document. (Approximately every fifth page was used in St Ann's and every tenth in St Botolph). An estimate of the total population within the sample is 23 per cent (St Ann) and 10 per cent (St Botolph).

The remainder of our five areas also pose a number of problems. Southampton is covered except for St Michael and part of All Saints but not all the lists come from the same year. Shrewsbury, on the other hand, lacks some, though not all, of the suburbs.[8] As for Wiltshire and Kent, it has to be remembered that although rural, they were not exclusively given over to farming. Ash in Kent, for instance, was a populous parish though not a market town, supporting a sprinkling of trades including five victuallers, three maltsters, a glazier and a tallow chandler. Similar minor urban functions may have existed at Wroughton in Wiltshire, though in the absence of precise occupational information it is impossible to be certain. The inclusion in our sample of Wroughton and Ash is justified in that they played a key role in the rural economy. In the context of our collection of rural lists, however, they may conceivably distort the balance between small and large settlements.[9]

With these points in mind we can now set out the principal components of the household in each of our five areas (Table 4.6). If any one area stands out, it is London with more lodgers and servants, but fewer children than the rest. In the Kent parishes a larger than average proportion of children in the household pushes up mean household size to 4.6, but generally mean household size is on the low side even in respect of communities enumerated between 1650 and 1749 (compare Table 4.3 above). Nowhere did kin constitute an important element in the household.

This is worth stressing as we turn to look at this group in more detail. The small numbers involved make it difficult to determine whether there were important differences between the five areas,[10] particularly in relation to the various categories of kin. All that can be said is that it would be very difficult to argue in favour of such variation from these figures. Instead it is the similarities that are noteworthy. Given that wives were frequently a little younger than their husbands and that the differential effect of mortality also tended to work in favour of females, there should be little cause for surprise that mothers more frequently feature amongst kin than fathers. That females should so heavily outnumber males among kin is more surprising.[11] In this connection it is interesting that no one relationship predominates. Most of the close kin (mothers, siblings and grandchildren) are all well represented, despite the fact that their proportion of the total is probably an understatement because there is a lack of precision about detailing kin relationships which swells the numbers of 'other' kin.

It is worth pausing for a moment to consider the rather different situation in the nineteenth century. The one clear example of differences in household structure between urban and rural areas is that which Michael Anderson has suggested for Preston and the rural Lancashire from which it drew its migrants. According to Anderson (1972, p. 224; 1971, pp. 44, 84), while households with kin were to be found in approximately equal proportions in both areas, Preston was characterised by stem families, defined as two or more lineally related married persons with their nuclear families, if any, and the countryside by composite families, that is other combinations of kin. Amongst

Table 4.6: Mean Membership of Households and Housefuls[a]:
5 Areas *c.* 1700

Household membership	Kent	Wiltshire	Southampton	Shrewsbury	London
Head (and spouse where present)	1.8	1.7	1.6	1.6	1.8
Offspring	2.0	1.7	1.6	1.7	1.2
Kin	0.1	0.1	0.1	0.2	0.1
Servants	0.7	0.3	0.5	0.5	1.3
Mean household size	4.6	3.8	3.8	4.0	4.4
Attached lodgers	0.1	0.1	0.2	0.5	1.7
Mean houseful size	4.7	3.9	4.0	4.5	6.1
Total households	455	292	435	1,112	771
Total persons	2,158	1,133	1,745	5,041	4,673

a. The houseful includes lodgers as well as all members of the household. See
Laslett and Wall, 1972.

Table 4.7: Size and Composition of the Kin Group: 5 Areas *c.* 1700

Percentage of Kin[a]	Kent	Wiltshire[c]	Southampton	Shrewsbury	London
Households with kin	5.5	7.9	7.4	8.3	8.3
Kin in population	1.6	3.4	3.0	2.6	2.2
Kin, mothers	26.4	0.0	15.4	8.5	13.5
Kin, fathers	8.8	0.0	0.0	3.1	2.9
Kin, siblings	17.6	21.4	23.0	14.6	23.0
Kin, son/daughter-in-law	2.9	10.7	3.8	5.2	2.9
Kin, grandchildren	29.4	32.1	23.1	42.3	8.6
Kin, other[b]	14.9	35.7	34.7	25.3	49.1
Sex ratio	30.8	81.0	52.9	52.9	65.1
Total kin	34	38	52	130	104

a. Kin are defined as the relatives of the head of the household apart from spouse
and offspring (including stepchildren). Terms such as 'fathers' do not therefore
represent the total number of fathers in the lists but the number with that
relationship to the household head.
b. e.g. kinsman, kinswoman.
c. In Uffcott all 10 kin relationships are ill-defined and are therefore excluded
from calculations relating to the various types of kin.

these, parentless grandchildren, in the sense that parents were not present in the same household, were particularly important. The water is somewhat muddied, however, by other urban areas that have been studied. Mid-nineteenth-century York, for example, lacked the son-in-law and daughter-in-law element that was such a prominent feature in Preston (Armstrong, 1974, p. 188). That leaves, therefore, the large number of grandchildren found in rural Lancashire as the sole candidate for a distinctive feature of rural society, since these levels have not been surpassed in any of the urban communities so far studied. Clearly, however, many more communities must be investigated before urban-rural differences in household structure can be identified.

The marital status of household heads and numbers of children in the household (Tables 4.8 and 4.9) have attracted relatively little of the attention that has been focused on kin, though involving much larger sections of the population. It is curious, therefore, that it is here that we begin to notice some differences between the five areas. In Southampton, for instance, almost a quarter of all households were headed by widows, whereas in the rural areas they amounted to less than 10 per cent of the total. In respect of those specifically said to be widows, urban-rural differences were quite marked. If, however, one looks at all the non-married heads of households, this ceases to be the case, although important differences between the areas remain.

These calculations take no account of widowers, and widows and persons of unknown marital status who headed lodging groups. Given that these groups were generally smaller than the households to which they were attached, it seems likely that a rather lower proportion of these groups compared to the household proper were headed by married couples. Reference back to Table 4.6, however, shows that it is only in Shrewsbury and London that lodgers form an appreciable section of the population. The effect of their inclusion, therefore, would be to increase rather than lessen urban-rural difference in respect of the proportion of 'domestic groups' headed by unmarried persons.

Much the same situation arises in the case of children. Southampton, Shrewsbury and Kent resemble each other closely in the percentage of households with children, as do the Wiltshire and London parishes. On the other hand, a study of the mean size of the sibling groups shows that the number of children at home was considerably higher in the country areas than in the towns.[12] Even though exact interpretation is impossible without information on fertility, mortality and age structure, it is tempting to seize on this factor as pointing to a considerable

Table 4.8: Marital Status of Heads of Households: 5 Areas c. 1700

Percentage of Households Headed by:	Kent	Wiltshire	Southampton	Shrewsbury	London
Married couples	80.2	66.7	58.6	67.5	74.1
Widowers	5.3	6.8	7.8	4.9	5.9
Widows	8.8	9.6	24.1	18.5	12.5
Single males	2.0	4.4	4.1	2.2	4.7
Single females	0.4	1.0	0.2	1.2	0.8
Males of unrecorded marital status	2.0	5.8	1.8	4.2	0.8
Females of unrecorded marital status	1.3	5.5	3.4	1.5	1.2
All non-married	19.8	33.3	41.4	32.5	25.9
Total households	455	292	435	1,112	771

Table 4.9: Comparison of the Child Population: 5 Areas c. 1700

Children	Kent	Wiltshire	Southampton	Shrewsbury	London
Percentage households with children	73.8	64.0	71.3	71.6	62.3
Percentage children in population	41.8	45.7	43.5	40.6	26.0
Percentage children + servants in population	58.4	53.3	55.6	51.5	46.9
Percentage offspring groups size 1	31.8	27.4	28.7	33.6	46.0
Mean size of offspring group	2.6	2.7	2.4	2.4	1.9
Mean experienced size of offspring group[a]	3.5	3.7	3.0	3.2	2.4
Total children	901	518	759	2,046	1,216

a. Obtained by weighting each size category by the number of children within it, see Laslett and Wall, 1972, p.409.

urban-rural difference in the experience of the growing child within the home environment. To some extent, however, it detracts from what deserves to be the main finding, which is the abnormally low percentage of children in the London population. Indeed it is so low that even with the addition of London's numerous servants the proportion of 'young' persons in the population fails to rise to the level of other areas (Laslett, 1977). It may perhaps be queried whether such proportions are genuine, or whether there has not been some omission of children as, for example, occurred in two of the Marriage Duty Act returns for Swindon. (That for 1697 was complete but those for 1701 and 1702 were not; Wall, 1976.) This is something which is impossible to settle without much detailed work linking together families in the lists with families in the registers. At this stage all that we aim to do is to emphasise that these figures are for individuals described as children by the list-maker and that they do not include surviving offspring when living elsewhere either as servants or lodgers. We also have a little evidence of certain families placing children and servants in lodgings in Kensington while they continued to reside in the heart of the city.[13] If this practice was at all common amongst wealthy families, it could help to explain some of the low figures for the child population of central London.

Finally we turn to servants (Table 4.10). Their importance in London's population is clear, but it is Kent that stands closest to London in regard to the percentage of servants in the population. However, it is too easy to be impressed by this overall similarity in percentages when in fact the composition of the servant group was subject to important variations. In Southampton and Shrewsbury, for instance, approximately a third of servants were solitary; in Kent only 7 per cent were. Secondly, within the towns the majority of servants were female. This is most noticeable in the case of Shrewsbury, whereas in Wiltshire the sexes were evenly balanced, and in Kent male servants outnumbered females by more than two to one. In respect of the percentage of servants solitary and percentage female, seventeenth-century urban areas seem to anticipate the servant keeping of the country as a whole in the nineteenth century. Yet the resemblance is largely superficial. Seventeenth-century London and Southampton had many more households with servants than did settlements of the nineteenth century, nor was the solitary servant so prominent as was to be the case later. There are signs, moreover, of considerable differences in the nature of the young work-force which would be worth exploring in more detail by looking at the sex ratios of both the

Table 4.10: Servants: 5 Areas c. 1700

Servants	Kent	Wiltshire	Southampton	Shrewsbury	London
Percentage households with servants	24.8	14.0	26.2	30.0	58.0
Percentage servants in population	16.6	7.6	12.1	10.9	20.9
Percentage servants in groups size 1	7.2	19.8	32.7	36.6	23.3
Mean size of servant group	3.2	2.1	1.7	1.6	2.1
Mean experienced size of servant group[a]	4.1	3.0	2.3	2.2	2.9
Sex ratio	226.5[b]	100.0	91.6	70.6	84.8
Total servants	359	86	212	551	976

a. See note to Table 4.9.
b. Sex specified for 271 servants. Excludes Barfristone, Guston, Little Mongeham and Wootton and 13 servants in Ash.

servant and child populations in the context of the employment
opportunities within and outside the parental home and the amount of
social differentiation in society. Unfortunately it is impossible to
proceed further with the present data because the Kent lists do not as
a rule distinguish children according to sex. One would expect, however,
that in an area where a high percentage of servants were males, there
would be rather more girls than boys at home (unless of course the
former had moved to other settlements). One important hypothesis to
test would be that the movement of servants from their home of origin
to the home of their employer represented the movement of labour
from where it was surplus, or incapable of full exploitation.

To conclude, it is necessary to urge caution. The limitations imposed
by areal coverage and reliability are obvious ones, but we should
perhaps add a third, because the data in Tables 4.6-4.10 are in the form
of overall means. To break down the various areas into their constituent
parts (parishes or tithings in the case of all except Shrewsbury, where
arbitrary divisions were imposed) does blur the differences between
them in that it is possible to find, for example, a Wiltshire hamlet with
a proportion of servants in the population that equals those in some of
the wealthier London parishes. In such a case the argument would
presumably be that distinctions in household structure within areas are
greater than those that occur between them. It is, however, worth
observing that our sole concern here is with the structure of the
household in each area considered as a whole, and that internal
differences between rich and poor are unimportant. This, of course, is
always assuming that the right balance between them has been
maintained during the process in which various lists were rejected on
the grounds of incomplete information. In the case of London and
Shrewsbury this should be so; but in Southampton some 1,000 people
were excluded in parishes where the surviving lists were of poor
quality. There are difficulties, too, with the rural areas in that the
correct balance between settlements of various sizes may not have
been achieved. The only way out of the impasse would be to examine
some of the other, more imperfect lists that survive for the various
areas, and how much useful information this would provide must be
uncertain.

4.4 Conclusion

In conclusion, it has to be decided whether the inter-area variations
ought to be regarded as significant. The evidence on this is equivocal.
Some key measures, size of sibling group, for example, show

variations between areas while others, such as percentage of children
in the population, do not, with the exception, of course, of London.
Indeed it seems to us that the only clear candidate for an area with a
distinct household structure is London itself, because of the relative
frequency of lodgers and servants and relative infrequency of children.

At the same time this should not be allowed to obscure the fact that
at almost the same time, mean household size was 4.6 in Kent and only
3.8 in Wiltshire; that less than two-thirds of the Wiltshire households
contained children compared with nearly three-quarters of the Kent
ones. This might seem unimportant viewed from a German perspective
where it has been shown (Berkner, 1977) that in 1689 in one large area
within Hanover 7 per cent of the households contained kin while in
another almost adjacent part, the comparable figure was 30 per cent.
This, however, requires one to rely on the frequency of kin to define
what constitutes important variation between areas, and there seems
no reason at present why some other factors such as the number of
children residing at home, for example, should not be accorded equal
consideration.

Rather similar issues are raised when we return to consider the
question of changes in the form of the English household between the
seventeenth and nineteenth centuries. No dramatic change seems to
have occurred and certainly nothing on the scale that Berkner (1976
and 1977) has found for a group of Hanoverian villages where, in less
than seventy years, households which included kin increased from 7 to
33 per cent. Nevertheless there was undoubtedly some change and this
involved children and servants as well as kin. In order to understand,
we must look in closer detail not just at the number of children who
left home but the age at which they made this break and the type of
households where they found positions as servants. Clearly the changes
are too great to be ignored. Even while it remains relatively robust
to the major demographic push of the eighteenth century, the
English household was not static. Nor, given the variations between
area and area, would it be correct to see English households as
variations on one basic type. At any one time, of course, the majority
of households consisted of parent(s) and unmarried children, but this
is far from being the most interesting or relevant fact about the
English household.

Appendix: List of Settlements Included in the Analysis of Variations in Household Structure in 1700

Settlement	Households	Population
East Kent. Enumerated 1705		
Adisham	22	125
Ash Chilton	150	728
Ash Overland	95	454
Barfreston	12	50
Buckland	19	107
Fronghamborough	27	100
Guston	20	80
Little Mongeham and Ashley Borrow	36	162
Shepherdswell	32	160
Womenswold	23	107
Wootton	20	85
East Wiltshire. Enumerated 1701 unless otherwise indicated		
Chiseldon (1705)	41	160
Elcombe	12	63
Liddington (1705)	61	230
Uffcott	20	91
Westlecott	24	111
Wroughton (1700)	134	478
Southampton. Enumerated 1697 unless otherwise indicated		
All Saints without Barr	101	376
Holy Rhood	185	730
St John (1696)	40	147
St Lawrence (1696)	62	300
St Mary (1695)	45	192
Shrewsbury. Enumerated 1698		
Castle Ward	442	1,999
Stone Ward	323	1,470
Welsh Ward	347	1,572
London. Enumerated 1695		
All Hallows Staining	148	847
St Ann, Blackfriars	85[a]	667[a]
St Botolph without Bishopsgate	176[b]	1,005[b]
St Ethelburga	131	644
St Mary Bothaw	56	324
St Mary Le Bow	106	693
St Mary Woolchurch	69	483

a. 23 per cent sample.
b. 10 per cent sample.

Notes

1. This chapter is a shortened version of my paper presented to the joint British Society for Population Studies and Institute of British Geographers Population Geography Study Group conference in Liverpool on 21-23 September 1977. My thanks are due to my colleagues in the Cambridge Group for their comments on an earlier draft, and in particular to Peter Laslett for permitting access to his computer runs of 1967 and to Margaret Escott, who, as research assistant to the SSRC Cambridge Group during 1975-6, analysed the data on regional variations in the household.

2. The median years of enumeration of all settlements (not just those involved in this particular calculation) are 1695 and 1787 (see note 4).

3. I would like to thank John Hajnal for drawing my attention to this point. The sex ratio of the child population would also be influenced by a change in the age gap between spouses on first marriage, but what evidence there is on this point suggests that in this respect the late seventeenth century differed little from the late eighteenth (Wrigley, 1976).

4. A full list of the settlements is to be found in Laslett and Wall, 1972, where they are divided into three periods. Periods I and II as defined in this paper appear as periods II and III in the earlier study. The median years of enumeration are 1695 and 1787 respectively. The inclusion of some London and Kent parishes in the period 1650-1749 but not in 1750-1821 causes problems. So does the large block of Westmorland parishes in the latter. Other biases probably exist but are not so obvious, although it will generally follow that the smaller the number of settlements for which information is available (in Table 4.3 the smallest numbers arise in the calculations involving kin in period II), the greater the chance of an unrepresentative result. The median year of enumeration is likely to experience similar variation.

5. Apart from lack of detail in the lists, not all characteristics were selected for analysis when the tables, completed by hand for each list then in the collection, were processed in the computer in 1967 (see Laslett and Wall, 1972). Since 1967 further lists have come to light and some new tables devised; also we have a much clearer idea of the key elements in the structure of the household. When time permits it is our intention to rework this data set in the light of current interests and in fact the material presented in section 4.3 is the outcome of such a revision.

6. Servants who were solitary (i.e. the sole servant in the household) rose from 21 to 35 per cent of all servants between periods I and II.

7. Every effort has been made to exclude lists of doubtful quality, particularly those which contain a number of persons whose relationship to the head of the household was not specified. In addition, lists which contained no reference to kin were excluded from any calculation relating to kin. Although there may be a danger in this of overestimating somewhat the numbers of kin, comparison over time should not be vitiated.

8. Included are the suburbs of Castle Foregate, Old Heath, Cotton Hill and Gravel Hill and excluded are the suburbs of Frankwell, Coleham and Abbey Foregate. Mr W.A. Champion of the University of Leicester, who has carried out an independent analysis of the Shrewsbury lists, has drawn my attention to the fact that the suburban households are on average smaller than urban ones and that in Abbey Foregate a lower percentage of households have servants than in the town as a whole. However, since no Middlesex parishes can be included in the analysis of London, comparison is perhaps best served by concentrating on the central area of Shrewsbury.

9. Ash has 245 households out of the Kent total of 455 and Wroughton 134

of the Wiltshire total of 292. A full list of the constituent settlements of each area is given in the Appendix.

10. The Kent figures, which are on the low side compared with the rest, might perhaps be revised upwards to take account of some grandchildren, nephews and nieces who cannot be distinguished from offspring (see below, note 12). For the same reason the sex ratio of kin is probably lower than would otherwise be the case.

11. A married son living with his parent(s) does not constitute kin for the purposes of Table 4.7. However, the relative infrequency of daughters-in-law should be noted.

12. Some caution is advisable in interpreting the figures on offspring for Kent because many of these lists named the household head but only provided a total for the number of children. Therefore a number of kin may be counted as offspring, e.g. grandchildren, nephews and nieces.

13. See, for example, Corporation of London Record Office MS. 40/114 Estreats, entries, 3, 22, 28.

References

Anderson, M. 1971. *Family Structure in Nineteenth Century Lancashire*, pp. 136-61. Cambridge: Cambridge University Press

Anderson, M. 1972. Household structure and the industrial revolution: mid-nineteenth century Preston in comparative perspective. In *Household and Family in Past Time*, eds. Peter Laslett and Richard Wall, pp. 221-4. Cambridge: Cambridge University Press.

Armstrong, A. 1974. *Stability and Change in an English County Town. A Social Study of York 1801-1851*, pp. 175-94. Cambridge: Cambridge University Press.

Berkner, L.K. 1976. Inheritance, land tenure and peasant family structure: a German regional comparison. In *Family and Inheritance. Rural Society in Western Europe 1200-1800*, eds. Jack Goody, Joan Thirsk and E.P. Thompson, pp. 71-95. Cambridge: Cambridge University Press

Berkner, L.K. 1977. Peasant household organisation and demographic change in Lower Saxony (1689-1766). In *Population Patterns in the Past*, ed. Ronald D. Lee, p. 63. New York, San Francisco and London: Academic Press

Census of Great Britain, 1851. *Population Tables*, I, Appendix to Census Report, Table 14, p. cii. Parliamentary Papers 1852-3 [1361] LXXXV

Ebery, M. and Preston, B. 1976. Domestic service in late Victorian and Edwardian England, 1871-1914. *Geographical Papers*, no. 42, Table 24, p. 66. University of Reading: Department of Geography

Glass, D.V. 1966. London inhabitants within the walls, 1695. *London Record Society*, 2, p. xxiii

Hall, R. 1974. Occupation and population structure in part of the Derbyshire Peak District in the mid-nineteenth century. *East Midland Geographer*, 6, p. 77

Laslett, P. 1969. Size and structure of the household in England over three centuries. *Population Studies*, XXIII, pp. 199-223

Laslett, P. 1977. *Family Life and Illicit Love in Earlier Generations*, pp. 31-5, 43-5, 193. Cambridge: Cambridge University Press

Laslett, P. and Wall, R. 1972. *Household and Family in Past Time*, pp. 24-32, 86-9, 129-31, 154, 409. Cambridge: Cambridge University Press

Lees, L. (forthcoming). Irish migration to London in the mid-nineteenth century

Mitterauer, M. and Sieder, R. 1977. *Vom Patriarchat zur Partnerschaft* pp. 94-119. München: C.H. Beck

Pearce, D. Ashford 1840-1870. A socio-demographic study. Undated typescript in the Library of the SSRC Cambridge Group for the History of Population and Social Structure, p.3

Robin, J. 1973. Elmdon: household composition 1861. Typescript in Library of the SSRC Cambridge Group of the History of Population and Social Structure, p. 2

Wall, R, 1976. Society and the sexes in an English town: Swindon in the seventeenth century. Unpublished paper in the Library of the SSRC Cambridge Group for the History of Population and Social Structure, Table 5, p. 10

Wrigley, E.A. 1966. Family limitation in pre-industrial England. *Economic History Review*, second series, XIX, no. 1, pp. 87, 89

Wrigley, E.A. 1968. Mortality in pre-industrial England: the example of Colyton, Devon, over three centuries. *Daedalus* (Spring), pp. 558, 560-2

Wrigley, E.A. 1976. Changes in the age of marriage. Paper presented to XIII International Congress of Genealogical and Heraldic Sciences, London, September 1976

PART TWO: FERTILITY

5 DEVELOPMENTS IN THE INTERPRETATIONS OF RECENT FERTILITY TRENDS IN ENGLAND AND WALES

John Simons

5.1 Introduction

While recent fertility trends in England and Wales have, like reproductive behaviour in general, defied attempts at definitive interpretation, some important contributions to understanding have been made. The trends and their relationships with other demographic phenomena have been the subject of illuminating analyses. In addition, some interesting exploratory work has been done on the nature of connections between fertility change and changes in circumstances and in prevailing ideas about childbearing. Some of the major developments are reviewed below. The chapter concludes with a consideration of the problem of analysing and interpreting changes in ideas about childbearing.

A fundamental point to be made at the outset is that any explanation of the course of recent fertility in England and Wales is unlikely to be valid if it cannot be applied to the many other countries which have experienced similar trends recently. Shown in Figure 5.1 is the behaviour of the total fertility rate in England and Wales since the Second World War. Also shown is the behaviour of the rates in Belgium, France, the Netherlands, Sweden and the two Germanies. The similarity of the curves, especially since the mid-1960s, is striking, and this phenomenon is not limited to Europe. Campbell (1974) identified 18 developed countries with populations of over 2 million which recorded a post-war rise in fertility above the levels of the 1930s, lasting at least to the early 1960s. These countries included those of Northern and Western Europe, Australia, New Zealand, Canada and the United States. During the later 1960s, declining fertility was almost universal among the eighteen countries.

5.2 Details of the Trends in England and Wales

Shown in Table 5.1 is the trend of completed family size for women married between 1861 and 1956. Fertility declined substantially in the period: from a mean of 6.2 children for women married in the 1860s to a mean of 2.1 children for women married in 1931. Mean family size

Table 5.1: Mean Completed Family Size (women married once only),
England and Wales, 1861-1956

Year of marriage	Mean completed family size	Year of marriage	Mean completed family size
1861-9	6.2	1911	2.8
1871	5.9	1921	2.4
1881	5.3	1931	2.1
1890-9	4.1	1941	2.0
1900-9	3.3	1951	2.2
		1956	2.3[a]

a. Marriage duration 17 years.
Sources: OPCS, 1976, and (for the 1956 figure) OPCS, 1975.

fell slightly for the marriages of the 1930s but began to rise for wartime marriages of the 1940s. The rise continued after the war.

Evidently, as far as average completed family size is concerned, there is very little trend to interpret between the 1930s and the 1950s, though these averages summarise a considerable range in fertility by age at marriage. For example, after 15 years of marriage, women marrying at ages under 20 in 1956 had a mean family size of 2.8 children. The comparable figures for those marrying at ages 20 to 24 and 25 to 29 were 2.3 and 2.1.

These figures for mean family size do not reveal the volatility in the annual rates for the period. To interpret this phenomenon, and to study fertility over a period too recent for ultimate family size to have been achieved, it is necessary to turn to measures of current fertility. As is clear from Figure 5.1, the main features of the English total fertility rate (the sum of the age-specific rates) since the war are the boom starting in the mid-1950s and the decline starting in the mid-1960s. Shown in Figure 5.2 are age-specific rates since the war. These show that the principal contribution to the 1950s boom was made by women aged 20 to 29. Rates for women in this age group rose rapidly after having moved downwards in the early 1950s. Women in the age group 30 to 34 also contributed modestly to the trend.

The changes in the age-specific rates have been associated with marked changes in the pattern of family formation. Marriage has become increasingly popular and has occurred at younger ages. Recent trends have been summarised by Leete (1976). The percentage of

Figure 5.1: Total Fertility Rate, England and Wales and Selected European Countries, 1946-76

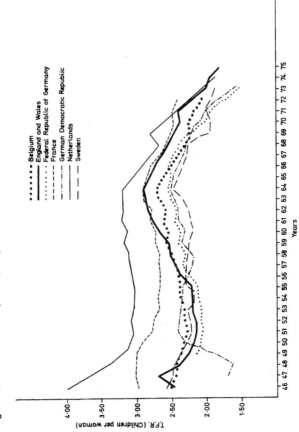

Source: Economic Commission for Europe, 1975, for most of the period.

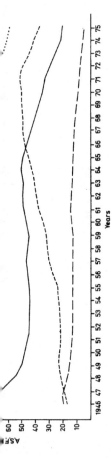

Source: Economic Commission for Europe, 1975, and *Population Trends* (OPCS, London), no. 7.

women aged 20 to 24 who had ever married almost doubled between 1939 and 1961: from 34 per cent to 59 per cent. Marriage rates in this age group reached a peak in 1970 but have subsequently declined.

The description of changes in the level and timing of marital fertility since the early 1950s falls naturally into two parts: first, the growth period between the mid-1950s and mid-1960s, and then the period of decline since 1964.

The cohorts of the middle 1950s had achieved higher family sizes after 15 years of marriage than the completed family size of any marriage cohort since 1925. Another important characteristic of the growth period was a tendency for childbearing to start earlier and to be concentrated into a shorter span. The shift to earlier childbearing was also apparent in the proportion of brides pregnant on their wedding day. From the mid-1950s, the proportion increased from 15 per cent of all spinster brides in 1955 to 22 per cent in 1967. (Campbell found, for the 18 developed countries he considered, that more than half the rise in the TFR from the lows of the 1930s to the highs of the late 1950s was due to increases in the TFR of women below age 25 years.)

The fertility patterns of women married in every single year since 1951 have been analysed in detail by Farid (1974). In the growth stage, there was a downward trend in the frequency of childless and single-child families, a significant shift to two- and three-child families, and even a slight shift to four-child families.

The analysis shows that the upward surge commenced in 1956 and affected most cohorts at childbearing ages. The analysis also shows the extent to which the childbearing period became compressed. For example, 45 per cent of one-parity women married under 45 years of age had a second child within 5 years of marriage in 1951. This figure rose to 52 per cent for the 1956 cohort and to 60 per cent for the 1963 cohort.

The upward trend reached its peak in 1964. From about 1963, the parity-specific rates stopped rising for nearly all cohorts and durations of marriage. In 1965 they began to fall, and continued to do so. The decline started with women in the older childbearing age groups, of longer marriage durations and higher parities, and subsequently spread to almost all groups. The decline at the longer durations could be at least partly explained by the tendency of earlier cohorts to complete their families earlier in marriage. However, there was also a general decline in parity progression ratios beginning with the 1964 cohort. Women married since the late 1960s have shown a tendency to postpone having the first child and to have longer intervals between

Table 5.2: Relationship of Regional to National Crude Birth Rate,
1931-1975

Year	Crude birth rate, England and Wales	Number of Standard Regions where local crude birth rate[a] differs by more than 5 per cent from national rate	Greatest difference (per cent) between any regional crude birth rate[a] and the national rate
1931	15.8	3	6
1941	14.9	2	11
1951	15.5	3	14
1961	17.6	1	9
1966	17.7	0	4
1971	16.0	2	7
1975	12.3	0	5

a. Adjusted rates, using area comparability factors, have been used where available: for all years from 1951 onwards. No adjustments have been made to take account of the several boundary changes made to the Standard Regions over the period.

Source: *Registrar-General's Statistical Review of England and Wales* for years 1931 to 1971 and, for 1975, OPCS, 1977.

successive births. The proportion of brides pregnant at marriage fell from 22 per cent in 1967 to 16 per cent in 1973. Between 1963 and 1970, the proportion of one-parity married women who had a second child within 5 years of marriage fell from 60 per cent to 54 per cent. In sum, the current evidence indicates a decline in mean ultimate family size and a slower pace of family formation.

Birth rates appear to have behaved similarly in all the regions of the country over the past few decades. Shown in Table 5.2 are the number of Standard Regions where the local crude birth rate has differed by more than 5 per cent from the national rate for various years from 1931 to 1975. In every year the number was 3 or fewer. Also shown in the table is the difference from the national rate of the region which differed most. Apparently the deviants have not been very deviant, and have become less so over the period.

5.3 The Relevance of Circumstances

One way of approaching the problem of interpretation is to seek connections between post-war and long-term trends. This is Campbell's (1974) approach. He points out that the long-term decline of marital fertility in the developed countries of Northern and Western Europe was a product of relatively late marriage, which restricted fertility at the younger childbearing ages, combined with the reduction in marital fertility in the nineteenth and twentieth centuries. The trends culminated in the relatively low rates at all childbearing ages during the 1930s. He sees the more recent trend towards sharply higher fertility rates at the younger childbearing ages as a result 'in part' of the continuation and acceleration of the long-term movement towards earlier marriage and reliance on the control of fertility within marriage by contraception, abortion and sterilisation. As another source of influence on post-war trends, he refers to improved economic conditions and the assumption of greater responsibility by national governments for many of the costs associated with parenthood:

> These social and economic supports for child rearing may not have increased completed fertility greatly, but they have probably made it possible for many couples to begin their families earlier and for higher proportions of couples to marry and have any children.

Campbell does not specifically address the problem of interpreting the decline since the 1960s.

Glass too interprets post-war trends in terms of historical trends. Comparing the marriage cohorts of 1931 and 1956, he says that while some 30 per cent of the increase in the average number of live births per married woman at 10 years' duration of marriage could be accounted for by the fall in age at marriage (a fall which continued after 1956), the remaining 70 per cent 'must reflect a rise in the number of children wanted by couples', for it occurred while increasing proportions of couples were using birth control, initiating its use at an earlier stage in married life, and shifting from less to more effective techniques of contraception. He suggests that the post-war trends in this country support Ryder's contention in respect of fertility trends in the United States during a comparable period: that there had not been a change in family size targets or norms, but rather a fulfilment of the norms which, but for a massive economic depression, would also have been achieved by the marriages of the 1930s (Ryder, 1969; Glass, 1976). He goes on to argue that this would imply that 'at least temporarily' the long-term decline in fertility had more or less exhausted itself by the 1930s, and that marriage rates could rise substantially and the rise be maintained just because small-family norms had become firmly established, with more effective means of achieving them, and a social climate in which the use of the means had become fully legitimate.

Glass reviews various factors which could help to explain fertility decline in England and elsewhere. These include easier access to more effective techniques of birth control, public discussion of birth control and population problems, expansion of secondary and higher education, continued increase in the employment of married women, and some amelioration of the poverty which tended to separate some groups from the rest of the community. For the future, he speculates that while there might be a further decline in fertility, it would probably not be large because childlessness was not attractive to many married couples and because the one-child family was also unpopular.

Writing in 1971, Tabah was more inclined to see post-war fertility trends as manifesting a fundamental change in the social structure of West European societies:

> it may be that a new kind of demography, a reflection of industrial and post-industrial societies is growing up before us and that the drop in fertility and its apparent homogeneity are only a stage in the transition from one to another (Tabah, 1971).

His view seems to have been prompted primarily by the apparently changing relationship in European countries between fertility and socio-economic level: from one that was clearly negative to a relation that was more U- or J-shaped, with higher fertility being characteristic of groups towards the top and at the bottom of the socio-economic scale. Tabah suggests that this could be an intermediate stage, and that eventually the relationship could become positive. The most recent findings for England and Wales are shown in Figure 5.3, which is based on 1971 census findings reported by Pearce and Britton (1977). According to them, all social classes have participated in the fertility decline, but there does not appear to have been a significant narrowing of differentials.

Tabah is confident that one reason for a fall in fertility among the lower-paid is the inverse relationship between family size and standard of living. The magnitude of the effect in this country has been demonstrated by analyses of data collected by the Family Expenditure Survey. The results of recent studies are summarised by Moss (1976). Taking as a standard an income equivalent to twice the Supplementary Benefit level[1] for each household, an analysis of the 1974 FES data showed that 65 per cent of households with children had incomes

Figure 5.3: Average Family Size after 15-19 Years of Marriage (women married once only) by Social Class of Husband, England and Wales, 1971

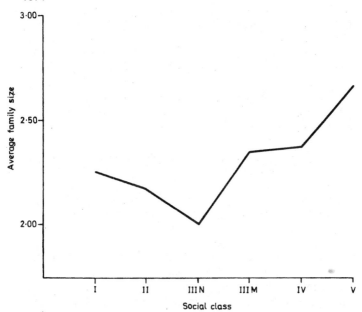

Source: Pearce and Britton, 1977.

below this standard, compared to 38 per cent of childless, non-pensioner families. Among households with children, 76 per cent of those with 3 or more children fell below the standard.

As Moss points out, in addition to the direct costs of children, there is often the indirect cost of earnings forgone by the mother. An analysis of the 1974 FES data showed that 70 per cent of childless wives earned over £20 a week, compared to 22 per cent with a child aged 5-10 and 6 per cent with a child under age 5.

It would be surprising if one factor contributing to the fertility decline was not the reluctance of many couples to bear the direct costs and loss of earnings imposed by child-rearing, especially in a period of economic difficulties. It is well established that 'economically active' women have relatively small families. The 1971 census showed that the mean family size of women married 15 to 19 years was 2.31 children;

those who were economically active had a mean family size of 2.08 children. The percentage of economically active married women who were still childless after 5 years of marriage (women married once only, at all ages of marriage under 30) rose from 56 per cent at the 1951 census to 81 per cent at the 1971 census (Britton, 1975).

The relationship between the economics of childbearing and trends and differentials in fertility has been the subject of considerable work by American economists. One of them, Richard Easterlin, is responsible for a theory that was first tested on post-war fertility trends in the United States and has subsequently been tested on trends in England and Wales and other countries. Recent developments and references to earlier work are reported in Easterlin, 1976[2] and Easterlin and Condran, 1976.

In essentials, Easterlin's argument is as follows. A major formative influence on the material aspirations of young adults is the standard of living achieved by their parents. Since this standard depends on the father's income, the material aspirations of young adults should reflect the earlier earning and employment experience of their fathers. The more the earnings of young husbands (the primary breadwinners) enable them to achieve these aspirations, the easier it will be for couples to have children and the less will be the pressure for the wife to work. Thus the fertility behaviour of young adults should depend on their affluence relative to that of their fathers.

Using ratios of income and employment rates as measures of relative affluence, Easterlin has demonstrated a close correspondence between trends in these measures and post-war fertility behaviour in the United States. In a further development of the argument, it is proposed that relative affluence is a function of relative cohort size: that the ratio of younger to older workers, 'though not itself a measure of the relative affluence of young persons, can be thought of as one of the important determinants of that variable'. Easterlin justifies this view as follows.

An upsurge in fertility tends eventually to raise the proportion of younger to older workers. This adversely affects the prosperity of the younger workers, and one consequence is that they have fewer children. However, the reduction in fertility will eventually mean a change in age structure that lowers the proportion of younger to older workers. This has a positive effect on the prosperity of the younger workers with the result that they increase their fertility, thus setting the process in motion again. The process results in waves in population growth of a generation or more in length. It is this version of Easterlin's theory that has been applied to England and other countries as well as the United States (Easterlin and Condran, 1976).

The test comprised a comparison of movements in the TFR with movements in the ratio of males aged 35-64 to those aged 15-34 over the post-war period. According to Easterlin, an upward movement in the curve of the age ratio should correspond to an upward movement in the fertility rate. Using American data, the curves for the two measures did in fact correspond quite closely. A comparison of the same two measures for England and Wales produced the result shown in Figure 5.4. Again the relationship seems close. A close relationship was also demonstrated for Canada and Australia. Unfortunately for the theory, their 'preliminary comparison' of age ratio and fertility for a number of European countries was much less successful: 'While in Belgium and France there is some similarity between the two series. there is little indication of a relationship in Denmark, Sweden, Germany, Italy and the Netherlands.'

This may not be the end of the age-ratio story. It is conceivable that a more generally applicable model could be developed by taking other factors into account. As Easterlin points out, besides relative age, the relative income of an age group is influenced by the state of aggregate demand and by relative education. However, he concedes that it may be that the relationships he found were purely coincidental, due perhaps to changes in other determinants such as a common 1930s depression and post-war boom, 'followed in the 1960s by the diffusion of a common fertility control innovation, the oral pill'. For a discussion of Easterlin's ideas and attempts to apply variants of them to British fertility behaviour, see Ermisch, 1977.

It is still a fairly common belief that the recent fertility decline is due largely to improvement in the availability of better contraceptives and abortion facilities. This view is inconsistent with a substantial body of relevant evidence. Most of the decline in fertility between the 1870s and the 1930s preceded the availability of modern forms of contraception and legal abortion facilities, and owed virtually nothing to public services. No doubt illegal abortions ended many unwelcome pregnancies in the period.

Among the countries of Europe with fertility as low or lower than that of England and Wales, surveys have shown considerable variation in the extent to which fertility is controlled by modern forms of contraception. Differences among twelve countries (the USA and eleven European countries) in the proportions using different methods of birth control are shown in Table 5.3, which is taken from a comparative

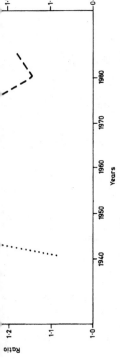

Source: Easterlin and Condran, 1976.

Table 5.3: Differences among 12 Countries in the Percentage of Survey Respondents Reporting Current Use, as a 'Main Method', of Each of Various Methods of Birth Control, in Surveys between 1966 and 1972

	Finland (1971)	Hungary (1966)	Denmark[a] (1970)	Czechoslovakia (1970)	Poland[b] (1972)	Yugoslavia (1970)	France (1972)	United States of America (1970)	Belgium[b,c] (1966)	England and Wales (1967)	Netherlands[d] (1969)	Turkey (1968)
Total fertility rate in survey year	1.7	1.9	2.0	2.1	2.2	2.3	2.4	2.5	2.5	2.6	2.6	5.3
Current users						Current use[e]						
As percentage of all respondents	77	64	67	66	57	59	64	56	76	69	59	35
As percentage of respondents exposed to risk of pregnancy[f]	83	70	84	–	–	62	71	67	83	84	–	40
Percentage distribution of users according to main method currently used												
Intra-uterine device	4	–	4	14	1	2	2	9	–	2	1	5
Pill	26	–	37	4	4	9	17	41	8	19	45	5
Condom	40	16	30	19	17	6	12	17	6	41	23	13
Diaphragm	–	7	9	–	–	–	1	7	–	6	2	–
Withdrawal	21	66	7	52	49	73	52	3	51	25	9	54
Rhythm	1	4	2	3	23	3	14	8	26	5	19	–
Other	8	7	11	8	5	8	2	16	8	2	1	23
Total	100	100	100	100	100	100	100	100	100	100	100	100

Notes: a. Excluding central municipalities of Copenhagen. b. Delay of 18 months in field work. c. Women under 40 years of age. d. 1958 and 1963 marriage cohorts only. e. Women reporting multiple methods (excluding abstinence and sterilisation) were assigned to the first of those methods as ordered in this table. f. Excluding pregnant and sterile women; but for Yugoslavia, excluding only pregnant women.

Source: Economic Commission for Europe, 1976.

analysis of surveys conducted around 1970 (Economic Commission for Europe, 1976). In some of the low-fertility countries (Hungary and France, for example) the main method currently used was withdrawal. Incidentally the authors of the comparative analysis demonstrate a relationship between estimates of legal abortion in some of the countries and dependence on withdrawal as a method of contraception.

Some of the common suppositions about the effects of contraception on fertility, and about other aspects of reproductive behaviour, are based on questionable assumptions about the meaning of responses to typical survey questions. Even if they were theoretically justified, concepts like 'wanting' or 'intending' a pregnancy would be difficult to operationalise satisfactorily. In practice the difficulties are often ignored and people are simply asked to say whether, for example, they were sorry they became pregnant. These and related issues are examined elsewhere (Simons, 1976).

5.4 The Relevance of Ideas

Circumstances can affect fertility in ways that have little or nothing to do with people's ideas about childbearing. For example, wars can diminish the number of available males. However, some notions about people's ideas about childbearing must form part (though not necessarily an explicit part) of any attempt to explain fertility trends in England and Wales, recent or long-term.

In most of the interpretive work on fertility trends, the stress has been on changes in the circumstances taken into account by people when they are determining their reproductive behaviour: changes in the resources available, and changes in the direct or indirect costs of parenthood. On the other hand, some writers have pointed out that fertility is also influenced by the way people interpret their circumstances, and have argued that changes in the way circumstances are interpreted, especially by women, are among the factors explaining recent fertility trends.

The authors of a survey of European demographic trends refer to the 'swiftly changing role and rights of women in both family and extrafamilial connexions' as one indication of a sharp discontinuity with the past (Economic Commission for Europe, 1975). At another point, they suggest that the desire of women for higher education and economic independence is likely to lead young women to postpone marriage and the initiation of childbearing after marriage.

Willmott (1976) refers to survey evidence of a change in the ideology of marriage. The common ideal used to emphasise the wife's traditional roles of housekeeper and mother. Over the past two decades there had been a change and the emphasis was now on the sharing of interests and activities. Most wives now went out to work and more husbands helped with the children and the housework. Couples did more things together whenever they could. The family was 'once more a unity as it had been before the Industrial Revolution, but it was now sharing in consumption rather than production'. However, according to Willmott, women do not seem to have a great deal of confidence in the permanence of this new unity and seek more independence outside the home, as a form of insurance. He argues that the growing instability of marriage had underlined the advantages of having outside interests, staying attractive and enjoying some degree of current and potential economic independence. In his view, the contemporary effect of feminism on fertility is similar to (what he assumes to be) the effect of economic difficulties on fertility in the 1870s:

> My reason for believing that a longer-term decline in average family size is likely is that I expect feminist aspirations to spread 'downwards' throughout the social class structure in a similar way to that in which economic calculation did from about 1870 to about 1940.

It is not clear from this account, and others like it, why fertility should have risen between the mid-1950s and mid-1960s or why the relationship between fertility and socio-economic group should be positive between the middle and upper strata. A more general weakness of such accounts is that, because changes in fertility behaviour are treated simply as inevitable concomitants of new ideas about the role of women, they offer little insight into the specific nature of changes in ideas about childbearing.

If change has occurred, what is its character? What types of ideas have prevailing ideas become less like or more like? And what evidence is there to justify the claim that ideas have become more like or less like the specified kinds? Unless questions like these are posed and answered, little progress is likely to be made in identifying the relevance of changes in ideas about childbearing to an understanding of fertility trends. Answers to the questions are needed not only to elucidate the way changes in ideas may affect fertility, but also to provide a better understanding of the way ideas mediate the effects of fertility of changes in exterior circumstances.

What follows is an attempt to suggest some answers. Specifically, it is an exploratory attempt to analyse the changes in ideas about childbearing that have accompanied recent fertility trends.

First, what kinds of ideas have prevailing ideas become less like or more like? Two opposed sets of ideas will be proposed, to define the extremes of a scale on which the prevailing ideas of real societies can be located. The two sets will be described as though they were those of two types (ideal types) of female individual. It is hypothesised that the differences in the ideas attributed to the two types have a characteristic essential to the validity of the typology: this is that they correspond to differences between the ideas that real people have about childbearing.

At one extreme of the scale is a type designated as Fundamentalist. The Fundamentalist's ideas have the following characteristics. She regards herself as a participant in a momentous drama, metaphysical in its origins and purposes. Conception occurs as a consequence of the performance of roles required by the drama. Thus childbearing is an end in itself. Any form of birth control is incompatible with competent performance. Consistently with these beliefs, the Fundamentalist aspires to marry someone who shares them, and to reproduce Fundamentalists. The aim is a family united in its commitment to a Fundamentalist ideology, including the idea that male and female roles are interdependent and fundamentally constrained by the complementary biological characteristics of the sexes. To the Fundamentalist, a way of life is unnatural if it fails to acknowledge the reciprocal needs and obligations of family members. To Fundamentalists, the status of parent is the foundation of self-image, and therefore of self-esteem. An essential characteristic of Fundamentalist thought is that it construes current behaviour and experience in terms of long-established custom or eternal truths.

At the other end of the scale is a type designated as Pragmatist. The Pragmatist differs from the Fundamentalist in respect of all the above characteristics. To the Pragmatist, human sovereignty over the processes of human reproduction is in principle absolute. Childbearing has no intrinsic merit. Childbearing is a natural phenomenon that owes any potential advantages it may have to the capacity of children to provide for the needs and gratifications of their parents. These needs and gratifications could include public esteem or economic benefits. Involuntary conception is a sign of incompetence if means of avoiding it are known and available. Pragmatists aspire to marry like minds, if marriage seems worthwhile, and to reproduce if it seems useful to do so. If it does, the aim will be a family that shares the Pragmatist's commitment to a utilitarian rationale of reproductive behaviour. This rationale includes the idea that physiological characteristics are to be regarded not as natural imperatives but, if they are impediments to valued ends, as problems to be surmounted as efficiently as possible. An essential characteristic of Pragmatist thought is that it construes current behaviour and experience in terms of its expected consequences.

It is suggested that real people in real societies combine the characteristics of Fundamentalist and Pragmatist types, but that the ideas of one type are normally dominant. The dominant type will be whichever of the two is generally perceived as demonstrating most understanding of current circumstances. The prevailing perception of which type this is will depend on the history and actual circumstances of the society. The effect of a change in this perception on fertility will depend on current fertility level and pattern. A shift in the importance of one type relative to the other would prompt a fertility trend, up or down, in the absence of counter influences.

The Hutterites are one obvious example of a real society that is well towards the Fundamentalist end of the scale, a fact which has been very useful to demographers in need of a community exhibiting the characteristics of natural fertility in benign circumstances. Contemporary Europe offers examples of societies that are nearer to the Pragmatist end.

So much for an attempted answer to the question: 'What types of ideas have prevailing ideas become less like or more like?' The next step is to try to produce a plausible interpretation of English fertility trends since the war in terms of shifts in the relative appeal of the ideas used to characterise the Fundamentalist and Pragmatist outlooks.

The dominant orientation of the decade or so following the war was Pragmatist. This was an era of institutional innovation: a new educational system, a new health service, new towns. It was a time for demonstrating that people could create institutions to a design of their own choosing, a design that could represent a total break with the past.

The fertility boom between the 1950s and 1960s could be seen as a Fundamentalist reaction against the Pragmatism of previous decades. While this was probably a pervasive reaction to the times, it may well have been led by the ideas of generations entering the main childbearing age groups in the mid-1950s. These generations had grown up during the war, in a world where the prospect of a secure family life seemed intensely attractive by contrast with the real or potential circumstances of the time. On the other hand, they had been too young to experience events in the way which had moulded the outlook of older generations.

In consequence, they were inclined to Fundamentalism, and eventually expressed this in relatively high fertility and a relatively low age of marriage and of childbearing. The increase in fertility at longer marriage durations might be explained as a response to the influence of the ideas of the new generation of parents.

By the mid-1960s, the parents who had been children during the war had moved out of the main childbearing ages, to be replaced by cohorts of parents born after the war. Prevailing ideas now shifted towards Pragmatism again. Post-war birth cohorts rebelled against what they saw as the failure of older generations to make social arrangements fit modern circumstances and needs. One manifestation of their sentiments was conflict in the universities between students and authorities. Also characteristic of the period was the extent of new legislation bearing on the family: legislation on divorce, homosexuality, the age of marriage, family planning services and abortion. Perhaps the most revealing phenomenon of the period was the vigorous and ultimately successful campaign to persuade Parliament that free family planning services would mean a major decrease in annual births and therefore in the burden on national resources and amenities (Simons, 1974). The agitation was itself an expression of the shift to Pragmatism that was already bringing about the fertility decline so anxiously desired by the campaigners.

Some further evidence for or against the proposed account can be sought in measures of the religiosity of the population over the period of interest. If fertility variation can be validly described in terms of the proposed typology, one concomitant of change in typical reproductive behaviour should be indications of a change in the appeal of at least some kinds of religious interpretations of experience. This should be especially so in the case of interpretations offered by the Roman Catholic Church, given the correspondence between the doctrine of the Church and the Fundamentalist doctrine described above. Among the relevant data available, annual totals of adult conversions seemed attractive and comparatively unambiguous as indications of the appeal of the Church's doctrine. The trend, expressed as a rate per thousand of the population of England and Wales aged five years[3] and over, is shown in Figure 5.5. The total fertility rate is also shown. There appears to be some correspondence between the two, with a rise in the conversion rate anticipating the rise in fertility in the 1950s and a fall in the rate from 1959, anticipating the fertility decline.

It might be objected that the Catholic conversion rate is subject to influences which might make it suspect as an index. However, its

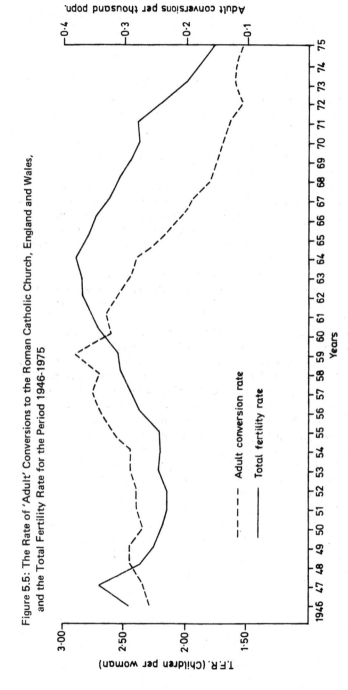

Figure 5.5: The Rate of 'Adult' Conversions to the Roman Catholic Church, England and Wales, and the Total Fertility Rate for the Period 1946-1975

Note: The adult conversion rate is the number of conversions per thousand of the population aged 5 and over
Source: (Number of conversions) *Catholic Directory*, various years.

reliability is supported by data on movements in the membership of the major Protestant churches. Protestants and Catholics have had a highly similar experience of getting and keeping members throughout the present century, including the period since the last war: Protestant church membership rose to a peak in 1956 and fell heavily after 1960 (Currie *et al.*, 1977).

Currie and his colleagues also reveal a phenomenon which might be interpreted as direct evidence that shifts in fundamentalism imply reverse shifts in pragmatism. Over the 25-year period 1940-1965 (though not subsequently) there was a very high negative correlation between membership of the major Protestant churches and membership of an explicitly secular organisation, the Rationalist Press Association. Membership of this organisation reached a peak in 1947, fell to its lowest point in the period in 1956, and then rose continuously until 1965. It has since declined.

As mentioned at the start, the foregoing account is a speculative one. Although parts of the interpretation are known to apply to some other countries which have had similar fertility trends, no attempt to test its generality has been made. In fact, it may not survive, without radical change, future confrontations with English data. Finally, it should be stressed that even if something like the interpretation survives, it is more likely to complement than to supersede types of explanation which concentrate on changes in circumstances. None of the following possibilities, among others, is excluded: that the Fundamentalism of the 1950s was, at least in part, a response to improving living standards; that subsequent Pragmatism was a response to economic difficulties or to a failure of the economy to keep pace with rising aspirations; that changes in the age structure of the population intensified the effects of other factors in some countries while moderating their effects elsewhere.

Acknowledgements

I am very grateful to Susan Evans for her help in assembling data and preparing the diagrams. I received helpful criticisms of an earlier draft from Kay Bispham, Tim Dyson, Colin Newell, John Osborn, Veronika Simons and Basia Zaba.

Notes

1. The Supplementary Benefit level is regarded as the income necessary for minimum subsistence and the avoidance of poverty. Twice the income is regarded as necessary for a 'modest but adequate standard of living'.

2. This paper is one of a set by various authors in the same issue of *Population and Development Review* presented as a symposium on the 'Easterlin hypothesis'.

3. 'Adult' is defined by the Church as aged seven or over, but with the statistics to hand, it was more convenient to use the population aged five years and over.

References

Britton, M. 1975. Women at work. *Population Trends* (London), no. 2, 22-5

Campbell, A. 1974. Beyond the demographic transition. *Demography* (Chicago), 11, no. 4, 549-61

Currie, R., Gilbert, A. and Horsley, L. 1977. *Churches and Churchgoers.* Oxford: Clarendon Press

Easterlin, R. 1976. The conflict between aspirations and resources. *Population and Development Review* (New York), 2, nos. 3 and 4, 417-25

Easterlin, R. and Condran, G. 1976. A note on the recent fertility swing in Australia, Canada, England and Wales, and the United States. In *Population, Factor Movements and Economic Development, Studies Presented to Brinley Thomas*, ed. H. Richards, pp. 139-51. Cardiff: University of Wales Press

Economic Commission for Europe. 1975. *Economic Survey of Europe in 1974, Part 2. Post-war Demographic Trends in Europe and the Outlook until the Year 2000.* New York: United Nations

Economic Commission for Europe. 1976. *Fertility and Family Planning in Europe around 1970: a Comparative Study of Twelve National Surveys.* New York: United Nations

Ermisch, J.C. 1977. The relevance of the 'Easterlin hypothesis' to fertility movements in Great Britain. *Working Papers on Studies in Population Change and Social Planning.* London: Centre for Studies in Social Policy

Farid, S.M. 1974. The current tempo of fertility in England and Wales. *Studies on Medical and Population Subjects*, no. 27. London: HMSO

Glass, D. 1976. Review lecture: recent and prospective trends in fertility in developed countries. *Philosophical Transactions of the Royal Society of London*, B, Biological Sciences, 274, no. 928, 1-52

Leete, R. 1976. Marriage and divorce. *Population Trends* (London), no. 3, 3-8

Moss, P. 1976. Beyond child benefit. *New Society* (London), 38, 351-3

OPCS. 1975. *The Registrar-General's Statistical Review of England and Wales for the Year 1973*, Part II, Tables, Population. London: HMSO

OPCS. 1976. *Variant Population Projections, 1974-2011*, Series PP2, no. 6. London: HMSO

OPCS. 1977. *Local Authority Vital Statistics*, Series VS, no. 2. London: HMSO

Pearce, D. and Britton, M. 1977. The decline in births: some socioeconomic aspects. *Population Trends* (London), no. 7, 9-14

Ryder, N. 1969. The time series of fertility in the United States. *International Population Conference*, Liège, 1969

Simons, J. 1974. Great Britain. In *Population Policy in Developed Countries*, ed. B. Berelson, pp. 592-646. New York: McGraw-Hill

Simons, J. 1976. Illusions about attitudes. In *Population Decline in Europe*,
    proceedings of a seminar held by the Council of Europe on the Implications
    of a Stationary or Declining Population in Europe, Strasbourg, 6-10
    September 1976. London: Edward Arnold
Tabah, L. 1971. *Rapport sur les relations entre la fécondité et la condition
    sociale et économique de la famille en Europe; leurs répercussions sur la
    politique sociale.* Second European Population Conference. Strasbourg:
    Council of Europe
Willmott, P. 1976. The Role of the Family. In *The Uncertain Future*,
    eds. M. Buxton and E. Craven, pp. 51-8. London: Centre for Studies in Social
    Policy

6 POPULATION CHANGES AND REGIONAL PLANNING IN A PERIOD OF FALLING FERTILITY

David Eversley, John Ermisch and Elizabeth Overton

6.1 Summary and Introduction

The three-part chapter which follows is part of the outcome of a larger research project, which is designed to investigate the nature and consequences of the cessation of population growth (and possibly incipient decline) in the United Kingdom since 1964, undertaken in close co-operation with a similar investigation in the Federal Republic of Germany. This particular part of the research is concerned with the validity of existing British regional policies in the light of changing demographic structure. Section 6.2 shows the changes in the distribution of the population of the UK during the last few years, and the pattern which results from a combination of differential migration and differential fertility. Section 6.3 investigates the possible interrelationship between rates of change in the size and structure of regional populations and their economic potential and output. It also examines the extent to which policies designed to correct inter-regional imbalances have produced population stabilisation as well as equality of employment opportunities. Section 6.4 summarises the history of UK regional policies and their connection with the concern with demographic variations, and questions how far policies conceived during a period of relatively rapid economic and demographic development are still applicable, during a period when these assumptions no longer apply and the focus of interest has now shifted to changes in intra-regional population distribution and income differences. In particular, the relevance of the available household projections for regional/local planning is assessed.

6.2 The Development of Regional Population since 1961

The growth of the UK population fell from 3½ per cent in the five-year period 1961-6, to only 1.6 per cent in the three years 1966-9 and then to 0.6 per cent between 1971 and 1974. In the first two periods growth due to natural change exceeded that due to migration in all but two regions: East Anglia and the South-West, both of which were receiving large, though ageing, groups of migrants. By the final period the

139

situation was reversed and migration accounted for the larger proportion of growth rates in all regions except Northern Ireland, Yorkshire and Humberside and the West Midlands, where fertility was still high enough to compensate for loss through migration. The longer-term pattern of migration has been from the old industrial areas of the north where unemployment was at its highest, particularly in Scotland and Northern Ireland, where both fertility and out-migration levels were high. The scene in Scotland has, however, undergone considerable change, with a fall in fertility and unemployment after 1967 until, in the year 1973-4, with investment in North Sea oil production, Scotland actually received more people from other areas of the United Kingdom than it lost to them.

The period over which these changes have taken place is also the period in which government has for the first time involved itself strongly in influencing regional planning decisions, primarily to arrest the exaggeration of income differentials between regions but also, indirectly, to reduce the higher levels of unemployment and out-migration of workers from the poorer regions. The Northern region lost people of all age groups until unemployment began to fall later in the 1960s. Wales, another slow-growing region, was losing a large proportion of its youngest workers whilst receiving people in the older and youngest age groups. However, by the late 1960s the loss had been confined to the youngest adults and many more people of working age were coming into the country. In both of these areas the improvements took place concurrently with the invigoration of regional policy in the 1960s (Champion, 1976). Two other slow-growing areas, Yorkshire and Humberside and the North West, had unemployment rates which increased during the 1960s and were losing population in all age groups. Intermediate Areas were designated much later in these regions, but out-migration was reduced, though later than in Wales and in the North. In contrast, the South West and East Anglia continued to gain large numbers of pensioners and an even greater number of people in other age groups; in both regions the majority of the migrants came from the South-East region.

However, some of the most significant recent migratory movements have been unrelated to or independent of government intervention. Some of the most significant trends do not even show up in the conventional analysis of administrative regions and are not yet integrated into our machinery for the projection of future population sizes. The population shifts out of the centre of conurbations (which increased in significance during the 1960s) were shown by Hall *et al.*

(1973), who re-aggregated the smaller units to create settlement areas in line with the regional employment patterns. Sub-regional reconstruction was seen, for example, in the North, where the population of Tyneside, Merseyside, Manchester, Sheffield and Hull declined through out-migration, and West Yorkshire, the Potteries and Tees-side fared only marginally better, whereas the areas separating these cores achieved higher than regional average growth rates.

The selectivity of the migration out of the city centres leads to social policy problems which may well be aggravated by the fall in the rate of natural growth. The older, poorer, less skilled parts of the population are left behind as the skilled workers and their families and retired people, who can afford to buy their own homes, move out.

Such a functional analysis cuts across regional boundaries used in traditional projection techniques and produces migration patterns which cannot be incorporated into the assumptions used, though they contain a stronger logic.

The fall in the United Kingdom birth rate began almost simultaneously in all countries and regions, reducing the rates of natural growth, so that these came to assume a relatively smaller role in the determination of population change than that played by migration in recent years (see Table 6.1). Regional fertility rates have shown little evidence of convergence, though levels have fallen overall by about a third since the fertility decline began. During the first few years of the decline, the rate of fall was only between a third of a per cent (in the North and Yorkshire and Humberside) and nearly 2 per cent per annum (in the South East region).

After 1970 there was a fall of around 25 per cent over the five-year period to 1975, with declines ranging from under 20 per cent in East Anglia and Northern Ireland to 27 per cent in the West Midlands and North West. In the most recent years all rates of fall seem to be slowing down again.

The slower rates of fall in Wales and East Anglia produced above-average fertility levels in the early 1970s for two regions whose fertility levels had been below the UK level in the early 1960s. On the other hand, faster rates of fall in fertility for the Northern and South Western regions brought their fertility levels from average in the North, and above average in the South West in 1961, to some of the lowest rates of all UK regions, once the overall decline had begun. By far the highest fertility rates were experienced in Northern Ireland, where in spite of a fall in the general fertility rate from 117 in 1964 to a provisional estimate of 88 in 1975, these rates increased in relation to the UK

North-West	+ 2.9	− 0.4	+ 1.46	− 0.67	5.5	− 3.7	+ 0.57	− 0.83	4.6	1.7
Wales	+ 2.2	+ 0.4	+ 1.00	− 0.33	5.2	− 5.2	+ 0.34	+ 0.88	6.2	3.1
Scotland	+ 3.7	− 3.7	+ 1.93	− 1.98	5.4	− 2.1	+ 0.73	− 0.77	13.8	4.0
Northern Ireland	+ 6.1	− 2.4	+ 3.59	− 1.28	11.8	+ 1.1	+ 2.41	− 2.31	10.6	4.4

a. Gross Domestic Product deflated by UK implied GDP deflator for total final expenditure (*National Income and Expenditure, 1967-74*, Table 17). English regional boundaries as of 30 June 1969.

Sources: *Abstract of Regional Statistics*, no. 6, 1970; *Regional Statistics*, no. 11, 1975, Tables 5 and 6; *Population Trends*, no. 7, 1977, Table 6; *Abstract of Regional Statistics*, no. 6, 1970, Table 7; D. Kent-Smith and E. Hartley, *Economic Trends*, November 1976, 'New Estimates of Employment on a Continuous Basis', *Department of Employment Gazette*, August 1976.

Table 6.2: General Fertility Rates 1961 and 1965 to 1975 by UK Region (live births per 1,000 women aged 15-44)

Region[a]	Average rates for the years:			Average rates as proportions of UK rates (UK = 100)			Per cent change in rates (annual average):		
	1961 and 1965	1966-70 inclusive	1971-5 inclusive	1961 + 1965	1966-70 inclusive	1971-5 inclusive	1961-5	1965-70	1970-5
North	91.5	83.3	71.8	100	94	98	-0.3	-2.1	-4.3
Yorkshire/Humberside	92.5	90.1	75.4	101	102	102	-0.3	-0.7	-5.6
East Midlands	93.0	89.3	74.4	101	101	101	-0.5	-1.4	-4.9
East Anglia	88.0	84.1	75.4	96	95	102	+0.8	-1.5	-3.8
South-East	87.0	83.9	69.2	95	95	94	+1.8	-2.3	-4.5
South-West	93.0	84.3	72.2	100	95	98	-0.5	-2.4	-4.7
West Midlands	92.0	91.1	75.6	100	103	103	+0.7	-1.2	-5.2
North-West	93.5	91.1	75.8	102	103	103	+0.8	-1.3	-5.3
Wales	88.9	84.9	74.4	97	96	101	+0.3	-1.3	-4.3
Scotland	96.7	91.5	74.2	105	103	101	-0.2	-2.0	-4.7
Northern Ireland	113.0	111.8	97.3	123	126	132	+0.7	-1.0	-3.9
United Kingdom	91.9	88.6	73.6	100	100	100	+0.7	-1.7	-4.9

a. 1961 data by 1965 boundaries, for later years data for boundaries as of year quoted.
Sources: Annual Abstract of Statistics, 1966 and 1976; Abstract of Regional Statistics, 1969, 1971, 1973, 1974; Population Estimates, PP1, no. 2; Registrar-General's Quarterly Return for England and Wales, nos. 484 and 469.

North-west	8.5	8.9	8.9	8.4	7.9	15.5	14.8	15.2	16.2	16.6	14.9	15.1	15.6	16.1	16.7
Wales	7.9	8.3	8.2	7.8	7.5	15.6	14.8	14.9	15.5	16.0	15.1	15.3	16.3	16.8	17.4
Scotland	9.1	9.3	9.2	8.7	7.9	16.7	16.3	16.8	17.5	17.5	13.3	13.8	14.5	15.1	15.9
Northern Ireland	10.4	10.6	10.9	10.5	9.6	18.6	18.3	18.9	19.5	19.8	12.7	12.7	13.1	13.2	13.4
United Kingdom	8.1	8.6	8.7	8.3	7.7	15.3	14.6	14.9	15.8	16.2	14.7	14.9	15.4	15.9	16.6

a. Men aged 65 and over, women aged 60 and over.
Sources: *Abstracts of Regional Statistics*, 1968, 1970, 1971, 1973, 1974; *Annual Abstract of Statistics*, 1966.

average. Scotland, on the other hand, which had the next-highest level
in 1962, began its decline before 1964 and had reduced its ratio to UK
rates by 1975.

Though the majority of regions did retain their relative level of
fertility *vis-à-vis* the UK throughout the three five-year periods
examined, the changes in rates of change of fertility within regions
were sufficient to make the projection of regional birth rates by past
trends a very difficult task. An average estimate over past years would
not allow for the changes in relative position seen for some regions,
especially for ten years into the future, and challenges the assumptions
underlying the UK projections that in the long term differentials could
remain constant.

The different levels of fertility have produced the expected
differences in the size of the child population of each region (see
Table 6.3). The differences are most marked in the proportions aged
0-4 but are still clearly evident in the proportions aged 5-14. By later ages
migration effects have taken their toll. The South West and East Anglia
received persons of all age groups during the 1960s, but particularly
large proportions of persons of pensionable age, raising the proportion
of people in these age groups to 19 and 18 per cent respectively by
1973. Between 1961 and 1971 persons aged over 60 continued to
account for a third of net migration to the South-West region. The
incorporation of any such apparently well established, long-term trends
into population projections is a precarious exercise since the predicted
population estimates may alert planners to the threat to their housing,
medical and social service budgets and they may then try to slow the
migration flow so as to prevent these from becoming over-burdened.

Although consultation takes place with central government
departments and regional authorities before regional migration
assumptions are made, the components are then integrated
arithmetically, not functionally; migration is estimated by net
movements and the population estimates for each sub-area in each year
are 'controlled' (Campbell, 1976) so that they sum to a predetermined
total for each larger region. Distortions in the estimates of gross flows
are thereby easily produced, because regional authorities exercise
varying control over the determinants of population movements, and
some of their statistical teams are in a worse position than others to
predict the migration flows between regions with which they trade
population and so errors become compounded.

6.3 Regional Economic and Demographic Change

In the preceding section the sources and nature of regional population changes since 1961 were discussed. The key factor in producing differences in population growth rates among regions is net migration: in the post-war period the correlation (across regions of Great Britain) between percentage total population increase and natural increase is not significantly different from zero, while the rate of total increase is positively correlated with the rate of net migration. An investigation of the relationship between economic variables and regional population growth therefore amounts to an investigation of the relationship between economic factors and migratory movements.

There are of course a multiplicity of motives for moving one's home, of which the attempt to secure more remunerative or stable employment is only one. Nevertheless, it seems reasonable to assume that net migration to/from a region is somewhat responsive to the growth of the regional demand for labour, and a major factor influencing the rate of change in the regional demand for labour is the spatial distribution of gross investment by firms selling their output in supra-regional markets (sometimes called 'basic industry'). While this formulation captures the essence of an important relationship between economic factors and population change, the quantitative impact of £1 of investment by such exporting firms upon the regional demand for labour depends upon the type of industry making the investment. In particular, the degree of labour intensity and the multiplier effect on industries almost exclusively providing goods and services for the regional market (i.e. 'non-basic industries') will vary among export industries, and the multiplier effect on regional employment will also vary among regions with different sizes and industrial structures.

In general, however, the investment and employment in industries serving only the regional market will depend upon the rate of investment in the exporting industries, and in the long run the rate of growth of regional gross domestic product (GDP) will be determined by the rate of growth of investment in the exporting industries. Given the latter rate of growth it follows that regional population growth is a function of the rate of growth of regional GDP, both observable magnitudes.

The regional location of exporting firms, and thus the growth of GDP, depends in turn upon the perceived economic attractiveness of the region. With the exception of extractive industries, the location decisions of firms in the vast majority of industries are primarily a function of the cost and availability of space, labour costs/availability, and the external economies of industrial agglomeration. Regional investment and the change in the regional demand for labour may therefore also respond to the rate of growth of labour supply, through the latter's effect on labour costs/availability and the rate of growth of regional investment and GDP may then be dependent upon the rate of population growth through its effect upon labour costs/availability. We shall attempt to disentangle the response and stimulus relationships between economic growth and population growth below. We then consider the demographic impact of regional policy.

Because of refinements in measurement methods from 1971 onwards there is a break in the regional GDP time series between 1970 and 1971. We therefore break the period into two sub-periods (1966-9 and 1971-4) for analysis purposes. Table 6.1 shows the growth rate of regional GDP for these two sub-periods. As noted above, regional investment and growth could be a response to population and labour force growth; if so, the adjustment mechanisms would work through changes in wages and/or labour availability. At least in the short term, there is no empirical support for this: in neither sub-period do we find any correlation between the growth rate of GDP and the wage rate at the beginning of the sub-period, the rate of increase in the wage rate, or the unemployment rate at the beginning of the sub-period. There is in fact little variation in wage rates and labour costs among regions; thus differences in the growth of labour supply are not reflected in differences in labour costs per employee. Furthermore, the skill composition of the unemployed labour force is probably much more important than the numbers of unemployed for industrial location decisions and regional investment. In this regard the attractiveness of a region may be affected by the process of selective migration. If the labour supply of a region is growing at a rate in excess of the regional demand for labour, the young and skilled workers may emigrate, leaving the less skilled behind and diminishing the attractiveness of the region. In this manner out-migration could have a negative impact on regional investment, even though aggregate unemployment in the region is substantial. This dynamic process could lead to a vicious circle of regional decline. Out-migration could also directly affect the willingness of mobile industry to invest by impairing confidence and increasing uncertainty about the region's future. It shall be assumed that regional investment in exporting industries and the rate of growth of GDP are exogenous variables, but the possibility of a dynamic feedback of out-migration on regional investment should be kept in mind.

Interpreting the rate of growth in GDP as exogenous implies that the rates of net migration and population change responded to the change in the regional demand for labour. The estimated regression coefficients are statistically significant in both sub-periods, and they suggest that in the period 1966-9 a percentage point increase in the GDP growth rate entailed a 0.5 percentage point increase in the net migration rate, while in the period 1971-4 a percentage point increase in the GDP growth rate implied only a 0.1 percentage point increase in the net migration rate. In the latter sub-period we also find evidence for the existence of a strong 'Verdoorn effect'. The 'Verdoorn effect' is the positive impact, through learning by doing and dynamic scale economies, that growth in output has upon productivity growth (Kaldor, 1970). The absence of the 'Verdoorn effect' and the larger effect of GDP growth on net migration in 1966-9 appears to be primarily the result of the regional GDP estimation method which implicitly tended to eliminate the systematic regional variation (with respect to GDP growth) in productivity among regions. In both sub-periods we find that a 1 per cent increase in employment increases the net migration rate by about 0.5 percentage points, and it is probably the case that a 'Verdoorn effect' existed in both sub-periods as well.

We define the 'autonomous rate of net migration' as the rate of net migration which would occur if there were *no differentials* in the rate of GDP growth among regions. The autonomous rate of net migration indicates the attractiveness or unattractiveness of a region which is independent of the rate of regional economic growth relative to the rate of economic growth in other regions. There is of course always some rate of regional economic growth which will produce zero net migration; Table 6.4 merely measures the rate of net migration to/from a region which would have occurred if the GDP of all regions had grown at the average rate for the period. Differences of the absolute autonomous rates between the two-sub-periods are not very meaningful, although changes in the relative rankings are.

We can make some general interpretations of these rates. The antipodal autonomous rates of the South East and East Anglia are to a great extent statistical freaks. In reality, the South East has been growing geographically as an economic region, and the growth has overspilled into the static statistical boundaries of East Anglia. The popularity of the South West as a retirement region at least partly explains the strong tendency for the South West to gain population independent of its economic growth performance relative to other regions. The North and Scotland are consistent losers of population independent of differences in regional economic growth rates, and they also rank as the bottom two in relative wage and salary levels. We may therefore be observing a long-run migratory drift from the regions with low relative earnings to regions with high relative earnings (e.g. West Midlands), but superimposed upon this long-run adjustment pattern are migratory movements in response to medium-run regional differentials in economic growth, which can correspondingly accelerate or decelerate net migration to/from a region in any given period.

As the discussion in the next section will demonstrate, a primary objective of regional policy in the UK has been a substantial reduction in net outward migration from the depressed areas by bringing about a net diversion of demand for labour away from the prosperous areas. Moore and Rhodes (1974) estimate that between 1960 and 1972 regional policy created about 250,000 to 300,000 jobs in development areas (i.e. the North, Scotland, Wales and Northern Ireland), and this was to a large degree accomplished by inducing moves of manufacturing firms to development areas (DAs). Critics have shown that their estimates of the number of manufacturing moves to DAs and the employment growth in DAs induced by regional policy are too high (Ashcroft and Taylor, 1977; Buck and Atkins, 1976). Employing the estimates of the regional policy impact in employment growth on the DAs by Moore and Rhodes as well as their critics, and utilising the relationship between employment growth and net migration derived above, we estimate that regional policy reduced the rate of net outward migration from the DAs by 30-50 per cent. A similar impact of regional policy is suggested by the migration figures for the North, Scotland and Wales from census data, in that 1966-71 is a period of strong regional policy relative to 1961-6 (see Table 6.5). Although the net migration figures indicate a 50 per cent reduction in net outward migration from three of the DAs, these figures do not control for differences in the rates of regional economic growth and employment growth between 1961-6 and 1966-71 which are unrelated to regional policy.

The above suggests that the impact of regional policy on out-migration from the DAs was not insignificant. Nevertheless, our analysis also suggests that the effectiveness of the traditional instruments of regional policy (in a programme run at a realistic cost) is quite limited in influencing demographic movements. Table 6.4 implies that it is very difficult to eliminate net out-migration from development areas such as Scotland and the North because a substantial proportion of the net out-migration from these regions is not a result of below-average rates of economic growth (i.e. the autonomous rate of out-migration is high). For example, in order to eliminate net out-migration from Scotland in

Table 6.4: Autonomous Rate of Net Migration[a]

Region	Autonomous rate of net migration[b]	
	1966-9	1971-4
North	−0.2	−0.3
	(6)	(8)
Yorkshire/Humberside	0.6	−0.2
	(3)	(6)
East Midlands	−0.3	0.2
	(7)	(5)
East Anglia	1.5	3.0
	(1)	(1)
South-East	−0.8	−0.3
	(9)	(8)
South-West	0.4	0.9
	(4)	(3)
West Midlands	1.4	0.6
	(2)	(4)
North-West	−0.3	0.3
	(7)	(5)
Wales	0.1	1.8
	(5)	(2)
Scotland	−1.6	−0.9

a. Estimates have been computed from the following equations:
$M(i,t) = A(i,t) + 0.5 g(i,t)$ for t = 1966-9;
$M(i,t) = A(i,t) + 0.13 g(i,t)$ for t = 1971-4.
The 'autonomous rate' for period t = $A(i,t) + 0.5 g(t)$ for t = 1966-9;
$A(i,t) + 0.13 g(t)$ for t = 1971-4.
$g(i,t)$ = the rate of GDP growth in region i during period t;
$M(i,t)$ = the rate of migration in region i during period t;
$\overline{g(t)}$ = the average rate of GDP growth during period t;
$A(i,t)$ = 'residual' rate of net migration in region i during period t.
b. Relative ranking in parentheses.

the period 1971-4, GDP would have had to have grown at an annual rate 3 percentage points higher than the average for Great Britain (i.e. 70 per cent higher). It would be quite difficult to induce such a large economic growth differential in a traditionally underdeveloped region such as Scotland; in the past the best regional policy had done was to keep the economic growth of the DAs close to the mean rate for Great Britain (see Table 6.1). Furthermore, the observed effects of regional

Table 6.5: Migration between the Regions of Great Britain within the Two Five-year Periods 1961-6, 1966-71

Region	Net migration flows (persons aged 5 or over)		1966-71 Gross Flows: per cent who were males aged 15-44	
	1961-6	1966-71	From other parts of GB into each region (1)	Who left each region for other parts of GB (2)
North	−48,320	−25,710	31.0	32.3
Yorkshire/Humberside	−16,680	−42,370	30.1	31.9
East Midlands	43,700	34,950	31.3	30.8
East Anglia	49,350	73,680	27.7	32.3
South-East	−16,870	−46,630	33.4	28.1
South-West	100,970	116,350	25.8	31.4
West Midlands	−16,060	−38,930	32.7	30.2
North-West	−17,750	−35,510	31.3	30.3
Wales	230	6,420	27.1	32.3
Scotland	−78,570	−42,250	31.8	34.0

Sources: *1966 Census Migration Summary Tables*, Part I, Table 2B; *1971 Census Migration Tables*, Part I, 10 per cent sample, Table 3B.

policy took place in a favourable environment of expanding productive capacity. Many more moves of firms are generated when the national rate of investment is high and spare capacity is low (Ashcroft and Taylor, 1977). We would therefore expect the effects of these same regional policy instruments on employment growth in DAs, and outward migration from them, to be of much lower magnitude in the stagnant UK economy of at least the next few years.

6.4 Regional Policy, The Distribution of Population and Housing Demand

In its origins, British regional planning policy was always population orientated, though under very different circumstances at its inception (before the Second World War), at its height (in the mid-sixties) and in the present period when there are grave doubts as to its efficacy. At the time of the Barlow Report (Royal Commission, 1940) Britain, in common with other European countries, had begun to experience a downturn in fertility, which at the time was interpreted as leading in the long run to a drastic overall decline. The Commission recognised that the combination of large-scale unemployment in the 'depressed areas' with reduced rates of population increase was rapidly shifting the centre of gravity of the settlement pattern into the growth areas. This was supposed to be due to the direct effect of the migration of unemployed workers and the indirect consequences of the resulting differential fertility, i.e. if the young and active populations in particular were mobile, then the economically stronger areas would also be areas of fast natural increase as well as immigration.

This fundamental view survived into the post-war years, when there was a temporary return to fairly high fertility. The relatively prosperous reconstruction and growth areas from the end of the war to the early sixties weakened the central government's commitment to regional policy, especially as fertility and consequently rates of projected population growth declined: there was fairly full employment in most areas, and even the less favoured regions were very much better off than the country as a whole had been before the war. Hence little was done to correct migrational imbalances, though officially the policy still was to prevent the overgrowth of the main conurbations and to encourage the spread of new manufacturing industry as far as possible into the endangered areas.

The situation changed again with the renewed rise in fertility after 1956, and signs of a worsening of regional differentials in economic growth rates. Gradually, policy became more stringent, culminating in the era of the short-lived National Plan (1965), which assumed that although there would be overall growth of the economy, this might accrue mainly to the already prosperous areas which could result in renewed inter-regional migration leading to gross overcrowding of the already most populous areas. Thus economic and population policies were strongly linked through: measures to steer manufacturing plant to the development areas; later also the attempt to steer office development away from the large cities; and special grants to improve the social and environmental infrastructure of the poorer regions. At the same time, the retention of population in the disadvantaged areas was supposed to make it easier to solve housing problems.

The position can be illustrated by the assumptions behind *The South East Study*, published in 1964. This still started from the idea that in the absence of strong countervailing measures, Greater London would, by 1981, have at least 9 million inhabitants, compared with just over 8 million at the time of publication; that this would happen within the framework of national population growth which might bring the British Isles to somewhere between 70 and 80 million people by the end of the century; and that these assumptions pointed to a tough policy of discouraging in-migration to London; of insisting even more strongly that growth should be directed to the areas which were also experiencing strong natural population growth, but less economic prosperity and would therefore tend to shed their surplus by internal migration towards the areas of greatest employment opportunity. This led to the view that a combination of strong measures might achieve a position, by 1981, in which London would be held at about 8 million people, and the remainder distributed to new and expanded towns and the East Anglian region, but predominantly kept where it was already settled, i.e. in the development regions.

Ten years after the hey-day of economic/demographic redistribution policies, economic growth had virtually ceased. Population growth slowed down after 1964, as we have shown. London had declined to less than 7 million people by mid-1977 and other conurbations suffered equal or greater losses in population. The combination of declining births and net emigration led to a reduction of the population of the UK in three successive years.

It is difficult to separate the economic and the demographic developments which are implied in this brief account. Whereas economic growth performance is susceptible to short-term influences, much of the demographic change is probably connected with longer-term behavioural patterns. The temporary reversals of long-term fertility decline of 1944-8 and 1956-64 will show up on the demographic map twenty to thirty years later as a renewed 'increase' in marriages and births even if nuptiality should fall and fertility continue its decline.

In section 6.3 of this chapter we discussed the evidence for any short-term connection between rates of population growth and economic performance, but as we show there, a high proportion of the rates of change in net migration and population growth is independent of economic growth. We must conclude that governmental measures designed to produce a balance between the available work-force and job opportunities are not very effective. This is not surprising. In the first place, there are doubts in some quarters whether official measures have really created many extra jobs in areas of high unemployment (Chisholm, 1974, 1975), though other investigators claim a higher success rate (Moore and Rhodes, 1973, 1974 and 1976). Certainly any idea that new private and public investment would have a positive multiplier effect began to be doubted a good many years ago (Wilson, 1968). As we showed some time ago (Eversley, 1971), past differential fertility has always created a corresponding differential of work-force entrants in the disadvantaged areas, and despite the general spread of contraception and liberalised abortion into these areas, the differential persists to some extent (see section 6.2). Northern Ireland especially (Compton, 1976), with its large Catholic population, exhibits one of the last clear examples of differential fertility in Europe; though we do not know how much of Northern Ireland's higher fertility is also due to its relatively large rural population and to the high proportion of families with heads in social classes IV and V. In the past at any rate, these have had noticeably higher fertility and, whatever the position may be in 1977, they are still contributing a relatively large number of potential labour-force entrants into a local economy which is incapable of absorbing the existing adult work-force, let alone newcomers, and whose opportunities to migrate to the British mainland have been considerably reduced.

As was shown some time ago (Holmans, 1964) true north-south migration in the sense in which the Barlow Commission had seen it was never an important factor in the situation. What had usually happened was that there was a 'ripple' effect which, by relatively slow movements, tended to tilt the balance of population from the heartlands of the Industrial Revolution towards the concentrations of the newer growth areas of the Midlands and the South-East. In addition, immigrants tended to concentrate where most employment existed in the late fifties and early sixties (i.e. mainly the Midlands and the South-East). To this can be added the differential fertility effect due to the age structure of the migrants, both external and internal. This moderated the natural increase rate of the less developed regions and increased that of the stronger regions.

The internal redistribution of the population within regions was proportionately more important, especially in those with the strongest economic potential, highest real incomes, and largest effective demand for housing. The 'flight' from the city accelerated in all regions and has been most noticeable in the South-East and adjoining growth regions.

These movements are differentiated, as our tables in section 6.2 show. Thus the movement to East Anglia has been predominantly that of the younger age group, which accords with the strong economic upswing of that region. But the coastal areas are also attracting the better-off retired age groups, as is the case in the South Eastern and Western regions, and in North Wales (Law and Warnes, 1976). Within the Western region there is a further differential: its eastern half (Wiltshire to Bristol) has received both population and industry on such a scale as to make it an area of high prosperity and virtually an extension of the South-East region, whereas the areas to the south-west of Bristol have received a high proportion of older and retired migrants, and very few new job opportunities, to such an extent that the westernmost parts of the British Isles have also become development areas. Similar sub-regional differences exist elsewhere, often due to the existence of preferred retirement areas (Karn, 1977). The simple division into 'prosperous' and 'development' areas had to be abandoned in favour of a more complex classification following the report of the Hunt Committee (Hunt, 1967).

Turning now to the detailed future population and housing projections for the regions, the assumed future distribution of the total between regions has been relatively stable. However, within these regions the share accruing to major agglomerations obviously cannot be uniformly projected.

Those with no or fewer children are more mobile and can exert a wider range of choices. In the public sector, priority is supposed to be given to families with children. In general, census results demonstrate that average occupancy rates in publicly owned housing are significantly higher than those in private housing. So, inasmuch as the greater part of the private development is taking place outside the conurbations and the greater part of the public development within them, we would expect the adult population of metropolitan areas to fall relatively faster than the child population in the public sector and the adult population in the areas outside conurbations. But all we can predict with some certainty is that, within regions, the balance between large urban agglomerations and small settlement areas will continue to shift in favour of the latter (Hall, 1973).

Such work as has been done until now in the field of household projections and housing demand analysis does not provide much by way of useful guidelines. Most of it dates back to the era of relatively high fertility and rising real incomes, and increasing proportions of a rising GNP devoted to investment in the residential sector and other parts of the built environment. Hence previous discussion has been dominated by the propensity to form separate households (household fission) by changing patterns of distribution of rising personal incomes and by the assumption of a continued high rate of supply in both the private and public sector. These assumptions are now largely outdated and fresh work remains to be done to assess both the real demand for future housing and future supply of new or improved dwellings.

Yet even the most recent regional plans have so far largely failed to take account of the new factors which will have an important effect on the total demand for housing and its composition. Officially, the basis of the projections continues to be the enumeration of households of different types in successive censuses. From these, headship rates are derived by estimating how many potential households formed actual separate entities (and therefore occupied a separate dwelling space). Changes in these headship rates are then projected forward by applying past trends in household formation to future populations broken down by planning region. This extrapolation has been performed by either plotting trend curves in a linear fashion, or exponentially, at the national level (i.e. by purely mathematical operations). For the regions, only one estimate is available *(Housing and Construction Statistics*, 1977; Department of the Environment, 1977; Harrison, 1977; Holmans, 1970; Macmillan *et al.*, 1976; Campbell, 1976). Critical commentaries have indeed been supplied, particularly by the Greater London Council (Hollis *et al.*, 1977) and the general principle of the link between the rate of household formation and economic changes has been examined (Byatt *et al.*, 1973).

Obviously the existing methods have only limited validity for planning purposes at the regional, let alone sub-regional, level. We already have four sets of population projections, based on different assumptions about fertility, at the national level and also for the Greater London area using two sets of assumptions about fertility levels and two about the volume of migration (Hollis *et al.*, 1977). We do not yet know how far these are connected with rates of growth of personal real incomes. In turn, each of these projections can be converted into household projections on a static, linear growth, or exponential growth basis, and these will certainly be dependent largely on assumptions about the relationship of purchasing power in the private sector to the trends in the costs of land and building. The general connection between demographic change and infrastructure investment, especially in housing, has been investigated by Ermisch (1977). To this we must add some social factors, e.g. the rate of formation of lone-parent households (actual or potential) which depends on divorce, separation and illegitimacy rates; the propensity of the 'hidden' one-person households (enumerated as sharers at each census) to form households of their own (which may be a function of changing preferences as much as purchasing power); and the policies with regard to institutional housing for special categories (the elderly, the mentally or physically handicapped, children in need of care, etc.).

Although these factors are mentioned in some of the literature cited, (e.g. Department of the Environment, 1977), they do not seem to have led to any conclusions on which regional planners could base their activity. Clearly, there is a maximum value (highest population projections, maximum trend towards household fission, minimum institutional population, etc.) and it appears that regional plans are often little more than the sum of the maximum estimates by constituent authorities as to their capacity for new building. It is certainly known (Campbell, 1976; Department of the Environment, 1977 that regional and local projections are mutually adjusted to fit the sum of national and regional projections respectively. However, when we turn to the detailed arguments of a region's own projections (Macmillan *et al.*, 1976) we find that despite the admitted uncertainties surrounding the projections, local planning authorities are still inclined to think in terms of the highest possible number of households which can be extrapolated on the basis of a static or even falling total population.

The reports usually draw attention to the fact that their operations do not touch the root of the matter — the imbalance between demand and supply at the local level, and the mismatch between dwelling stock and household size. They also indicate that a large surplus of houses for sale in the desirable residential locations of each region is quite compatible with a continued shortfall of family dwellings, especially in inner urban areas. Yet the approach to policy is still that of the

'numbers game'; housing authorities are encouraged to think that if
some theoretical total supply of dwellings exists, administrative means
can be found to fit those in need of housing into this stock. However,
there is no evidence for this.

Thus, despite the identified preponderance of urban problems for
family-type households, especially in the lower-income groups, the
stress is usually shifted on to the most striking aspect of the household
projections: the growth of one- and two-person households (Northern
Region Strategy Team, 1976). This encourages trends which would
quite possibly have undesirable side-effects: a concentration of scarce
resources of local authorities on the construction of very small
dwellings, continued encouragement to the private sector to build only
small flats in urban areas and family housing for the upper-income
groups outside them.

The situation has changed in part, in most recent times through
government initiatives to shift resources from the areas of profitable
growth (to both local authorities and the private sector) back to the
inner cities where a large proportion of acute housing problems exists
(Inner Area Studies, 1977). This departure, if successful, will have
fundamental effects on inter-regional and intra-regional policies. Within
regions, it will continue the shift from new building to rehabilitation,
but now the main aim will be to house priority groups. But continued
'gentrification' is not ruled out (Shankland, Willmott and Jordan,
1977). As for the rest of the relatively prosperous regions, attempts
may well be made to slow down the growth which has favoured the
small and relatively affluent household, as far as this can be done by a
shift in the application of national subsidies and grants. But so far
this has not gone beyond the limitation of tax relief to a main dwelling
and an upper limit on mortgages.

In the development areas, whereas the stress until recently has been
mainly on the need to provide additional workplaces, it is now
increasingly realised that unless housing is also improved considerably,
especially within their own old urban sectors, industrial investment
may well not succeed in promoting higher living standards. Again this
housing will have to be predominantly of the family type, whatever the
household projections may indicate *(Strategic Plan for the North West,*
1973; *Change or Decay,* 1977).

In the past thirty years, over eight million houses have been added
to the available stock, more to cater for additional households and for
those displaced by slum clearance than for a growing population. Yet
this process has still left many severe cases of need in a state which the

authorities find cannot be altered by existing policies (Eversley, 1977). In view of this, strategic housing plans have to start from the needs of existing under-housed family units (as do the Inner Area Studies) and not from the projections. Plans need to identify what households are inadequately housed and where they can be rehoused with a chance of keeping or finding employment. Public resources need to be concentrated on schemes which meet this need. Starting from this point, local, sub-regional and national/regional plans will have to be rewritten accordingly. The small households will have to take care of themselves (except for sections of the elderly population) by moving to areas where the infrastructure already exists and where there are unused planning permissions. It would have been different if the population had in fact continued to grow as it did until the late 1960s, and a much greater number of family-type houses had been required from the late eighties onwards. As this is not now likely to be the case, the shift in emphasis seems to follow logically from the criticism of the mechanical projections, and the lack of emphasis on the economic and social conditions on which they depended.

It would be useful if the Department of the Environment, in its promised future county household projection estimates, co-ordinated their statistical exercises with the intentions of their inner city and public housing divisions so as to show that at the most local level the fitting of curves to trends observable between 1961 and 1971 may have (or should have) little relevance to the planning of housing supply of various kinds. To show, as do the latest available projections, a 10 per cent fall in London households between 1971 and 1991, a rise of 30 per cent in the Outer Metropolitan Area, and of 50 per cent in the Outer South-East, is to write the absence (or failure) of new policies into regional planning. The present lack of comparable data in these tables for Scotland and Northern Ireland compounds the difficulty. If planners are to be able to use these projections, they must be less based on past events but, on balance, it is probably safer to use such figures only as a starting-point for much more drastic intervention in market forces (Eversley, 1978).

References

Ashcroft, B. and Taylor, J. 1977. The movement of manufacturing industry and the effect of regional policy. *Oxford Economic Papers*, 29

Buck, T.W. and Atkins, M.H. 1976. The impact of British regional policies on employment growth. *Oxford Economic Papers*, 28

Byatt, I.R.C., Holmans, A.E. and Laidler, D.E.W. 1973. Income and the demand
for housing: some evidence for Great Britain. In *Essays in Modern Economics*,
ed. M. Parkin. London: Longmans

Campbell, R. 1976. Local population projections. *Population Trends*, no. 5

Champion, A.G. 1976. Evolving patterns of population distribution in England
and Wales, 1951-71. *Transactions, Institute of British Geographers*, new series,
1, 401-20

Chisholm, M. 1974. Regional policy for the 1970s. *Geographical Journal*,
CXL, 2

Chisholm, M. (ed.). 1975. *Regional Economic Policy, a Time for Re-appraisal*,
various contributors. London: Regional Studies Association

Compton, P.A. 1976. Religious affiliation and demographic variability in
Northern Ireland. *Transactions, Institute of British Geographers*, new series,
1, Part 4

Environment, Department of the. 1977. Revised estimates and 1974-based
projections of households for England and Wales and the regions, 1961-1991.
SH (77) 10, Department of the Environment

Ermisch, J.F. 1977. *The Impact of Demographic Change upon Public
Expenditure and Infrastructure Investment*. PCSP–WP-4, Studies in
Population Change and Social Planning. London: Centre for Studies in Social
Policy

Eversley, D.E.C. 1971. Population changes and regional policies since the war.
Regional Studies, 5

Eversley, D.E.C. 1977. Are we better housed? *New Society*, 40, no. 758

Eversley, D.E.C. 1978. The falling birth rate – implications for urban and
regional planning. Discussion paper no. 10. London: Regional Studies
Association

Hall, P. *et al*. 1973. *The Containment of Urban England*. London: George Allen
and Unwin

Harrison, A.E. 1977. Demographic and economic trends. *Proceedings of the
Royal Town Planning Institute, Annual Conference, 1977*, pp. 7ff. London:
The Royal Town Planning Institute

Hollis, J., Henderson, A. and Congdon, P. 1977. *Population and Household
Projections for London*, 1976, Parts I, II, and III, Research Memoranda 506,
507 and 509. London: Greater London Council

Holmans, A.E. 1964. Restriction of industrial expansion in South East England –
a re-appraisal. *Oxford Economic Papers*, 16

Holmans, A.E. 1970. A forecast of effective demand for housing Great Britain
in the 1970s. *Social Trends* (1970), 33-42. London: HMSO

Housing and Construction Statistics, no. 21, 1st Quarter, 1977

Hunt, Sir John (Chairman). 1969. *The Intermediate Areas*, Cmnd. 3998.
London: HMSO

Inner Area Studies. 1977. *Liverpool, Birmingham and Lambeth, Summaries of
Consultants' Final Reports*, Department of the Environment. London: HMSO

Kaldor, N. 1970. The case for regional policies. *Scottish Journal of Political
Economy* (November 1970)

Karn, V. (1977). *Retiring to the Seaside*. London: Routledge and Kegan Paul

Law, C.M. and Warnes, A.M. 1976. The changing geography of the elderly in
England and Wales. *Transactions, Institute of British Geographers*, new
series, 1, Part 4, 453-74

Macmillan, A., Duguid, A. and Young, S. 1976. Strategy for the South East:
1976 review. *Report of the Housing Group* and *Appendices*. London:
Department of the Environment/HMSO

Moore, B. and Rhodes, J. 1973. Evaluating the effects of British regional policy.

Economic Journal, 83

Moore, B. and Rhodes, J. 1974. The effects of regional policy in the United Kingdom. In *Regional Policy and Planning for Europe*, ed. M. Sant. Farnborough: Saxon House

Moore, B. and Rhodes, J. 1976. Regional economic policy and the movements of manufacturing firms to development areas. *Economica*, 43

National Plan, The. 1965. Ch. 8. London: HMSO

Northern Region Strategy Team. 1977. *Final Report.* London: HMSO

Northern Region Strategy Team. 1976. *Technical Report*, nos. 15 and 16. *Housing.* Newcastle-upon-Tyne: RSI

Royal Commission on the Distribution of the Industrial Population. 1940. *Report.* Chairman: Sir Montagu Barlow. London: HMSO

Shankland, G., Willmott, P. and Jordan, D. 1977. *Inner London, Policies for Dispersal and Balance, Final Report of the Lambeth Inner Area Study.* London: HMSO

South East Study, The. 1961-1981. 1964. London: HMSO

Strategic Plan for the North West, 1973. 1974. London: HMSO

Wilson, Hugh, Womersley, Lewis *et al.* 1977. *Change or Decay. Final Report of the Liverpool Inner Area Study.* London: HMSO

Wilson, T. 1968. The regional multiplier, a critique. *Oxford Economic Papers*, XX, no. 3

PART THREE: MIGRATION

7 MIGRATION WITHIN AND BETWEEN THE METROPOLITAN ECONOMIC LABOUR AREAS OF BRITAIN, 1966-1971[1]

Stephen Kennett

7.1 Introduction

This chapter attempts to indicate some of the principal population shifts attributable to migration for urban Britain in aggregate and for some British cities in more detail between 1966 and 1971. It reports some findings derived from a Department of Environment funded research project at the Geography Department, London School of Economics, which attempted to evaluate these and many other aspects of urban change in Britain.[2] It is hoped that some of the following comments contribute to providing a national and a regional as well as more local perspective on migration. Crucial to the achievement of these aims, however, is a comprehensive and consistent areal definitional base for urban Britain. It can be argued that a purely physical definition of urban areas neglects much of what many would regard to be of urban character. This research uses a definition which is based upon principles developed for the United States census as early as 1940, and which have since been used in several major studies.[3]

For the functional definition of urban areas a central concept must be that of an urban field or daily urban system linking places of work and residential areas. Basically such a definition provides for areas which are employment cores and those which are commuting hinterlands. The cores are made up of contiguous local authority areas with employment of over twenty thousand. The commuting hinterland is divided into two areas: first, a metropolitan ring comprising local authority areas having more than 15 per cent of their economically active population commuting to the core: second, an outer metropolitan ring area (OMR) defined as comprising all other contiguous local authorities having more economically active population commuting to a particular core than to any other core. The core and metropolitan ring defines the Standard Metropolitan Labour Area (SMLA) which normally has a population exceeding seventy thousand. The SMLA and the outer metropolitan ring area define the Metropolitan Economic Labour Area (MELA). Together the 126 MELAs constitute the total urban system. The remainder of the country is exhausted by rural or unclassified areas. The present project has updated the PEP team's areas by using a combination of 1966 and 1971 census data.[4]

The advantages and disadvantages of the use of MELAs and their constituent zones with specific reference to migration have been discussed elsewhere (Kennett, 1975). It is important to stress that all types of migration are of concern to this paper. Moreover, the assumption that movers between MELAs are labour migrants is avoided. Implicitly the relationship between distance and probability of being a labour migrant is positive. However, it is not tenable to assume that all migrants who cross MELA boundaries are labour migrants and equally that all movers within MELAs are non-labour migrants.

The completed analysis of net migration change for the whole 1961-71 decade has been published elsewhere (see Urban Change Project, 1974b and 1974c, and Department of the Environment, 1976). These results coupled with those for differential migration have been presented more fully (Urban Change Project, 1978a). This analysis is used here as a setting for the present study of migration flows between 1966 and 1971, and 1970 and 1971. The flows are restricted to movements within Britain. The essentially descriptive study has tended to concentrate upon the five-year, rather than the one-year interval, because more detailed data are available relating to socio-economic and age structure of migrants. Problems with migration census data have been dealt with elsewhere (see, for example, Willis, 1974, and Kennett, 1978) and need not concern us here. In the context of this essay it is especially important to remember that comparison of the five-year and one-year migration figures in order to derive trends in the changing patterns of movement is usually not a viable exercise.

7.2 Net Migration and Population Change

Study of population change in urban Britain during the 1961-71 decade has revealed several distinctive features: the inter-regional variation in SMLA growth performance; the regional variation of rapidly expanding small and medium-sized SMLAs (and the decline of associated large SMLAs, usually centred on the conurbations), and intra-SMLA decentralisation of population from cores to rings. Such aggregate shifts of population can be attributed only to variations in natural change and net migration. What is the relative importance of these two components in explaining the variation in population change?

The study has examined the relationship between natural change, net migration and population change for all labour markets and their constituent zones. If natural change is taken as a constant (in the SMLA case 6.18 per cent; their mean natural increase rate) on a graph of net migration change (Y) and total population change (X), then deviations from this line will indicate urban areas with above- or below-average rates of natural change. The remaining population change is attributable to variations in the net migration rate. Figure 7.1 exemplifies the striking conformity that was found for SMLAs. An almost identical pattern was found for the labour market constituent zones (cores, rings and outer rings) as well as for the MELA aggregates. The great majority of areas vary only slightly on either side of the mean rate. Additionally the exceptions are easily identified. Those to the far left of the mean natural change line are principally retirement centres; conversely, those with relatively high levels of natural increase are almost all New Towns or Expanded Towns. These extreme levels of natural change can in themselves be viewed as being at least partially attributable to differential net migration between labour markets or their constituent zones. It can be seen that with the exception of predictable deviations net migration rates can readily be equated with population change rates (and vice versa) for areal units employed by this study.

A convenient spatial summary of most of the variations of net migration and natural change characteristics occurring between labour areas during the 1961-71 period is provided using an eight-way classification following Webb (1963).

Figure 7.2 shows that when the classification is applied to MELAs, clear-cut regional and sub-regional variations emerge in the relationship between the two components. Urban areas with net in-migration greater than natural increase (class 1) are concentrated in the South-East (outside London), much of East Anglia together with parts of the South-West region, and other MELAs peripheral to the main conurbations. The larger cities themselves reveal the contrasting position of net out-migration exceeding their natural increase. Elsewhere natural increase tends to play a more important role in population change, especially for MELAs in the West Midlands and Yorkshire and Humberside regions, where often natural population growth either offsets net out-migration or exceeds levels of in-migration. Again, the resorts stand out, incurring net in-migration coupled with a natural decrease.

This classification based on net migration and natural change is thus successful in summarising the variable spatial impact of net migration upon population totals for city regions as a whole. However,

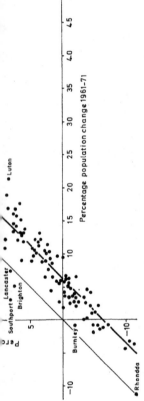

Named places are those having a rate of natural change greater than one standard deviation from the mean rate of natural change.

Figure 7.2: Natural Change and Net Migration Classification for Metropolitan Economic Labour Areas, 1961-71

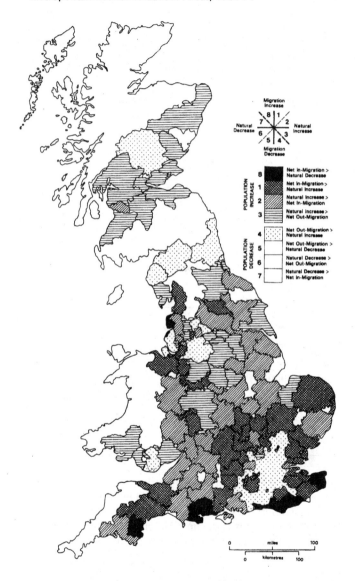

Table 7.1: Proportions of Movers by Origins and Destinations
(1966-1971)

Type of Movers	Number	Proportion of all movers (per cent)	Proportion of inter-zonal movers (per cent)
Movers in Great Britain	17,444,170	100	
Movers within local authorities	9,075,540	52.03	
Movers between local authorities	8,368,630	47.97	
Movers within urban zone but between local authorities	1,549,980	8.89	
Movers between urban zone including unclassified areas	6,818,650	39.09	100
Movers within MELAs but between urban zones	2,092,250	11.99	30.68
Movers between MELAs	4,179,400	23.96	61.29
Movers between MELAs in same planning region	2,128,900	12.20	31.22
Movers between MELAs in different planning regions	2,050,500	11.75	30.07
Movers between MELAs in non-contiguous planning regions	866,630	4.97	12.71
Movers between MELAs (including unclassified areas)	4,726,400	27.09	69.32
Movers between MELAs (including unclassified) in same planning region	2,365,690	13.56	34.69
Movers between MELAs (including unclassified areas) in different planning regions	2,360,710	13.53	34.62
Movers between MELAs (including unclassified areas) in non-contiguous planning regions	996,080	5.71	14.61

movements within MELAs and the differential strength of the streams
on an origin-destination basis cannot be depicted by such information
Detailed local authority data for the one- and five-year periods
preceding 1971 have been made comparable with the urban system
framework as outlined, and some of the results are presented below.

7.3 Migration and the Areal Units Adopted by the Study

The inter-local authority migration flow matrix was first used to assess the relative importance of movements within and between the study areas. Table 7.1 shows that between 1966 and 1971 nearly 17.5 million people moved within Britain — some 36 per cent of the population. During 1970-1, just under 5.9 million (or more than 12 per cent of the population) are recorded as changing residence. It is, of course, no surprise to find a negative relationship between migration and distance, but it is useful to discriminate the proportion of migrations falling within and between the urban units employed here. Table 7.1 and Figure 7.3 show that just about half of the total moves remained in the same local authority area and a further 10 per cent moved between local authorities but remained in the same urban zone. Thus 40 per cent of migrants traversed zonal boundaries and remain of interest here. In absolute terms, inter-zonal movement is represented by 6.8 million migrants between 1966 and 1971 and 2.3 million in the final year.

Of these inter-zonal migrants almost exactly 30 per cent remained in the same MELA. The inter-MELA movers may be broken down into those moving within and between economic planning regions. Table 7.1 indicates similar totals for these two groups, although very slightly more did migrate between labour markets in the same region. Additionally, over 8 per cent of inter-zonal migrants moved into, out of or between unclassified areas.

7.4 Migration and the Redistributive Effects on Population in the Urban System

Analysis concerning net migration trends between 1961 and 1971 revealed a considerable redistribution of population within the nation's cities. The average net migration growth for urban cores in the decade was only 0.6 per cent (Table 7.2), but this figure hides a considerable dispersion of values, and that the largest cities suffered net out-movement which, in absolute terms, far outweighed the net in-movement principally recorded by New Towns and Expanded Towns. Altogether cores lost about 2.5 million people due to net out-migration between 1961 and 1971. In contrast, metropolitan rings experienced a mean population growth of 14.7 per cent attributable to net migration. Unlike the urban cores, the rings were uniformly characterised by high rates of net in-migration. Outer rings, while having an average population increase of 5.1 per cent due to net migration, exhibit a slightly higher degree of variation in this

Migrants within MELA's

| | within E.P.R. | Migrants* |

Intra Planning Region Migrants*

Inter Regional: M_2 Migrants

0   20   40   percent   60   80   100

M₁ Migrants between Local Authorities remaining in same Urban Zone

M₂ Inter Regional Migrants moving between non-contiguous Planning Regions

* Includes moves to, and from, and between unclassified areas

E.P.R. - Economic Planning Regions

Table 7.2: Summary Statistics of Mean Relative Net Migration Change
by Urban Zones, 1961-1971

	Mean	Standard deviation	Coefficient of variation
Urban cores	0.6	12.6	21.0
Metropolitan rings	14.7	11.5	0.8
SMLAs	5.5	9.5	1.7
Outer metropolitan rings	5.1	9.0	1.8
MELAs	5.4	9.2	1.7

characteristic than rings.

Using the more detailed migration flow data it is possible to review
the origins and destinations of inter-zonal moves. Overall, Table 7.3
indicates a similar pattern of redistribution between 1966 and 1971 to
that which was identified for the whole decade: net movement out of
cores and net in-movement for the other zones but with principal gains
at the rings. However, the net decentralisation of 900,000 people
within SMLAs is achieved by an outflow of 1.9 million, outweighing
the inflow of almost one million. Moves 'inward' from rings to cores
thus represent the second-largest inter-zonal flow and the proportion of
the rings' 1966 population that moved to cores (6 per cent) is, in fact,
only slightly less than the proportion of cores' 1966 population that
moved to rings (7 per cent).

The volume of migrations within the SMLA tends to submerge some
of the other interesting features of Table 7.3. An evolving population
pattern may be suggested as the outer rings made substantial net gains
from *each* of the other three zones. In the five-year interval these areas
grew by some 250,000 people due to net migration, of which almost
80,000 originated in ring areas. Additionally, the unclassified areas as a
whole, which traditionally had suffered out-movement, are now
growing by net in-migration from both of the constituent SMLA zones.

How do patterns of population redistribution caused by migration
vary when comparing movement within and between labour markets?
Analysis of Tables 7.4 and 7.5 reveals the following major points:

(1) That both within and between MELAs the most important zonal
reallocation of population is outward from cores to rings. Clearly the
process of decentralisation from urban cores is not confined to the
same city region. Often considerable distances are involved.

Table 7.3: Inter-zonal Migration, 1966-1971

Origin		Destination						Destination				
		C	R	O	U	T		C	R	O	U	T
	C	794	1,865	530	115	3,304	C	11.6	27.3	7.8	1.7	48.5
	R	963	640	494	90	2,187	R	14.1	9.4	7.2	1.3	32.1
	O	335	416	235	87	1,072	O	4.9	6.1	3.4	1.3	15.7
	U	82	76	87	10	255	U	1.2	1.1	1.3	0.1	3.7
	T	2,175	2,997	1,345		302 6,819	T	31.9	44.0	19.7	4.4	100

(a) Absolute flows (thousands)　　　(b) Percentage of total flows

Table 7.4: Inter-zonal Migration within MELAS, 1966-1971

Origin		Destination					Destination			
		C	R	O	T		C	R	O	T
	C	—	1,136	136	1,273	C	—	54.3	6.5	60.8
	R	479	—	141	620	R	22.9	—	6.8	29.7
	O	82	117	—	199	O	3.9	5.6	—	9.5
	T	561	1,254		277 2,092	T	26.8	59.9	13.3	100

(a) Absolute flows (thousands)　　　(b) Percentage of total flows

Table 7.5: Inter-zonal Migration between MELAS and
Unclassified Zones, 1966-1971

Origin		Destination						Destination				
		C	R	O	U	T		C	R	O	U	T
	C	794	729	393	115	2,031	C	16.8	15.4	8.3	2.4	43.0
	R	484	640	352	90	1,567	R	10.2	13.6	7.5	1.9	33.2
	O	253	298	235	87	873	O	5.4	6.3	5.0	1.8	18.5
	U	82	76	87	10	255	U	1.7	1.6	1.8	0.2	5.3
	T	1,614	1,744	1,067		302 4,726	T	34.1	36.9	22.6	6.4	100

(a) Absolute flows (thousands)　　　(b) Percentage of total flows

C — Core　　R — Ring　　O — Outer Ring　　U — Unclassified　　T — Total

Figure 7.4: Inter-zonal Migration within Labour Markets, 1966-1971

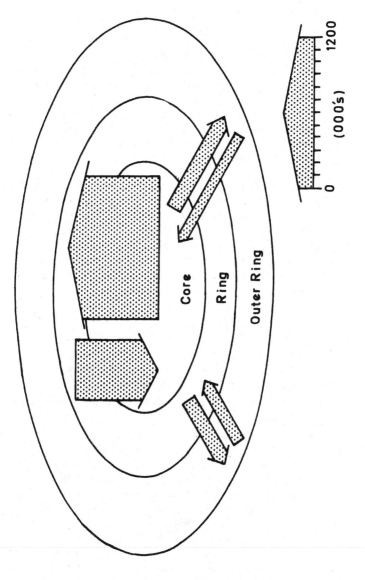

(2) 'Counter-currents' of migrants toward the centre, although significant both within and between MELAs, show increased importance with the longer migrations. Within SMLAs, centralisers were in proportionate terms 42.4 per cent of the number of decentralisers (see Figure 7.4). Between SMLAs as a whole the rate was 67 per cent. This may be broken into movement between MELAs in the same planning region for which 65 per cent was the proportion of inward to outward migrants, and inter-regional migrants – 69 per cent. Finally, for the very long-distance moves – those between non-contiguous planning regions – the proportion of inward to outward movement was 71 per cent.

(3) Both within and between labour markets the outer rings gained by net migration from both cores and rings. The growth of the OMR, unlike the inner rings was, in absolute terms, greater by inter-MELA migration. Additionally, despite its smaller population base, the OMRs' inter-MELA increase of migrants exceeded that accruing to metropolitan rings (194,000 compared with 177,000 in 1966-71). Much of this growth can be accounted for by the decentralisation from the big cities, particularly London, into neighbouring city regions' OMRs.

It is now possible to develop these themes and review some of the regional and local variations of these national patterns.

7.5 Some Regional and Local Variations in the Redistribution of Population by Migration within the Urban System

7.5.1 Redistribution of Population between Urban Zones Aggregated to Planning Regions

In view of the figures quoted earlier concerning the dispersion around national average net migration rates for cores, rings and outer rings, it is perhaps useful to note a remarkably consistent pattern accruing to urban zones in different parts of the country. Using the 1961-71 figures as a starting-point, Table 7.6 and Figure 7.5 show that urban cores in all regions suffered a net loss of population by out-migration in the sixties, although the figures do vary between –1 per cent in East Anglia and –12.9 per cent in Scotland. Highest rates of net in-migration occur for each region in the metropolitan ring, with the exception of the South-East, where the very high rate of OMR growth can be attributed to the large net migration increase by London's outer zone.

In general, although rankings do vary, Table 7.6 indicates that a

Figure 7.5: Relative Changes in Migration for the Constituent Zones of Metropolitan Economic Labour Areas Averaged for Economic Planning Regions, 1961-1971

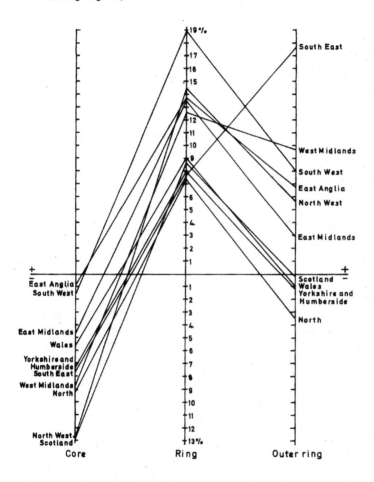

Table 7.6: Relative Net Migration Change by Urban Zone Summed for
Economic Planning Regions, 1961-1971

Economic Planning Region	Urban Core	Metropolitan Ring	Outer Metropolitan Ring
South-East	− 7.7	7.6	17.6
West Midlands	− 8.7	12.5	9.6
East Midlands	− 4.7	13.5	2.8
East Anglia	− 1.0	13.7	6.7
South-West	− 1.8	19.0	8.0
Yorkshire and Humberside	− 7.5	7.9	−1.2
North-West	−12.8	14.5	5.6
Northern	− 9.3	7.3	−3.5
Wales	− 5.7	9.1	−1.1
Scotland	−12.9	8.8	−0.3

higher rate of core decrease due to migration is associated with a
generally lower rate of migration gain in the metropolitan ring and
possibly migration loss in the outer ring.

Turning to flows in terms of their origins and destinations, each
region reveals clear decentralisation within SMLAs between 1966 and
1977 (Table 7.7). However, the strength of this outward push varies.
In terms of the mean rate of outward to total moves within SMLAs the
West Midlands' city regions indicate lowest mean propensity toward
decentralisation with an average 59 per cent of moves between core and
rings being outward. The North-West region has the highest outward
push with almost 70 per cent of migrations within the SMLA taking the
core to ring form.

Although each region presents a picture of overall intra-SMLA
decentralisation, some urban centres, mainly found in locations
peripheral to 'Megalopolis Britain', are still centralising. Decline of the
metropolitan rings occurs in the most rural of such areas, for example
King's Lynn and Hereford, causing problems for local economies no less
severe than those resulting from more common patterns in other parts
of the urban system.

Regarding net shifts of population to the outer ring, an even greater
variation between the regions emerges (Table 7.8). In the South-East,
the mean for the outward proportion of SMLA-OMR moves within
city regions is as strong as decentralisation within the SMLAs at

Table 7.7: The Proportion of Intra-SMLA, Inter-zonal Moves
Decentralising from Core to Ring Averaged for Economic Planning
Regions (1966-1971)

Economic Planning Region	Per cent
South-East	61.5
West Midlands	59.4
East Midlands	64.7
East Anglia	60.8
South-West	62.0
Yorkshire and Humberside	65.7
North-West	69.6
Northern	60.9
Wales	63.2
Scotland	60.7

Table 7.8: The Proportion of Total Movement between SMLAs and
Outer Rings Decentralising, Averaged for Economic Planning
Regions (1966-1971)

Economic Planning Region	Per cent
South-East	60.0
West Midlands	54.6
East Midlands	53.2
East Anglia	50.3
South-West	52.1
Yorkshire and Humberside	52.1
North-West	58.8
Northern	50.2
Wales	47.0
Scotland	42.2

Table 7.9: Proportion of All Intra-Regional Inter-local Authority
Migrations Taking Place between MELAS (1966-71)

Economic Planning Region	Per cent
South-East	22.0
South-West	16.9
North-West	14.9
Great Britain	14.1
Scotland	14.0
East Anglia	13.4
East Midlands	13.1
Yorkshire and Humberside	10.7
Wales	10.6
West Midlands	8.0

62 per cent. In absolute terms, because the exchanges between SMLAs and outer rings are less than those between cores and rings, the net redistributive effects of net movement to the OMR are considerably smaller in the South-East and elsewhere.

Other regions record much lower rates of decentralisation to the outer ring than for their SMLAs. Only 'outward' movement in the North-West exceeds an average of more than 55 per cent of all exchanges between SMLAs and outer rings. At the other extreme Wales and Scotland reported a majority of their systems to be centralising between 1966 and 1971. In Wales the outer ring incurred net losses with both ring and urban cores and in Scotland the OMRs' net loss to rings outweighed the number of migrants relocating in the OMR from cores. By the final year of the period, Wales as a whole appeared to have started to decentralise out of SMLAs, and the mean inward and outward proportions for Scotland were virtually in balance. In other regions the outer rings also revealed an apparent 'improvement' in interaction with the SMLAs. This is best exemplified in the Northern region, where the OMR as a whole suffered aggregate five year deficits for both inter-MELA migration within the region and inter-regional migration, but reported net gains for both these streams during the final year. Thus Scotland is the only remaining region where for both the 1966-71 and 1970-1 intervals metropolitan rings were gaining in net terms from the other three zones in the region.

The fortunes of unclassified areas also vary regionally. As with the outer rings, the peripheral regions tend to fare relatively poorly in terms of net migration compared with the more industrialised regions. The unclassified zones of Scotland, Yorkshire and Humberside, the North and Wales still direct migrants in net terms to urban Britain, but in these examples net gains are accomplished from cores (and usually rings) offset by a greater net loss out of unclassified areas to the OMR.

In the other regions the unclassified areas are growing in terms of net migration, although their interaction with the OMR always results in a net loss. Interestingly, a local pattern of centralisation within East Anglia and the South-West can still be detected, but these small deficits are easily offset by inter-regional in-migration, principally from the South-East. These in-migration flows contain a high proportion of elderly, the retirement migrants, and again such influences are likely to cause a new type of demand with regard to local authority service provision.

7.5.2 Movements Concerning 'Million Cities'

The South-East was the only region where the proportion of the total number of migrants between MELAs was significantly in excess of the national average (Table 7.9). This is mainly due to decentralisation out of London labour market to neighbouring MELAs. In total, London lost some 408,180 people to the rest of the urban system, including 322,720 to rest of the South-East between 1966 and 1971. Figure 7.6 reveals the importance of London's decline to the population change of the 37 other labour areas in the region. Thirty-five MELAs grew by net in-migration during both periods from the region as a whole, but this total is reduced to only 13 of the region's peripheral MELAs if the net gain from London is excluded. Figure 7.6 suggests two related themes. First, that the population in the region is moving gradually away from the capital in the form of a 'ripple-effect' – a view enhanced when the net loss of population of even the South East's peripheral MELAs to their contiguous neighbours just outside the region is taken into account. Secondly, this process appears to affect the New Town labour markets as much as the other 'established' city regions. This suggested the New Towns may be vulnerable to a shift in the direction of net migration should the supply of migrants from London in any way diminish. That the New Towns might quickly begin to lose population by net migration is supported by the fact that those areas have not only the highest in-migration rates per thousand population, but also the highest out-migration rates, probably due, amongst other factors, to their relatively young populations.

As indicated earlier, London is not the only large city to be experiencing loss of population by inter-metropolitan decentralisation. Although London is the only city region to possess a truly national migration field, the fortunes of the other great cities have implications concerning the redistribution of population within regions, if not wide areas. Each of the other six cities with SMLA populations exceeding one million (Birmingham, Glasgow, Leeds, Liverpool, Manchester and Newcastle) have directed considerable numbers into contiguous systems. Altogether 63 MELAs received at least one-quarter of their in-migrants from a 'million city'. Of those, 39 are orientated towards London, 5 towards Birmingham, 4 towards Manchester, 5 towards Liverpool, 4 towards Leeds, 1 towards Newcastle and 5 towards Glasgow. The bulk of migration from million cities to these satellite areas is likely to stem from the decentralisation of both population and workplace, reflecting the desire for better conditions and less congestion. Out-migration of those in the higher-income groups, who can afford relatively long and expensive journeys to work, will still be represented in these totals. The analysis of migration flows between million cities and the rest of the country has been dealt with in more detail elsewhere (Kennett, 1977),

Figure 7.6: The London MELA's Impact on Net Migration Flows
within the South-East Region

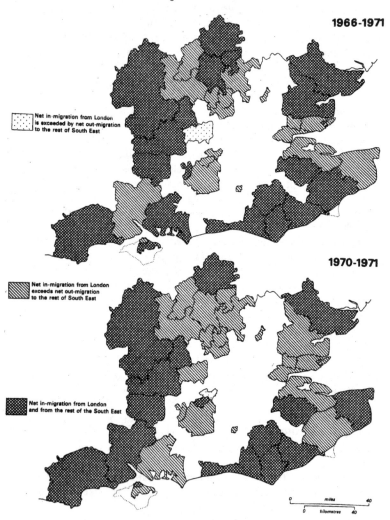

as has the differential decentralisation by individual socio-economic groups from conurbations to the rest of the regions (Kennett and Randolph, 1978).

It is interesting to note that a much higher proportion of out-migrants from London's core chose other cores as destinations compared with out-migrants from the capital's ring (59 per cent compared with 47 per cent). Conversely, higher proportions of out-migrants from the London ring chose other rings rather than cores compared with out-migration from the capital's core (42 per cent against 34 per cent). The London outer ring directed an almost identical proportion into satellite MELAs' constituent zones to those leaving the whole MELA. Similar results were also obtained from decentralisation of Newcastle, Birmingham, Glasgow and Liverpool, but two million cities, Leeds and Manchester, recorded the reverse relationship. This is probably an indication of the depressed nature of their relatively small satellite markets.

Decentralisation into the New Towns from the capital depicted a much stronger version of the relationships described above. New Town cores, virtually synonymous with the designated areas, imported as much as 70 per cent of in-migrants from the London MELA from its core.[5] But paradoxically the New Town rings show a much lower proportion of in-migrants from the core (42 per cent) with correspondingly greater emphasis upon London's ring as a source (38 per cent).

The importance of the seven million cities upon migration in Britain is emphasised when it is noted that 52 per cent of migrants between labour areas were involved with one of the MELAs. About 4 per cent of all inter-city region migration passed between the seven areas, about 17 per cent arrived in the conurbations from the rest of Britain and 31 per cent left the major areas for the rest of Britain: compared with proportions of population accounted for by million cities these elements are relatively low. In terms of inflow, 106 MELAs received their largest stream from one of the seven systems. London is the source of the largest inflow to 68 of these. Fifty-eight labour markets directed their largest outflow to the London MELA.

Not surprisingly, of all inter-MELA migration streams, in absolute terms, those between the million cities are the largest. However, while the most important origins of flows to the conurbations tend to stem from the other six areas, their most important outflows are likely to be directed to more desirable areas or the satellite systems discussed above. The migrations between the largest systems were predominantly inter-core. Inter-million city decentralisation between cores and rings was about the same strength as the nation, but the rate of out-migration from SMLAs to other million city outer rings appeared lower than that for Britain. This is of course in marked contrast to the pattern *within* the 'big cities'. Here the out-migration to the OMR was probably stronger than anywhere else, particularly in London and Birmingham, superseding decentralisation from cores to rings.

The traditional population relocation southward via the million cities could still be detected. In spite of London's overall loss, net gains were derived from exchanges with each of the other six areas, and Birmingham showed net surpluses when interacting with its five northern counterparts. In contrast, Glasgow incurred net migration loss in each of its six migration exchanges and Newcastle recorded net gains only from the Scottish million city.

7.6 Summary

The objective of this paper was to attempt to determine some of the principal population shifts attributable to migration within and between functional areas in Britain. The areal units adopted are sufficiently flexible to allow analysis of intra- and inter-city region migration in either national aggregate terms or for individual areas (or subsets of areas).

The analysis indicates that for both labour market areas as a whole and their constituent urban zones, with some predictable deviations, migration was by far the more important component of the changing distributions of population.

By use of the relationship of the two components of population a summary of the net redistribution characteristics between MELAs was presented. Direction of these movements and population shifts within labour markets, however, remained outstanding.

Using the five-year and one-year inter-local authority area migration tables and net figures relating to the whole decade, it was shown that urban cores were losing considerable numbers of migrants in net terms and that, although each of the other three zones was growing by net in-migration, by far the largest increases were directed to the metropolitan rings.

When the direction of migrants was considered, although, as expected, the largest inter-zonal flow was that from urban cores to metropolitan rings, the absolute size of the 'inward' component of intra-SMLA moves easily surpassed any of the remaining inter-zonal streams. On a proportionate basis only slightly lower levels of the ring's population moved to urban cores than made the reverse move.

Decentralisation was shown to be taking place from both zones within the SMLA to outer rings. Absolute net growth of population by net in-migration for the OMR was still less than that recorded for metropolitan rings. Unclassified areas were also in receipt of net influxes from the SMLAs which nationally offset losses incurred with the interaction with outer-rings.

Patterns of inter-zonal migration within and between labour areas were compared and contrasted. The principal findings were:

(1) decentralisation from cores to rings was clearly in evidence for both, although the proportion of 'inward' to 'outward' movers increased with the length of the migration;

(2) decentralisation from SMLAs to outer rings was also evident both within and between MELAs. Inter-MELA growth of OMRs by migration in absolute terms exceeded the equivalent growth by metropolitan rings.

Some of the regional and local variations of population distribution were considered. The major points were:

(1) The consistency of net out-migration from cores in all regions with major net gains associated with rings and lesser gains to the OMR.

(2) The decentralisation within SMLAs was evident within each region, although the strength of this trend varied.

(3) Some regions still indicated an overall centralisation of the OMR population between 1966 and 1971. A general 'improvement' in the outer ring's position regarding population change could be detected in these regions by the final year.

(4) The unclassified areas revealed a division between those regions containing most of highland Britain where continuing loss of population through migration persisted and those in more southerly regions where net in-migration was recorded.

(5) In absolute terms million city MELAs reported the largest inter-MELA inflows and outflows of migrants. However, there was a tendency for these cities to receive their largest inflows from other big cities whilst they directed principal outflows to 'more desirable' cities, or satellite areas.

(6) New Towns continued to record net in-migration during the late 1960s but solely due to net gain from the capital. Since of all city regions the New Towns have the highest in- and

out-migration rates per thousand population, any reduction in the supply of in-movers *could* result in a transfer of the problem of out-migraton to the New Towns. New Town cores received a disproportionately high proportion of in-migrants from London's core, possibly exemplifying success of their objectives. However, their rings recorded very low proportions of in-migration from London's core and this is likely to have implications concerning the social balance of these areas.

(7) Although London is the only MELA to suffer net out-migration in the South-East in both the five- and one-year periods, a deconcentration of population moving away from the capital within the whole South-East and beyond was identified.

This chapter has dealt with net changes of population attributable to migration and migration streams for total populations. Clearly in reality the position is more complex. Not only is migration the main determinant of population change at the spatial scales employed here, it is also the main factor in the changing age structure of an area's population and a considerable influence on its socio-economic characteristics (though here social mobility also plays a major role). The Urban Change Project at the London School of Economics has investigated such trends in detail with regard to both the composition of changing total populations and also the specific influence of migrants. Results from this analysis are available from two research reports (Urban Change Project, 1978a, 1978b). Thus, whilst the work presented in this essay casts considerable light on inter-regional as well as intra-regional population change, it should be set within this more complex reality.

Notes

1. This chapter is published with the permission of the Department of the Environment. It summarises part of some research undertaken by the Department of Geography, London School of Economics, under contract to the Planning Intelligence Directorate of the Department of the Environment. The other members of the team were J.R. Drewett, A.E. Gillespie, J.B. Goddard and N.A. Spence. The full results of the study are published in two research reports — Department of the Environment, 1976, and Urban Change Project 1978a.

2. The project covered such topics as population change, employment change, migration and natural change, socio-economic group change, age structure change and work-travel change.

3. For the United States see Berry, 1973; for Great Britain refer to Hall *et al.*, 1973, and Urban Change Project, 1974a.

4. 1966 Journey to Work data were used, since the 1971 tables were not available at the time. Population data referred to 1971.

5. The success of New Towns in aiding the decentralisation from congested central areas is implied, but note that urban cores cannot be equated with inner-city areas.

References

Berry, B.J.L. 1973. *Growth Centres in the American Urban System. Volume 1, Community Development and Regional Growth in the Sixties and Seventies.* Cambridge, Mass.: Ballinger Publishing Co.

Department of Environment. 1976. *British Cities, Urban Population and Employment Trends 1951-71*, Research Report 10

Hall, P. *et al.* 1973. *The Containment of Urban England, Volume 1. Urban Metropolitan Growth Processes or Megalopolis Denied.* London: George Allen and Unwin

Kennett, S. 1975. A classification of the components of intra-urban and inter-urban population change in England and Wales, 1961-71. Graduate School of Geography Discussion Papers, no. 54. London: London School of Economics

Kennett, S. 1977. Migration and 'million city' labour markets, 1966-71. Working Report no. 52, Urban Change in Britain Project. London: Department of Geography, London School of Economics

Kennett, S. 1978. Census data and migration analysis: an appraisal. Department of Geography, London School of Economics, unpublished paper

Kennett, S. and Randolph, W. 1978. The differential migration of socio-economic groups, 1966-71. Graduate School of Geography Discussion Papers, no. 66. London: London School of Economics

Urban Change Project. 1974a. Standard Metropolitan Labour Areas and Metropolitan Economic Labour Areas, Part 1. Definitional notes and commentary. Working Report no. 1. London: Department of Geography, London School of Economics

Urban Change Project. 1974b. Additional perspective on population change in the urban system. Working Report no. 9. London: Department of Geography, London School of Economics

Urban Change Project. 1974c. Net migration, natural change and density of population in the urban system. Working Report no. 10. London: Department of Geography, London School of Economics

Urban Change Project, 1978a. British cities: migration trends. London: Department of Geography, London School of Economics, mimeographed paper

Urban Change Project. 1978b. British cities: socio-economic trends. London: Department of Geography, London School of Economics, mimeographed paper

Webb, J.W. 1963. The natural and migrational components of population changes in England and Wales, 1921-1931. *Economic Geography*, 39, 130-48

Willis, K.G. 1974. *Problems in Migration Analysis.* Farnborough: Saxon House

THE RELATIONSHIP BETWEEN GEOGRAPHIC
AND OCCUPATIONAL MOBILITY IN THE
CONTEXT OF REGIONAL ECONOMIC GROWTH

David Gleave and Derek Palmer

8.1 Introduction

There are a number of reasons why the migration of labour should be
evaluated within a framework which also incorporates the process of
occupational mobility. This chapter will consider two particular reasons
why this should be so.

First, there is a need to carefully define both the *processes* and the
problems which require analysis. In the field of applied social science
research the policy-maker is concerned with developing policies aimed
at ameliorating specific, well defined problems. It is often the case that
problems represent the particular states that a number of processes
generate *simultaneously*. For example, what is comprehensively
referred to as the inner-city problem defines the present state of a
number of economic and social processes concerned with housing
supply and demand, the location of the firm (employment
opportunities), journey to work, land-use planning and many others.
The researcher, on the other hand, will often be concerned with the
analysis of discrete process which may, according to their various
instantaneous states, be associated with quite different problems. In
this case, the process of the location of the firm might be associated
with problems of unemployment in the inner city or the declining
region or with 'overheating' in rapidly expanding areas. There is
therefore considerable utility in developing a framework of analysis
which is more agglomerated than is often utilised in order to
understand interrelated processes and problems. Such an approach
would reject the analysis of labour migration as a comprehensive whole
and require a more generic approach. What types of problems are
associated with labour migration? What other processes are
determinants of such problems? These are the questions we need to
answer.

The analysis of labour migration has thrown up a number of
methodological problems, one of which may serve as a starting point
for developing the comprehensive systematic approach which we favour.
The delineation of appropriate spatial units has been achieved by a

number of different approaches, depending upon the terms of reference of the analyst. From the perspective of the journey to work *process* the concept of labour market areas has been devised as being useful for examining geographic labour mobility (see for example, Fielding, 1971; Johnson, Salt and Wood, 1974). However, the policy-maker, who might be more concerned with the unemployment *problem*, would find a classification based on employment opportunities within commuting distance of place of residence to be more relevant (see Hyman and Gleave, 1976). These two approaches to defining appropriate spatial units are largely conditioned by the questions posed by researcher or policy-maker, but both are adopted with a view to understanding aspects of the worker-job matchmaking system. The fact that research problems do not usually arise out of the state of single, simple processes, or that such processes rarely generate single problems, suggests that a spatial taxonomy should be defined which is conditioned by the need to analyse interrelated processes and their associated interrelated problems. In the case of the example cited, an appropriate classification (albeit an imperfect one) has been developed by Smart (1974). Each region he delineates meets a certain threshold requirement concerning the proportions of workers (and jobs) which are tenured with local jobs (and workers). In the next section we develop a framework which composites a number of processes and problems which are related to the employment matchmaking system. Vacant jobs are not only filled by geographically mobile workers but also by those who develop or become equipped with new skills. Our approach integrates occupational and geographic mobility in analysing the dynamics of the labour market.

Secondly, we are suggesting that the analysis of migration should be carried out in a way which explicitly recognises a dynamical dimension. This is because the processes which determine the state of the labour market at any one time develop at a variety of rates and cannot be analysed satisfactorily by adopting a cross-sectional approach. However, having made this point, the dynamics of the matchmaking system are discussed in this paper in a methodological and theoretical context rather than empirically. We now spell out our comprehensive, dynamic framework of analysis.

8.2 A Dynamic Framework of Analysis

No satisfactory theory of why workers change their jobs, their occupations and their places of residence has been forthcoming to date. Similarly, there have been no adequate explanation or good predictions about the numbers, locations and types of job which employers will create or destroy. The majority of papers in the field of labour market dynamics have adopted a single-discipline, partial approach and thereby treated many relevant variables as exogenous. However, the stocks and flows mentioned previously are all of major importance to our analysis. We commence, therefore, by adopting a very broad accounting framework within which to study the processes and problems of the labour market. Our initial premise is that the absence of a good comprehensive theory of the matchmaking system suggests that a completely deterministic analytic approach would be unrealistic. Our second premise is that there are, at the macroscopic level, a number of statistical regularities associated with labour market processes. For example, the interaction effect in migration (distance decay) is well established empirically, as is the relationship between mobility and age. Such regularities may well be confounded in aggregate mobility data, but their isolation into a number of identifiable concepts and the definition of an appropriate classification of labour market stocks and flows enables us to proceed with a stochastic analysis of our system of interest. Our framework of analysis is reproduced as Figure 8.1. This representation is primarily concerned with identifying stocks and flows rather than specifying the form of the process which explains the flows. Put another way, we describe the state space of our system in terms of stock variables and measure their derivatives, the flow variables, without specifying the theoretical form of the equations of motion. It is possible to assume initially that the rates of change in stock variables,, dX_i/dt, function to the existing values of all stock variables, $X_i...X_n$ described by Rosen (1970), i.e.

$$\frac{dX_i}{dt} = F_i (X_1 \dots \dots X_n) \quad i = 1, n.$$

The first requirement in adopting this approach is to derive a measure of the rates of change and in this paper we focus attention on the rates of change in two principal dimensions affecting labour supply, occupational change and geographic change. We shall demonstrate that not only do empirical regularities obtain in the case of these two simple processes, but that the two processes are fairly complementary in providing the appropriate labour supply in a specific location in order to meet the requirements of employers.

Figure 8.1: The Matchmaking System

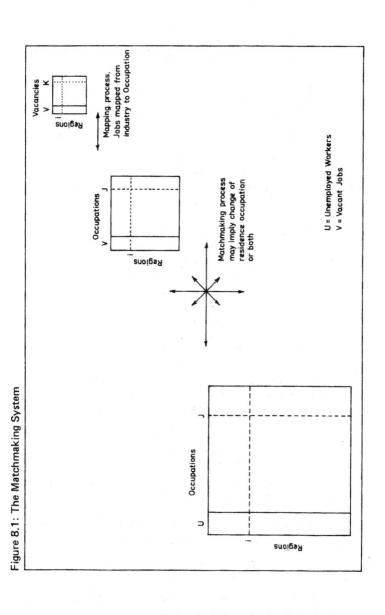

Vacancies
V   K
Regions

Mapping process.
Jobs mapped from
industry to Occupation

Occupations
V   J
Regions

Matchmaking process
may imply change of
residence occupation
or both

Occupations
U   J
Regions

U = Unemployed Workers
V = Vacant Jobs

8.3 The Changing Local Labour Force

An analysis of the demographic and occupational characteristics of the labour force at the *regional scale* does not adequately probe supply conditions within a local labour market. None the less, a provisional analysis at regional level can be used to illustrate the processes which bring about a change in the skill characteristics of the region's labour supply. Four major factors are relevant:

(1) the career profile learning process;
(2) entrants to and exits from the labour market;
(3) occupational mobility;
(4) geographic mobility.

The changing skills of labour are an important determinant of the economic well-being of a region, but it is not uncommon to see analyses which disregard one or more of these components of change simply because their system of interest is defined very narrowly. (See, for instance, Greenwood, 1973.)

The career profile learning process represents a simple concept, but one which is virtually impossible to measure unless it results in occupational or geographic mobility. It is simply concerned with acquiring skills whilst in employment which may well contribute towards increasing regional income. It is most easily identified through the apprenticeship system, but is probably more significant when associated with changes in skill inputs due to technological innovation. The ability of labour to adapt to new production processes without requiring formal retraining or needing to pass through a sequence of redundancy and re-employment is possibly the most important adjustment process relating the supply of labour to a qualitative changing demand.

The second adjustment factor is measurable and is again of extreme importance in changing the occupational structure of the regional labour market. This important dynamic component is not reported in detail in this paper; it is the subject of a separate analysis (Palmer and Gleave, 1977). However, some of our observations are summarised as follows:

(1) The local labour market is constantly changing so that at the start of any one year around 2½ to 5 per cent of the initial stock will cease to be economically active at the end of the year. This

Figure 8.2: Age Distribution of Males in Occupation Group 2 (Miners) and Group 6 (Electrical/Electronics)

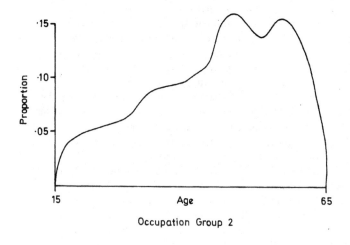

Occupation Group 2

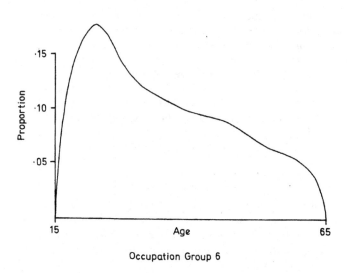

Occupation Group 6

proportion is mainly comprised of women producing children and retirements.

(2) The long-run changes in demand for particular skills are accommodated by differing marginal entry rates into the various occupation groups. The natural wastage principle operates not only in the form of agreements between trade unions and employers, but also as a natural market process. Occupations which are declining do not proportionately reproduce themselves by definition. However, conditions do fluctuate on a cyclical and less regular short-run-basis. These points are best illustrated by comparing the age distributions of two contrasting occupation groups (see Palmer, 1977). Mining is an occupation group which has for many years been in general decline, a fact which is illustrated in Figure 8.2 and indicated by the low proportions of workers in the age cohorts below 40 years. In contrast, electrical and electronics workers are disproportionately concentrated in the cohorts aged less than 35 years. These two density functions, which are significantly different at the 95 per cent confidence level (Kolmogorov-Smirnof 'D' statistic 0.329, n_1 = 25,623 n_2 = 52,914), illustrate how important the process of exits and entries is in defining the changing skill composition of the regional labour market.

However, the dynamic nature of regional economies is such that not all changes in demand for labour can be accommodated by 'on the job training' or by differential recruitment and retirement rates to and from the various occupation groups. There are, for instance, significant changes in skill requirements demanded in areas with strongly specialised and rapidly evolving local economies, such as North-West England. Secondly, there are also changes required due to overall net growth or decline in the demand for labour. The next section will deal with the interrelations between occupational and geographic mobility which tend to bring about these adjustments. There will not be a discussion of how labour demand is affected by supply characteristics, even though section 2 hinted at the importance of feedback mechanisms.

8.4 Geographic and Occupational Mobility: their Interaction

In attempting to explain the more subtle relationships and interactions of the matchmaking process there are two bounds outside of which analysis cannot be usefully developed at a macroscopic scale. Analyses at a highly aggregative level may develop an understanding of the general structural relationships between regional levels of employment, unemployment, vacancies and activity levels. But such analyses may fail to provide concrete input into the policy debate (aimed at minimising unemployment levels and maximising output or welfare functions) simply because of the failure to take account of, say, types of unemployment (see Thirlwall, 1974), vacancy flow processes (see Leicester, 1973), or other factors which militate against an easy matching of supply stocks with demand stocks. At the other extreme, disaggregated approaches may fail to develop anything but a temporary description of labour dynamics because of the unsuitability of concepts and classifications which are used or because of the non-stationary nature of transition parameters.

We do not aim at this stage to define an intermediate classification or level of disaggregation which maximises both our understanding of the processes involved or the utility of research findings for the policy-maker. Instead we shall examine, at the occupation order level of disaggregation, how two important 'simple' processes relate in affecting the matchmaking process.

Diagramatically, our focus of interest is as shown in Figure 8.3. We are concerned with two major sets, their intersection and their intersection with two other sets. We cannot satisfactorily measure the size and therefore the relative importance of the intersecting sets. At this stage we are only able to consider the superficial relationships at the disaggregated occupation order level between the occupation mobility set and the geographic mobility set.

It has been demonstrated elsewhere (Gleave and Cordey-Hayes, 1977) that the spatial restructuring of labour takes place according to a well established but slow process. A positive linear relationship exists between inter-regional in-migrants and out-migrants such that regions characterised by net population growth due to spatial mobility experience high rates of both immigration and emigration. It has also been shown that regional rates of out-migration relate fairly well to occupation structure and occupation-specific rates of migration (Gleave, 1976). In the remainder of this section we wish to probe:

(1) whether the inter-regional linear relationship obtains for the various occupation groups;

(2) whether regions experiencing growth attract migrants in specific occupation groups (or lose migrants from specific occupation occupation groups);

(3) how spatial mobility by occupation relates to occupational

Figure 8.3: Factors Contributing to the Changes in Skill and Location of the Economically Active

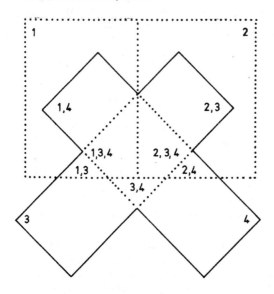

1. The career profile learning process
2. Entrants to and exits from the labour market
3. Occupational mobility
4. Geographic mobility

mobility;

(4) whether workers with different skills are more prone to migrate over different distance ranges.

The first of these enquiries can be tackled in either of two ways, depending on whether the emphasis is placed on occupational mobility, in the case of all regions, or geographic mobility, in the case of each occupation. These options are discussed in turn.

The positive linear relationship between regional out-migration and regional in-migration (see Figure 8.4) which was referred to above produced a correlation coefficient of $r_c = 0.933$ and has previously been explained in terms of a regional turnover process. It is not clear whether we are dealing with systematic behaviour which can be dichotomised as a mover-stayer process (see Blumen, Kogan and

Figure 8.4: Relationship between Out-migration and In-migration

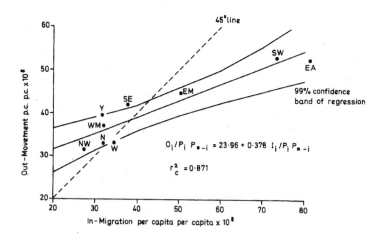

Figure 8.5: Occupational Mobility: Relationship between Out-movement and In-movement

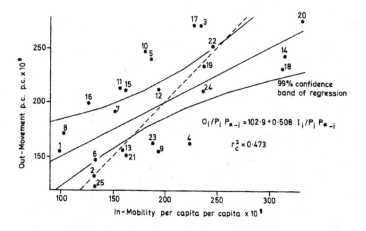

McCarthy, 1955) (implying that the same subset move on time and time again), or whether a different class of persons move out from those who move in. This detail will be taken up later, but at present the central point of interest is that the linear relationship is attributable to differential turnover rates with relatively small net changes. The important question to pursue is whether this process obtains in the case of occupational as well as geographic mobility. The relationship between the gross rates of occupational decline and growth, reproduced as Figure 8.5, are plotted by standardising for the numbers in the occupation concerned and the numbers in all other occupations. This latter component controls for the size of origin and destination pools and is of importance because some occupations, such as clerical workers, service workers and engineers account for a disproportionately large quantity of all employees whilst others, such as glass-, ceramics- and leather-workers, are tiny. It was hypothesised initially that the 'turnover process' would not obtain in the case of occupational mobility. A negative monotonic relationship was thought most likely, or, alternatively, it was anticipated that movement out of the various occupations might be random but that movement into occupations would favour a limited, small number of fast-growth groups. When we regressed occupation out-movement against occupation in-movement, the following relationship obtained:

$$\frac{O_i}{P_i \, P_{*-i}} = 102.9 \times 10^{-8} + 0.508 \; \frac{I_i}{P_i \, P_{*-i}}$$

where O_i and I_i represent the flows out of and into occupation i and P_i and P_{*-i} are the standardisation components mentioned above. The correlation coefficient of 0.687 was significant at the 95 per cent level of confidence. Whilst this was not so impressive as that concerning the components of geographic mobility, it did reflect an increase in the number of observations (up from 9 to 25) and strongly indicated a positive relationship. However, we were not able to state with such confidence that the fastest growing occupations due to mobility were also the occupations which also lost the greatest proportion of workers. Whilst this was generally true, the r_c^2 value of 0.473 indicated a broader distribution around the regression line than was the case with geographic mobility. Consequently, some net growth occupations, such as professional and technical workers, were characterised by low mobility levels, whilst some declining groups, such as utilities and transport workers, were generally highly mobile. Having affirmed a positive relationship in the case of occupational and geographic mobility, we then went on to establish whether the migration linear relationship occurred for each occupation.

An examination of the geographic mobility of each of the 25 occupations under analysis revealed that the spatial restructuring process did not conform to the positive linear turnover pattern which was exhibited macroscopically by all occupations (and all regions in the case of occupational mobility). Broadly speaking, each of the three previously mentioned relationships occurred in one or more of the occupation groups. Above anything else, this indicated that whilst restructuring at the aggregated macro scale exhibited a singular positive linear characteristic, at a disaggregated level a variety of processes and a variation in the rates of restructuring obtained. For example, occupation group 1, agriculture, exhibited no regularity whatsoever; the restructuring process appears to be totally random with Wales characterised by low rates of in- and out-migration, South-East England by high rates in both cases, the East Midlands by high out-migration rates but low in-migration rates, and East Anglia by the reverse pattern. Secondly, another set of occupations, notably gas, coke and chemicals makers, exhibited the negative monotonic relationship associated with the traditional economic push-pull theory. There was also evidence that the Lansing and Mueller (1964) hypothesis, which postulates random out-migration and differential rates of in-migration, obtained in the case of occupation 8, woodworkers (see Lansing and Mueller). Whilst most occupation groups did conform to the positive linear relationship, there was one interesting variant on the theme. Coal-miners and quarrymen produced a migration relationship with a coefficient of regression greater than unity. This indicated the regions characterised by net in-migration in this occupation experienced low rather than high levels of gross mobility.

The different rates at which restructuring took place amongst the occupation groups, however, did suggest that other regularities might occur. Fast-growing regions may be expected to 'attract' large proportions of the geographically and occupationally mobile population. Because certain occupations are in a long-run decline trajectory, it was hypothesised that the growth regions, besides attracting a disproportionately large share of the mobile population as a whole, might further attract an even larger share in those occupations which were growing. (The growth occupations in this context are those which are expanding due to occupational mobility rather than those whose growth is attributable to high entry rates of school leavers. In fact, these two components are strongly positively correlated.)

Figure 8.5 indicates that eleven of the occupation groups were growing as a result of occupation mobility. The groups were:

IV	glass and ceramics workers;
IX	leather workers;
XIII	paper and printing workers;
XIV	makers of other products;
XVIII	labourers not elsewhere classified;
XIX	transport workers;
XX	warehousemen, storekeepers, packers and bottlers;
XXI	clerical workers;
XXIII	service, sport and recreation workers;
XXIV	administrative and managers;
XXV	professional and technical workers.

Given their observed turnover rates and the empirical relationship between the directional components of occupational mobility, groups IV, IX, XIII, XVIII, XXI and XXIII were selected as growing most significantly. We might therefore expect the rate of geographic in-migration to be disproportionately high in the fast-growth regions, East Anglia, South-West England and the East Midlands, for these particular occupations. The rates of in-migration to our fast-growth regions rank 1, 2 and 3 for the system as a whole, but in the case of the occupations we have identified they rank in that order only in the cases of occupations XXI and XXIII. Only in the case of occupation XVIII is that order transposed. In each of the other occupations a lower ranking obtains for at least one of the regions, as can be seen from Table 8.1. There are, of course, nine regions overall.

Table 8.1: Occupation-specific Ranking of Regional In-migration Rates

Occupation	Rank of region's in-migration rate		
	East Anglia	South-West	East Midlands
IV	3	1	6
IX	1	2	4
XVII	7	1	2
XVIII	2	1	3
XXI	1	2	3
XXIII	1	2	3

All occupations were then examined to isolate those particular skill groups in which the three 'growth' regions ranked from 1 through 3 in any particular order. The following occupation groups emerged: VI, VII, XIV, XVI, XVIII, XIX, XXI, XXII, XXIII, XXIV and XXV. This collection includes all the occupations identified from Figure 8.5 as growing, with the exception of orders IV, IX and XIII. In addition, electrical and electronics workers, engineers, painters and decorators, and salesworkers were included.

This list of occupations which were producing high rates of in-migration to the growth regions was checked to ascertain whether they were attracting disproportionately large numbers of persons given their relatively fast growth rates. An expected rate of in-migration was determined on the basis of regional employment structure in 1970 and occupation-specific migration rates. For each region the observed number of migrants in each occupation was divided by the expected number and these ratios were further divided by the ratio for the region as a whole. The latter calculation was performed to standardise for variations in regional employment growth. All resulting ratios with a value greater than unity indicated a disproportionate attraction of migrants. The results which are reproduced in Table 8.2 showed that workers in the following occupation groups were attracted to the three growth regions: VI, VII, VIII, XI, XIII, XVI, XVIII, XIX, XXI, XXII, XXIV.

These results may be summarised as follows. Not all of the growth occupations are associated with growing regions, the notable exceptions being glass- and ceramics- and leather-workers. However, most of the growing occupations are growing disproportionately fast in such regions, as are some other occupations. The package comprises occupations in the quaternary sector plus electrical and electronics, engineering and 'other' manufacturing from the secondary sector, along with some associated service occupations such as construction and clerical workers.

Concerning the relationship between geographic mobility and occupational mobility, we hypothesised that there would be some sort of trade-off between the two types of mobility which would produce a negative monotonic relationship. This would be true whether geographic mobility was related to movement into the various occupations or to movement out of the various occupations for the simple reason that these two variables were positively correlated (see Figure 8.5). This exception was based upon notional mobility at the skill extremes of the occupational classification. Those workers with the greatest skills, perhaps the professional workers, would find that the

Table 8.2: In-migration by Occupation, 1970-1971

Occupation	N	Y	NW	EM	WM	EA	SE	SW	W
I	1.058	0.833	0.993	0.656	1.409	0.727	1.145	0.924	0.700
II	1.345	0.924	1.870	0.585	2.292	4.150	1.212	0.972	0.610
III	0.667	0.987	1.234	0.952	2.002	3.414	0.321	0.854	1.558
IV	1.553	1.805	1.057	0.666	0.697	0.998	1.000	2.410	0.509
V	1.111	0.735	1.576	0.802	0.752	3.423	1.103	1.343	1.496
VI	0.850	0.792	1.088	1.074	0.859	1.290	0.859	1.544	1.088
VII	1.092	0.791	0.902	1.252	0.794	1.892	0.940	1.188	1.339
VIII	0.469	1.062	0.746	1.195	0.828	1.895	0.625	1.323	1.832
IX	1.279	1.367	0.759	0.643	1.544	1.132	1.122	0.829	0.672
X	1.972	0.376	1.981	0.846	0.838	0	1.339	1.647	0.546
XI	1.099	0.723	1.191	1.099	0.738	1.518	0.943	1.027	1.563
XII	0.942	0.671	1.249	0.984	1.309	0.749	0.888	1.161	1.328
XIII	1.257	0.908	0.591	1.418	0.462	2.031	0.825	1.364	0.760
XIV	0.780	0.674	0.924	0.829	0.774	1.662	1.149	1.268	1.134
XV	0.770	0.870	0.992	0.968	1.130	1.098	0.828	1.165	1.494
XVI	0.969	0.822	0.890	1.255	0.369	1.015	0.836	1.875	1.359
XVII	0.882	1.176	1.251	0.855	1.120	1.081	0.970	1.439	0.529
XVIII	1.142	0.933	1.181	1.088	1.064	1.008	0.949	1.093	0.965
XIX	1.067	0.844	1.178	1.338	0.927	1.353	0.854	1.066	1.036
XX	1.163	0.716	1.057	0.673	0.937	1.932	1.050	1.060	1.194
XXI	0.924	0.750	0.899	1.053	0.925	1.407	1.028	1.213	1.127
XXII	0.747	0.869	0.929	1.096	1.091	1.431	0.915	1.231	0.960
XXIII	0.953	0.756	0.984	0.909	0.985	0.944	1.093	1.197	1.077
XXIV	1.047	1.036	1.186	1.065	1.028	1.226	0.888	1.013	1.135
XXV	0.970	1.841	0.981	0.988	1.043	0.974	0.997	0.875	0.838
XXVI	1.221	1.038	0.864	0.776	1.445	0.508	1.133	0.717	0.886
XXVII	1.188	1.220	1.021	1.237	0.671	1.567	0.950	1.221	0.976

Standardised regional attraction rates derived from estimates by occupation-
specific migration rates. Cell values represent O_{ij}/E_{ij} where O and E represent
observed and estimated in-migrants and subscripts i and j refer to region and
occupation.

The regions are labelled as follows: N = North; Y = Yorkshire and Humberside;
NW = North-West; EM = East Midlands; WM = West Midlands; EA = East
Anglia; SE = South-East; SW = South-West; W = Wales.

gross number of jobs which required their expertise would be relatively small and sparsely distributed through space. In addition, highly skilled and professional workers tend to be associated with career profiles which require, at least in the early working life, a significant turnover of jobs occupied. Thirdly, the majority of workers in these categories are owner-occupiers and therefore not geographically restricted in their search for jobs by housing constraints. We therefore expected professional workers on changing jobs to be unlikely to change occupation but highly likely to change location. The same type of reasoning led us to expect workers in unskilled and semi-skilled occupations to be occupationally mobile but geographically immobile. The occupational mobility, we argued, would be between groups with similar low-skill requirements and might be associated with the concept of the secondary labour market. If unskilled and semi-skilled workers are geographically constrained by housing tenure factors they must, we argued, have a high propensity to change occupation rather than location.

The scattergrams of migration rates against occupation mobility rates are reproduced as Figure 8.6. The data were standardised in the manner outlined earlier in this section. Neither plot exhibited the negative relationship which we hypothesised, although three of the four occupations with the highest geographic mobility exhibited low occupational mobility (XXI, XXIII, XXV). Similarly, two of the three least geographically mobile groups were characterised by high occupational mobility (III, V). Whilst there were a small number of occupations characterised by low mobility of both types (I, II, VIII) and high mobility of both types (XXII, XXIV), it was not these obvious exceptions which questioned the hypothesised relationship. The fact is, the majority of occupations displayed little variation in terms of geographic mobility but great variation in terms of occupational mobility. There are three possible explanations for the poor relationships. The first, quite simply, is that the hypothesis is incorrect. The second, is that the occupational classification produces spurious measures of occupational mobility, and the third is that the mobility rates are affected by the geographic distribution of employment opportunities.

Leaving aside the first explanation, the second suggests that rates of occupational mobility would be underestimated in large heterogeneous occupation groups because relevant within-group mobility would go unrecorded and that it would be overestimated in small, precisely defined occupation orders. The size of the order presents an additional

Figure 8.6: Scattergrams Relating Geographical and Occupational Mobility

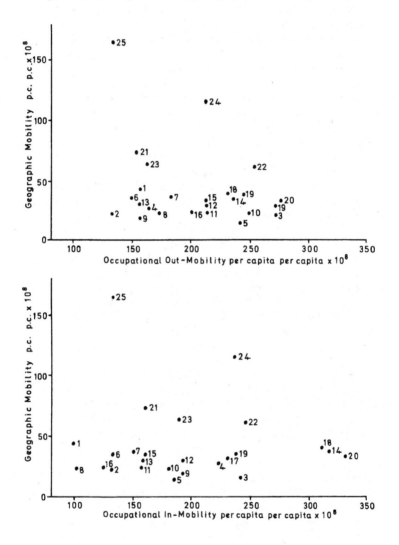

problem. It may be large either because there are a large number of almost *identical jobs* or because there are a large number of *similar job types*. For example, occupation XXII, sales workers, is large for the former reason, whilst occupation XXV, professional and technical workers, is large for the latter reason. However, this consideration aside, we would expect high occupational mobility in the case of small (homogeneous) groups and low mobility in the case of large (heterogeneous) groups. This was not in fact the case. There was no significant relationship between occupation, size and in-mobility. Therefore, without taking account of the homogeneity (or otherwise) of the occupation orders, the absence of a negative relationship between geographic and spatial mobility could not be attributed to the size variations between occupations.

The third explanation suggests that rates of occupational mobility will be low in regions characterised by a narrow employment base and could not be rigorously tested without examining the distribution of jobs amongst occupations and between regions. A provisional test of this hypothesis might indicate high mobility in the ubiquitous service sector and low mobility in highly localised occupations. Inverting the hypothetical explanation, we asked whether those occupations with the lowest in-mobility rates were especially localised and whether those with the highest in-mobility rates were ubiquitous. An inspection of Table 8.3 indicates that this hypothesis cannot be supported. The potentially localised occupations such as mining, gas coke and chemicals, glass- and ceramics- and textile-workers were characterised by intermediate rather than low levels of occupational in-mobility. Therefore we provisionally concluded that our original hypothesis relating geographic and occupational mobility was systematically incorrect.

There was, however, one relationship connecting geographic and occupational mobility worthy of note. The relationship between migration and net occupational movements suggested quite conclusively that the highly geographically mobile occupations experienced low net occupational mobility whilst those groups which were rapidly growing or declining through occupational mobility were characterised by low geographic mobility. The connection between geographic and occupational mobility suggests that the former is negatively related to absolute net changes in the latter. Only four occupations do not behave in this way — miners, leather-workers, paper- and printing workers and transport workers. Each of these groups had low geographic and low net occupational mobility. The

XV	397	2,532	1,910	52,505	33.2	212	160
XVI	155	1,256	782	27,288	24.7	200	125
XVII	205	1,858	1,566	29,766	30.0	272	229
XVIII	942	5,525	7,463	107,815	39.4	231	312
XIX	1,052	6,992	7,079	136,080	35.3	234	237
XX	567	4,678	5,621	75,558	33.3	275	330
XXI	5,038	10,550	11,046	348,715	73.0	153	160
XXII	2,852	11,721	11,343	219,463	61.7	253	245
XXIII	3,709	9,428	11,000	284,602	63.8	162	189
XXIV	2,336	4,261	4,762	90,210	116.0	211	236
XXV	9,058	6,841	7,320	269,328	163.4	123	132

pattern which emerges from these aspects of mobility is one that partially supports the general notion of higher occupational turnover in occupations characterised by low spatial mobility. This is especially true of lower-skill occupations. For jobs in the middle- and lower-skill occupations, it would appear that occupational mobility is a more important factor than geographic mobility in affecting labour supply in the regional labour market. The occupations with greater geographic mobility are more complex in terms of occupational turnover. They are populated with persons with higher rates of occupational turnover than anticipated, but the higher occupational turnover is attributable to different causes. In the case of occupation XXIV, administrators and managers, it is rarely the case that the occupation is entered at the same time as joining the labour market. Most workers in occupation XXIV enter it from another group and this fact boosts the rate of occupational mobility. Occupations XXI, XXII and XXIII each have high proportions of female labour. The incidence of high mobility in these groups could be a combination of two factors. First, the high concentration of female labour in these groups might reflect high geographic mobility rates because of the fact that wives migrate with husbands. Put another way, when husbands migrate, the associated mobility of their wives would be most concentrated in those occupation groups employing large numbers of female labour. Secondly, because female activity rates are most volatile through the economic cycle, their high rate of entries and exits to the labour market would provide greater scope for occupational mobility, especially if the occupation-specific demand for labour is changing. These two factors could affect different females within the occupation orders mentioned, but also both factors could affect a subset of females in these groups. The first of these two explanations for high mobility in the female-dominated occupations is supported by our final analysis of the distribution of distances moved.

Our analysis of distances migrated by persons in the various occupation groups was based upon a very unsatisfactory data mix. Because our previous analysis was based on 1970-1 census data, our data on occupation-specific migration data came from the same source. The only data available for distance moved were to be found in the 1961 census, so that the variables which were related reflect behaviour at two different time periods. However, this exercise was intended to be indicative rather than rigorous. Besides, it is extremely unlikely that the empirical distance distributions would alter radically over a ten-year period. Our measure of distance moved was the area beneath the log transformed distance distribution of migrants. The distance was transformed to reflect the exponentially decreasing number of migrants moving over longer distances. This variable, which has a low value for occupations with high mean migration distances and vice versa, was related to occupational mobility rates for 1970-1. A negative monotonic relationship was expected for the following reasons:

(1) The increased specialisation and credential requirements associated with some occupations would spread suitable job opportunities thinly over the national employment space. The job search process would, for such groups, result in a higher proportion of suitable jobs being located beyond commuting bounds. This would associate both migration and distance moved. In the case of less skilled occupations even if a suitable vacancy were not to be found within commuting distance it would probably still be located relatively closer to the existing place of residence than in the former case. (We might expect females in occupation orders XXI, XXII and XXIII to be associated with longer rather than shorter distances moved if the explanation in the previous paragraph was sound.)

(2) Because the distribution function dealt with moves between LAs rather than between regions then some non-employment migrations were confounded in the data. The highly mobile occupations are also associated with longer commuting behaviour which ought to reinforce the first reason.

A negative monotonic relationship did indeed obtain. When the geographic mobility variable was also log transformed, a significant correlation between distance moved and migration propensity obtained ($r_i = 0.76$). Of the three female occupations, occupations XXII and XXIII exhibited distance distributions similar to the highly mobile groups XXIV and XXV. Only occupation I, agriculture workers, and XVIII, labourers, moved over longer distances. In the case of occupation XXI only two additional occupations moved over longer distances. This is not surprising in an occupation with less wives and more single females than most other 'female' occupations. There was one paradox to this relationship. The occupation migrating over the shortest distances was also female-dominated. The explanation in this case is to do with the occupation, textile workers, the types of alternative job opportunities in areas with high employment, and the social structure in such areas. Succinctly, it is probable that females working in this occupation group are likely to be married to males with low spatial mobility.

8.5 Summary

We have shown in this chapter that there are some similarities at a macroscopic scale between occupational mobility and geographic mobility, but have found it quite difficult to relate geographic and occupational mobility directly. However, the positive relationship between the directional components of occupational mobility leads us to believe that this component of changing labour supply can be modelled in the same way as geographic turnover. That is to say that components concerned with intrinsic attraction effects, interaction effects and repulsion effects can be identified. This standard conception of the migration process was used to generate a linear relationship (Gleave and Cordey-Hayes, 1977) by assuming differential propensities to migrate based upon the cumulative inertia phenomenon. Similarly, a model based upon a mover-stayer dichotomy or cumulative inertia could satisfactorily explain the linear relationship in the case of occupational movement. This firmly suggests that an area for further work comprises an analysis of occupational durations. The faster-turnover occupations ought to be characterised by shorter durations than the slower-turnover occupations. This suggestion might also translate itself through durations in individual jobs rather than in occupation orders. There are at least two problems in carrying out such an analysis. First, the different age distributions of workers in the various occupation orders must be standardised, otherwise those with a high proportion of older workers will display a large proportion of longer durations. Secondly, the effects of firm size will have to be countered if occupations dominated by small firms are not to reveal disproportionately high turnover (and hence short duration) rates.

Although in this paper we have failed to substantiate a firm negative relationship between occupational and geographic mobility, we have firmly established a positive relationship between distance moved and mobility rate. This indicates that there is substance in the job search theory approach to explaining migration and indicates that workers in mobile occupations have a less dense job distribution in which to seek employment. Their labour markets are national, as opposed to being local. What we were unable to show explicitly was that high-turnover occupations were associated with low geographic mobility, perhaps because of housing constraints to migration. In fact, there are empirical grounds for suggesting that there are three relationships rather than one relationship between geographic and occupational mobility. In

Figure 8.6, if occupations XXIV and XXV are isolated as a subset and occupations XIV, XVIII, XX, XXI, XXII and XXIII isolated as second subset, a third subset of other occupations remains such that all three subsets exhibit different negative relationships between geographic and occupational mobility. It is interesting to note that the first two subsets contain almost all of the occupations of the primary labour market (see Gleave and Palmer, 1977). A further area of work, related to our initial summary observations, would require us to test the proximities of occupations in the three subsets. Could we justify a threefold classification in terms of the distances between occupations in behaviour space?

References

Blumen, I., Kogan, N. and McCarthy, P. 1955. *Industrial Mobility of Labour as a Probability Process.* Ithaca: Cornell University Press

Fielding, A.J. 1971. Internal migration in England and Wales. London: Centre for Environmental Studies, CES UWP 14

Gleave, D. and Cordey-Hayes, M. 1977. Migration dynamics and labour market turnover. *Progress in Planning*, 8, Part 1. Oxford: Pergamon Press

Gleave, D. and Palmer, D. 1977. Labour mobility and the dynamics of labour market turnover. Paper presented to the 17th European Congress of the Regional Science Association, Krakow

Greenwood, M.J. 1973. Urban economic growth and migration. *Environment and Planning*, 5, 91-112

Hyman, G. and Gleave, D. 1976. A reasonable theory of migration. *Transactions of the Institute of British Geographers*, new series, 3, no.2, 179-201

Johnson, J. Salt, J. and Wood, P. 1974. *Housing and the Migration of Labour in England and Wales.* London: Saxon House and Lexington Books

Lansing, J.B. and Mueller, E. 1964. *Residential Location and Urban Mobility.* Ann Arbor, Michigan: Institute for Social Research, University of Michigan.

Leicester, C. 1973. Vacancies and the demand for labour. *Monitor*, 3, no.2

Palmer, D. 1977. The application of Markov methods to the analysis of labour turnover: the open model. CES Working Note 474

Palmer, D. and Gleave, D. 1977. Labour market dynamics: a stochastic analysis of labour turnover by occupation. Paper presented to the Regional Science Association, British Section, Tenth Annual Conference, London

Rosen, R. 1970. *Dynamical Systems Theory in Biology*, New York, Wiley

Smart, M. 1974. Labour market areas: uses and definition. *Progress in Planning*, 2, Part 4. Oxford: Pergamon Press

Thirlwall, A.P. 1974. Types of unemployment in the regions of Great Britain. *The Manchester School of Economics and Social Studies*, XLII, no. 4 (December), 325-39

9 CHARACTERISTICS OF YOUNG PEOPLE WHO MOVE INTER-REGIONALLY: A LONGITUDINAL STUDY

Kathleen Kiernan

9.1 Introduction

Most migration analyses focus on net migration and are concerned with areal redistributions of population. Migration may also be studied as an event in the life-cycle of an individual. Thomas (1938), in relation to the problem of classifying persons according to migrant status, stated that 'the most satisfactory classification is one which preserves the time sequence of migratory acts during the life-span or during part of the life-span of the individuals studied.' In the years since then, the need for longitudinal studies of migration has been expressed by many others: Folger (1958), Shryock and Larmon (1965) and Taeuber (1966). In the absence of a complete population register, which permits analyses such as those of Wendel (1953), Neymark (1963) and Goldstein (1964), residential histories can be sought retrospectively, for example Harris and Clausen (1967) and Johnson, Salt and Wood (1974).

Analysis of migration through residential histories introduces an explicit emphasis on individual behaviour through time. If longitudinal data on employment status, occupation, education, marital status and so forth are also obtained as parts of life histories, or at dates for which residence is also obtained, migration can thus be set in the context not only of a person's current characteristics but also of prior characteristics and behaviour. The National Survey of Health and Development, a longitudinal study of a sample of a birth cohort, provides a data source for pursuing such a methodology.

9.2 The National Survey of Health and Development

The National Survey of Health and Development was born out of a study originally set up to investigate the cost of childbearing and the use of maternity services in the early post-war years. The population used for this study was all the mothers who had given birth to a child in the first week of March 1946 in Britain; 13,687 mothers were interviewed in this original study. As resources were limited, it was not possible to follow up the whole cohort. Consequently a stratified sample was drawn from this original population, including all children whose fathers were classified as being in non-manual occupations or agricultural work, but only 1 in 4 of those children whose fathers were in manual occupations. Illegitimate children and twins were excluded. This exercise produced a sample of 5,362 children who have been followed up at intervals of 2 years or less up to age 26. There have been 21 contacts in all, consisting of home interviews by professional interviewers and health visitors, interviews by youth employment officers, postal questionnaires, teachers' assessments and medical examinations by school doctors. In these ways a wealth of information has been collected about the family of origin and about the children themselves.

For the family of origin there is basic demographic information on size of the family, the age of its members, the ages at which the parents married as well as dates of death, divorce and separation. There is also information on the housing circumstances and the occupational histories of both parents. For the children themselves there are complete medical histories. From the age of entering the educational system there exist regular assessments such as IQ tests as well as examinations taken and passed, information on the number and types of schools attended, age at leaving school and, where applicable, the type of tertiary education received. Besides these relatively hard data, there is documented information on parental aspirations and interest in the education and future careers of their children, as well as the child's own ambitions with respect to future employment. After the children left the educational system the focus turned to their employment histories. Type and number of jobs have been monitored and periods of unemployment noted. Information on apprenticeships, day-release schemes and professional qualifications have been collected, as well as data on amount of income earned and satisfactions and dissatisfactions with their work. As the members of the survey have married and started families of their own, dates of these events have been collected as well as their housing circumstances and some information on their spouses' occupation and educational qualifications.

Obviously over the 26 years there have been losses from the sample, inevitable ones through death and emigration, and others resulting from unwillingness to co-operate and difficulties in tracing in time to meet an interview deadline. By age 26, 5.3 per cent (282) of the original sample were dead and 11.8 per cent (631) had emigrated. Of the remaining sample (4,449), 87 per cent were interviewed, 7 per cent were refusals and 6 per cent were untraced. These two latter groups have been of this status for varying lengths of time, some from as far back as 1948 when the first follow-up occurred. The state of retention of the sample over the 26-year period may be summarised by saying that between 70 and 90 per cent of the sample alive and living in Britain have provided information at each contact, although the same group of people were not necessarily successfully contacted on every occasion. Further information on the survey can be found in Population Investigation Committee (1948), Douglas (1964 and 1976) and Douglas *et al.* (1968).

9.3 Residential Histories

A by-product of these frequent contacts are the addresses at which the survey members were living. These provide a residential history for each survey member and a partial register of residential change for this sample, partial in that not all moves would have been included, for example, if the survey members moved more than once in the intervals between questionnaires, the intervening addresses would not have been recorded. So far, the residential histories of the 4,706 survey members born in England and Wales have been coded. The 21 possible addresses for each member have been allocated a 6-digit grid reference, a code for region, county, conurbation, type of local authority (using the pre-1972 classification) and size of population of the administrative unit. Complete residential histories from birth to age 26 are available for 79 per cent of the sample born in England and Wales and still living in Britain at age 26.

Unfortunately no direct questions on migration have ever been put to the sample so there is no information on reasons for moving. Insights into migration behaviour can only be obtained by aligning the residential histories to the wealth of available non-spatial data in order to isolate differences between movers and non-movers.

The analysis of this array of residential histories is still at an early stage. This chapter will concentrate on the period 1963 to 1972 when the survey members were aged between 17 and 26.

9.4 Results

Before discussing the characteristics of inter-regional migrants, some preliminary tables are given on how frequently these young people have moved and on the proportions moving within and between different types of administrative areas. In Table 9.1 a move is taken to be a change of address between one questionnaire and the next, regardless of distance moved. The maximum number of moves possible

Table 9.1: Frequency of Moves between Ages 17 and 26 by Sex

Number of moves	Males Per cent	Females Per cent	Total Sample Per cent	Total Sample Number
Not moved	15.7	7.0	11.4	344
1 move only	31.7	27.8	29.8	899
2 moves	25.6	31.8	28.6	865
3 moves	14.5	19.9	17.2	519
4 moves	7.3	9.3	8.3	251
5 moves	4.1	3.6	3.9	117
6 moves	0.9	0.5	0.7	21
7 moves	0.2	0.1	0.1	4
Number on which percentage based	1,525	1,495	3,020	

between the ages of 17 and 26 were seven.

The figures for the total sample in Table 9.1 show that 88.6 per cent of the sample had moved at least once in the preceding nine years. This figure compares favourably with that of Harris and Clausen (1967) who found that 86.1 per cent of the 25-30 age group had moved at least once during the decade 1953-63. The majority of the National Survey sample had only moved once or twice; the proportions who had moved more than three times tails off rapidly. With regard to sex differences, the only major difference in frequency of move was between the proportions who had never moved which probably reflects the later age at marriage of men as compared to women.

Further, in relation to frequency of move, it was of interest to know whether young people who had moved frequently as children were more likely to move more frequently in adulthood. Table 9.2 shows that there was a direct relationship ($Sr^* = 0.15$, $p < 0.001$) between frequency of move during childhood and frequency of move at the young adult ages.

Distance has a large influence upon the decision to migrate. Not only is the cost of moving greater the longer the move but, with increasing distance, knowledge of opportunities may be less and the potential disruption of family and community ties may be greater. For the National Survey sample a direct measure of distance was calculated from the grid references. In addition, a traditional census-type coding

*Sr = Spearman's rank order correlation coefficient.

Table 9.2: Mean Number of Moves from Birth to Age 16 by
Frequency of Move, 17 to 26

Number of moves 17 to 26	Mean	SD	N
Not moved	1.23	1.18	344
1 move only	1.26	1.17	899
2 moves	1.45	1.33	865
3 moves	1.67	1.32	519
4 moves	1.75	1.48	251
5 or more moves	1.82	1.35	142
Total sample	1.45	1.29	3,020

was used, defining distance of each move in terms of whether the areas
of origin and destination were in different administrative divisions.
These were:

(1) same local authority — intra-local authority;
(2) different local authority, same county — intra-county;
(3) different county, same region — inter-county;
(4) different region — inter-regional.

Tabulating actual distance moved gets round the problem of the
different sizes, shapes and lengths of border of administrative areas of
the same class. Using a census-type classification permits comparisons
to be made with census statistics and other studies, especially as few
studies in the field of migration research have recorded actual
distances moved. A cross-tabulation of the two measures enables one
to evaluate the proportion of moves that would traditionally be
regarded as long-distance on the proxy coding but are short-distance
in reality. Table 9.3 is one such cross-tabulation for the National Survey
sample for the move made between the questionnaires of 1971 and
those of 1972. One of Ravenstein's (1885) original laws of migration
was that 'the great body of our migrants only proceed a short distance'.
As the horizontal marginal totals show, this was the case for this
sample, 63 per cent of the total having moved less than 10 miles.
Looking at the body of the table, it would appear that the distance
categories fall readily into three broad groups, moves of < 10 miles
(short-distance moves), moves of 10-50 miles (medium-distance moves)
and moves of over 50 miles (long-distance moves). Overall, 80 per cent
of the sample had moved distances of 50 miles or less, whilst 85 per

cent of the inter-regional movers had moved distances of 50 miles or more. Of the total sample moving 50 miles or more, 85 per cent were inter-regional movers, so in this instance there is a 15 per cent misclassification error either way. If actual distance data are unavailable, it seems that taking inter-regional movers as long-distance movers is not an unreasonable proxy.

9.5 Inter-regional Movers

Between the ages of 17 and 26, 11.4 per cent of the sample had never moved, 26.4 per cent had moved only within their local authority of residence, 24.6 per cent had moved out of their local authority of residence but to a destination in the same county, 14.2 per cent had moved between counties in the same Standard Region, and 23.3 per cent of the sample had moved inter-regionally.

How do these inter-regional movers differ from their peers who did not move inter-regionally? On an initial screening of the data, the variable most highly correlated with propensity of the young people to move inter-regionally between the ages of 17 and 26 was another spatial variable, namely frequency of movement between 17 and 26 ($r = 0.55$, $p < 0.001$). As Table 9.4 shows, those who moved at least once inter-regionally were much more likely to have moved 3 or more times than non-regional movers.

Table 9.4: Type of Move by Frequency of Move

Number of moves 17 to 26	Non-regional movers	Regional movers
1 move only	42.2	9.1
2 moves	36.1	21.8
3 moves	15.1	31.5
4 moves	4.9	21.8
5 moves or more	1.6	15.8
Number on which percentage based	1,971	705
Overall percentage of movers	73.7	26.3

9.5.1 Background Characteristics

Many background characteristics have been explored and many more remain to be explored. Table 9.5 shows there were no differences between the sexes, with the young men and women being equally likely to move inter-regionally. Young people from upper non-manual families

Table 9.5: Background Characteristics of Inter-regional Movers

		Percentage moving inter-regionally	Number in total sample
Sex	Male	23.7	1,525
	Female	22.9	1,495
	Total	23.3	3,020
Social class of family of origin	Upper non-manual	48.8	338
	Lower non-manual	29.1	929
	Upper manual	19.3	524
	Lower manual	13.8	1,229
	Total	23.3	3,020
School leaving age	15 years	11.8	1,671
	16 years	20.9	618
	17 years	33.9	254
	18 years or later	58.8	466
	Unknown	27.3	11
	Total	23.3	3,020
Highest qualification attained	None	11.5	1,734
	'O' level	25.9	704
	'A' level	48.6	290
	Degree	77.7	224
	Unknown	13.2	68
	Total	23.3	3,020

were 3.5 times more likely to move inter-regionally than their peers from lower manual families. The social class of the family of origin of the survey members is a complex variable amalgamating not only information on father's occupation but also the educational experiences of both parents. A fuller description of its derivation is given in the Appendix to this chapter. The young people who left school at age 15, the minimum school-leaving age for this sample, were the least likely to move inter-regionallyand those leaving at 18 or later the most likely. Similarly, highest academic qualification attained, which to a large extent reflects school-leaving age, showed a similar pattern except that those survey members who subsequently went on to attain a degree were more likely to move inter-regionally (78 per cent) than those whose final academic qualifications were 'A' levels (49 per cent). The

very high proportion of inter-regional migrants amongst the graduates is partly a reflection of the coding scheme used, in that moves to university were counted, unlike the census, which re-allocates students to their home address. If moves to and away from university are ignored by taking only moves made since age 23 (which excludes the majority of university moves) one finds that the overall pattern remains, although there has been a scaling-down of the proportions. The proportions of young people who moved inter-regionally at least once between the ages of 23 and 26 were, with no qualifications, 6.8 per cent, with 'O' levels 15.1 per cent, with 'A' levels 25.9 per cent and 51.8 per cent with degree.

These findings in relation to social class and education confirm or expand what has been found by other researchers. Friedlander and Roshier (1966) and Harris and Clausen (1967) both found educational level to be strongly associated with geographical mobility. Friedlander and Roshier further found that father's occupation showed as strong a relationship with the male respondent's mobility before marriage as his own occupation did after marriage.

The advantage of a longitudinal study over a cross-sectional study is that information has been collected on past characteristics that are difficult to ascertain retrospectively. Examples of such items, now considered in relation to subsequent migration behaviour, are tests of ability and levels of ambition.

The children in this survey were given a battery of educational tests at ages 8, 11 and 15 measuring their reading ability, vocabulary, mathematical ability and intelligence. A test of general intelligence (Douglas, 1964) was given at age 11. This test has a mean of 50 and a standard deviation of 10. As boys and girls differ on some of the scores given in Table 9.6, the results have been shown separately for males and females on all items. Boys and girls who subsequently moved inter-regionally had higher average ability scores at age 11 than those who did not move inter-regionally and the differences for both sexes were found to be statistically significant at $p < 0.001$ when a t-test was applied. This is not an entirely unexpected finding given what we know about the relationship between educational attainment and inter-regional movement — and that ability and academic qualifications are highly correlated. However, at a later stage in this chapter it will be shown that ability scores are important in differentiating people with no qualifications.

The occupational interests of the young people in this survey were assessed by their scores on the Rothwell Miller Interest Blank (Miller,

1968) given at age 15. This inventory required the survey members to rank nine lists of 12 job titles. The scores on the interest inventory were subjected to a component analysis and three main components extracted (Cherry, 1974). The one we are concerned with here is the 'ambition' component which has a mean of 50 and a standard deviation of 10. A high score on the component indicates an interest in working in jobs of high status but not necessarily the will or ability to achieve them. The results given in Table 9.6 show that inter-regional migrants of both sexes had higher levels of ambition than their peers who did not move inter-regionally. Again the differences between the two mean scores for each sex were statistically significant at $p < 0.001$.

Table 9.6: Scores on Intelligence and Ambition Schedules for Non-regional and Regional Migrants, 17 to 26

Variable	Males			Females		
	$\bar{X}$	SD	N	$\bar{X}$	SD	N
General Intelligence (age 11)						
Non-regional movers	49.5	10.1	1,051	51.3	9.9	1,045
Regional movers	56.0	9.1	330	56.9	9.6	316
Ambition (age 15)						
Non-regional movers	48.4	9.6	1,000	48.4	9.7	979
Regional movers	54.4	9.4	318	54.1	9.9	307

Table 9.7: Proportion (per cent) Moving Inter-regionally by Social Class at Age 26

Social Class	Males		Females	
	Per Cent	N	Per Cent	N
Professional etc. I	57.4	155	41.7	12
Intermediate II	36.4	316	49.3	203
Skilled III NM	22.7	198	13.2	272
III M	10.5	484	10.8	37
Partly skilled IV	13.9	166	14.4	90
Unskilled V	3.8	26	0.0	22
Unknown or not working	21.1	180	21.5	859

Table 9.8: Proportion (per cent) of Men Moving Inter-regionally by Socio-economic Group at age 26

Socio-economic Group		Social class	Inter-regional movers Per cent	Number in sample N
4	Professional workers-employees	I	55.9	145
5.1	Intermediate occupations	II	51.4	142
1.2	Managers in central and local government, industry, commerce etc., large establishments	II-III	30.6	98
2.2	Managers in industry, commerce, etc., small establishments	II-III	26.1	46
6	Junior non-manual workers	III-IV	22.0	182
5.2	Foremen and supervisors non-manual	III N	21.1	19
8	Foremen and supervisors manual	III M	19.5	41
10	Semi-skilled manual	III M	13.0	115
2.1	Employers in industry, commerce, etc., small establishments	II-V	12.2	49
12	Own account, excluding professional	II-V	9.6	52
9	Skilled manual workers	III M	8.9	381
11	Unskilled manual workers	V	4.8	21
Agricultural workers				
13	Farmers — employers and managers	II	15.4	13
14	Farmers — own account	II	0.0	4
15	Agricultural workers	III M or IV	15.0	20
3	Professional workers — self-employed	I	80.0	10
7	Personal service workers	II-IV	50.0	4
1.1	Employers in industry, commerce, etc., large establishments	II-III	0.0	3
	Unknown or not working		21.1	180

9.5.2 Recent Characteristics

Let us now consider some of these young people's more recent characteristics. Social class of origin has been shown to have an influence on whether the survey members moved inter-regionally or not at young adult ages, and as Table 9.7 shows, current social class was also strongly related to propensity to move inter-regionally.

Social class in this instance is derived from occupation at age 26 and grouped into the usual census categories (OPCS, 1970). As over 50 per

cent of the women were not working at age 26, and given the tendency
for the social class of women to be more concentrated than it is for
men, the results have been shown separately by sex.

Only 11 per cent of the males in manual occupations had moved
inter-regionally by age 26, and within this broad category the unskilled
group had moved least. Thirty-seven per cent of the men in non-manual
occupations had moved inter-regionally and there was a noticeable
decrease in the proportions moving inter-regionally the lower the social
class category. For the young women who were working, the largest
differences were between those in social classes I and II and the rest.
None of the women in unskilled occupations had moved inter-regionally

The proportions moving inter-regionally may vary within these
broad social class categories, so socio-economic groupings (again based
on the census classification, OPCS, 1970) were examined for the men
in the sample. This classification is given in Table 9.8 ordered by the
proportions moving within the categories. The categories with very
small numbers have been placed at the bottom of the table. To
facilitate comparisons with Table 9.7 the social class categories for
these groups have also been shown.

Of the two groups that constitute social class I, the self-employed
professionals appear more likely to have moved inter-regionally than
the employed professionals. However, too much reliance should not
be put on this difference as the numbers in socio-economic group 3 are
small. It is interesting to note that the men who were classified as
being in social class II, in intermediate occupations socio-economic
group 5.1 (that is non-manual occupations, ancillary to the professions,
not normally requiring qualifications of university degree standard such
as teachers, study engineers, technicians), were as likely to have moved
inter-regionally as their professionally employed peers in social class I.
The remainder of social class II, mainly managers and employers in
industry, commerce and local and national government, were less likely
to have moved inter-regionally. Similar proportions of junior non-
manual workers, such as clerical and sales staff and foreman and
supervisors, moved inter-regionally; the semi-skilled manual were more
likely to have moved than the skilled and again the unskilled were the
least likely to have moved inter-regionally.

Income level is likely to be correlated with both socio-economic
group and age and it might be expected that higher-income groups are
more mobile because the cost of movement forms a smaller proportion
of their total wealth or income. Detailed income data were collected in
the interview at age 26. Examination of total household income showed

Table 9.9: Proportion (per cent) Moving Inter-regionally in
Qualification Groups by Sex, Social Class of Origin and Social Class
at 26

Variable	Highest Qualification Attained							
	None		'O'		'A'		Degree	
	Per cent	N	Per cent	N	Per cent	N	Per cent	N
Sex								
Males	9.9	857	25.7	311	41.1	151	76.8	168
Females	13.0	877	26.0	393	56.8	139	80.4	56
Social class of origin								
Upper non-manual	32.3	34	35.2	122	50.0	90	73.0	89
Lower non-manual	14.9	362	24.0	317	47.2	123	80.8	99
Upper manual	10.8	342	23.4	111	45.9	37	78.3	23
Lower manual	9.7	996	24.0	154	52.5	40	84.6	13
Social class at 26: males								
I	16.7	15	40.6	32	40.7	27	76.5	81
II	11.9	84	24.1	87	41.1	73	78.8	66
III N	15.5	71	25.0	88	26.9	26	71.4	7
III M	9.7	424	13.7	51	50.0	4	—	—
IV	8.6	140	41.2	17	60.0	5	—	—
V	4.0	25	50.0	2	—	—	—	—

differences between inter-regional migrants and the rest. Of the men
who had moved inter-regionally, 19.5 per cent were earning over
£3,000, the highest income category, as compared to 11.2 per cent of
those who had not moved inter-regionally.

9.6 Qualifications in Relation to Other Characteristics

In the preceding sections some characteristics which differentiated
those who moved inter-regionally from those who did not were studied.
From this preliminary analysis it appeared that education was one of
the most, if not the most, important variable. Most analyses usually
conclude at this level, although it is clearly of interest to go beyond
this and look at within-group differences. For example, some of the
young people with no qualifications moved inter-regionally (in
numerical terms nearly as many as with degrees) and one would like to
know what differences, if any, there were between them and their peers

who did not move. Table 9.9 shows the result of examining sex, social class of origin and for the males their social class at 26, within the qualification categories. There were no sex differences between the proportions moving inter-regionally and the rest taken as an aggregated group (Table 9.5). However, within the qualification categories, women with no qualifications or 'A' levels were more likely to have been inter-regional movers than the men. Explanations for these differences need to be sought by studying other attributes of these females, for example their occupations or those of their spouses. The young people with no qualifications from upper non-manual families were noticeably more likely to move inter-regionally than those from the lower non-manual or manual groups. A similar pattern emerged for the young people with 'O' level qualifications. There was no well-defined social class trend for the young people with 'A' levels or degrees. It seems that above a certain level of qualification social class of origin is no longer important in relation to the propensity to move inter-regionally. Turning now to the results in relation to social class at age 26 for the young men in the sample, it is immediately apparent that, within each social class, the likelihood of having moved inter-regionally increases with level of qualifications. The trends within the qualification groups are not so clear-cut, there being no apparent trends.

Intelligence and ambition scores were also examined within the qualification groups. With reference to differences in ability scores at age 11 between inter-regional migrants and the rest, the only significant difference was for the group with no qualifications. Men and women who moved inter-regionally having higher scores ($\bar{x}$ = 47.5; SD = 7.8; N = 84 (men) and $\bar{x}$ = 50.4; SD = 9.1; N = 107 (women)) than the rest ($\bar{x}$ = 45.5; SD = 8.7; N = 697 (men) and $\bar{x}$ = 47.5; SD = 8.5; N = 698 (women)). There was little difference in the ambition scores at age 15 of inter-regional movers and the rest for the young people with no qualifications, 'A' levels or degrees. But the young people with 'O' levels who moved inter-regionally were more ambitious (men: inter-regional migrants: $\bar{x}$ = 55.8; SD = 7.8; N = 72; non-regional movers: $\bar{x}$ = 58.8; SD = 8.9; N = 202; women: inter-regional migrants: $\bar{x}$ = 56.3; SD = 7.8; N = 89; non-regional movers: $\bar{x}$ = 53.8; SD = 9.4; N = 252).

9.7 Discussion

The age period 17 to 26 largely represents the peak ages of geographical mobility in the life-cycle. Young adults are leaving their families of origin to find jobs, to continue their education and to marry and set up their own homes. The findings of this chapter indicate that those young people who moved inter-regionally are a highly selected group from families of a higher socio-economic position, with educational levels, occupational status and ability scores above the average. These are highly interrelated factors and should be seen more as a collective process in stimulating migration than as isolated factors. This chapter is only a preliminary analysis reflecting a fraction of the relationships that can and will be examined, if cell size permits, in order to isolate differentials. Further analyses will be done, for example, on the relationship between inter-regional movement and social mobility, earnings, occupation and industry, etc. The attributes of return, migrants and chronic inter-regional movers will be studied, as well as regional variations isolated.

This is a particular cohort of people moving through time and space in a specific era subject to the prevailing social and economic values. The experiences of birth cohorts in nineteenth-century Britain or in more rural societies of Western Europe, for example Ireland or Third World societies, would be different. The major shifts in population observed in the past when the British economy was changing from a predominantly agricultural (rural) to a predominantly industrial (urban) one are now complete. The nature of migration and the role it plays in the economic life of the country have altered. Most people now grow up in urban environments, or close to them, and have available the services that previously constituted a major benefit of migration. Urban areas have a more varied job structure, whereas people raised in agricultural communities were generally impelled to move if they wished to do anything beyond a very narrow range of occupations. Given these changes in the economic structure of the country, the benefits of moving long distances are not so readily apparent for the majority of people. However, the situation may be different for those whose backgrounds or educational opportunities have put them in professional and administrative occupations for which there is a national labour market. For these occupations, career and economic advancement may depend on willingness to move long distances. Many people, especially the younger ones, in these status categories will have had higher education which may have brought an initial break with home ties that facilitates later moves. So, among certain segments of the population, migration remains an important option. The evidence seems to indicate that long-distance migration is and perhaps will be increasingly confined to certain identifiable social and economic groups within a population.

Appendix: Social Class Classification in the National Survey

The classification is based, for the most part, on the 1957 occupation of the father of the Survey child; where this is not known, on the 1946 occupation.

Upper-middle Class

The father is a non-manual worker, and:
- (a)   both parents went to secondary school and were brought up in middle-class families; or
- (b)   both parents went to secondary school and one parent was brought up in a middle-class family; or
- (c)   both parents were brought up in middle-class families and one parent went to secondary school.

Lower-middle Class

The rest of the non-manual workers' families.

Upper-manual Working Class

The father is a manual worker and:
either the father or mother or both of them had a secondary school education, and/or one or both of them were brought up in a middle-class family.

Lower-manual Working Class

The father is a manual worker, and:
both the father and the mother had elementary schooling only, and the father and the mother were brought up in manual working-class families.

References

Cherry, N. 1974. Components of occupational interest. *British Journal of Educational Psychology*, 44, 22-30

Douglas, J.W.B. 1964. *The Home and the School.* London: MacGibbon and Kee

Douglas, J.W.B. 1976. The use and abuse of national cohorts. In *The Organisation and Impact of Social Research*, ed. M. Shipman, Chapter 1. London: Routledge and Kegan Paul

Douglas, J.W.B., Ross, J.M. and Simpson, H.R. 1968. *All Our Future.* London: Davies

Folger, J.K. 1957. Models in migration. In *Selected Studies of Migration since World War Two, Proceedings of the 34th Annual Conference of the Milbank Memorial Fund, New York*, pp. 155-64. New York: Milbank Memorial Fund

Friedlander, D. and Roshier, R.J. 1966. Internal migration in England and Wales, Part II: Recent internal migrants – their movements and characteristics. *Population Studies*, 20, no. 1, 45-59

Goldstein, S. 1964. The extent of repeated migration: an analysis based on the Danish Population Register. *Journal of the American Statistical Association*, 59, 1121-32

Harris, A.I. and Clausen, R. 1967. *Labour Mobility in Great Britain 1953-1963*. London: Government Social Survey

Johnson, J.H., Salt, J. and Wood, P.A. 1974. *Housing and the Migration of Labour in England and Wales*. England: Saxon House

Miller, K.M. 1968. *Manual for the Rothwell-Miller Interest Blank*. London: National Foundation for Educational Research in England and Wales

Neymark, E. 1963. Migration differentials in education, intelligence and social background: analysis of a cohort of Swedish males. *Bulletin of the International Statistical Institute*, 40, 350-79

OPCS. 1970. *Classification of Occupations 1970*. London: HMSO

Population Investigation Committee. 1948. *Maternity in Great Britain*. London: Oxford University Press

Ravenstein, E.G. 1885. The laws of migration. *Journal of the Statistical Society*, 48, 167-235

Shryock, H.S. and Larmon, E.A. 1965. Some longitudinal data on internal migration. *Demography*, 2, 579-93

Taeuber, K.E. 1966. Cohort migration. *Demography*, 3, 416-22

Thomas, D.S. 1938. *Research Memorandum on Migration Differentials*. SSRC Bulletin (New York), 43, 165

Wendell, B. 1953. A migration schema. *Lund Studies in Geography*, Series B, Human Geography, no. 9

PART FOUR: PROJECTIONS

10 FORECASTING THE COMPONENTS OF POPULATION CHANGE, WITH SPECIAL REFERENCE TO MIGRATION[1]

John Hobcraft

10.1 Introduction

All population projections contain some quite critical assumptions, especially when continued for more than one projection period as is usual. The most important implicit assumption is usually one of population homogeneity. That such an assumption is critical is obviously the case with an attempt to project total numbers without any disaggregation. To take an extreme example, consider a population equally divided between two strains at the start of the projection, one strain of which is doubling every ten years and one of which is halving every ten years. The current growth rate would be zero, the long-term growth rate would be doubling every ten years. Such considerations have been implicitly recognised by most projectors since the earliest component projections. Much of the heterogeneity with respect to mortality is removed by taking age and sex (and perhaps racial characteristics) into account. This is routinely done in most projections. However, it is well known that mortality is strongly associated with other characteristics, such as regular smoking. Why do projections not control for this characteristic? One obvious reason is a paucity of data. A further reason is that smoking habits are not immutably fixed, whereas date of birth is, as is sex to all intents and purposes. The introduction of smoking status would lead to the need to specify the ways in which such status changed. This would probably make the projection process less efficient. Thus the desire for homogeneous sub-groups is tempered by the fixity of the characteristics involved. If occupation and education were roughly equivalent in terms of reducing heterogeneity, education would be preferred as being a relatively more fixed attribute, at least for adults.

Both Keyfitz (1972) and Brass (1974) refer to the need for such sub-classification for projection purposes. Much recent fertility research has been partially directed to such problems. Ryder (1965), in one of his many stimulating papers, has suggested that the important background variables for fertility are population membership, marital status and parity, with each being subdivided by a duration variable, namely age, duration of marriage and birth interval. Such a sub-classification, which has a very large number of cells, is not available for England and Wales. It is extremely unusual for a projection to include more than age, sex and marital status as classifications. Page (1977) has produced some quite strong evidence that much of the variation of fertility within marriage is explained by age and marriage duration. Again fertility varies substantially with other characteristics such as race, occupation, income, social class, contraceptive usage, etc. It is clearly not possible to control on all these variables for any analysis, and for projections the choice must come down to an 'efficient sub-classification' (Brass, 1974). To be efficient relatively fixed characteristics should be preferred, to avoid the problems of projecting the characteristics themselves (parity is acceptable as a birth always raises parity); the minimum number of sub-categories to give acceptable levels of homogeneity should be used.

Even after control on several background variables it is not at all reasonable to presume absolute fixity of rates within each relatively homogeneous group. The choice of an efficient sub-classification should reduce variability within the group. Ideally the variation within such relatively homogeneous groups should be well behaved but random variation. As such, there is at least the possibility of controlling for the variability (see, for example, Spilerman, 1972a).

Even assuming perfect population homogeneity (an unachievable aim), the projector is always confronted with the question of projecting rates over time. The simplest, but usually unsatisfactory, solution is to presume time — homogeneity as well as population homogeneity — this leads to stable population theory (see, for example, Keyfitz, 1968). More usually rates are not presumed constant over time. Information is then required on the variations of the relevant rates for each sub-classification used over time in the past. Some extrapolation procedure is then required. At this stage there are powerful arguments for making use of the natural structure of the rates across the various categories through the use of parametric or relational models (see, for example, Brass, 1974; Page, 1977; Duchene and Gillet-de-Stefano, 1974; Coale and Trussell, 1974, etc.; see also in a different way, Spilerman, 1972b, or Ginsberg, 1972b).

Additional problems arise which are worthy of note. The first of these is the problem of consistency (Brass, 1974). Almost always some reconciliation will be necessary between numbers of events for different sub-categories of the population; the numbers of newly married men and women must be equal; the numbers of widows and newly dead married men must be equal, the numbers of in- and out-migrants must be equal, etc. Until ways are found to better specify either the marriage process or the migration process, such problems will inevitably occur. Another set of problems arises through problems of rate definitions and deficiencies in available data (Rees and Wilson, 1977).

Finally, all component projection procedures implicitly or explicitly depend upon an assumption that the process is Markovian (for a formal reconciliation of stable population theory to a Markov Chain see Sykes, 1969). A process is Markovian if the transition rates for each sub-category depend only upon the current state of the category and not on its members' history of previous moves from state to state. Thus, for example, in most population projections fertility is not controlled by parity, or migration by number of previous moves. It is then implicit to the projection procedure that the pattern of previous births or moves does not impinge upon the current rates of birth or movement. If duration of residence is strongly related to propensity to move, or time since last birth is strongly related to fertility rates, then the Markovian rule is violated, and typical projection procedures go wrong. Although all these are exceptions to the Markovian rule it does seem to this author at least equally valid to regard them as violations of the population homogeneity assumption. It is hard to conceive of a violation of the Markov assumption which is not also a violation of the population homogeneity assumption, although the reverse is quite possible. The idea of dealing with violations of this sort by further sub-classification is not at all new: in projections, age, which is essentially a temporal variable which implies differing fertility, mortality and migration rates, has long been used as a categorisation variable; in the stochastic processes literature ideas such as the mover-stayer model and its extensions, and the Cornell Mobility or Retention Model essentially create new population sub-categories, which are attempts to get a more homogeneous population structure, allowing reformulation of the process as Markovian. We shall return to some of these ideas later.

10.2 Regional Projections and Migration

So far we have paid little attention to the special problems associated with migration and regional or multi-regional projections. Although regional projections can be made without taking account of migration, this is not a sensible approach, and any serious attempt to project at the regional level must allow for migration. This is even more true at the sub-regional level. Adoption of a traditional projection approach through some kind of population accounting or component projection method requires treatment of fertility, mortality and migration. We are already aware that projections involving mortality require disaggregation by age (as the most important variable) and sex (variations by sex are less extreme). Often such analysis would be conducted for five-year age groups giving 36 sub-categories (many projections are required by single years of age, necessitating some two hundred sub-categories). Again, for projection purposes, fertility should at the very least be disaggregated by age and marital status, and possibly marriage duration as well (Page, 1977). Because of substantial difficulties which arise with a true two-sex treatment of fertility, births are usually attributed to the mother. The introduction of marriage also causes substantial, if not insuperable, difficulties for a genuine two-sex analysis (see McFarland, 1976; Henry, 1972; Das Gupta, 1972; Bartlett, 1973, etc.). (However, two one-sex analyses with a mutual reconciliation can usually be carried out.) It should be noted that this really requires the introduction of four marital status categories, namely single, married, widowed and divorced. (Although fertility differentials are not great between the single, widowed and divorced categories, there are such substantial differences in marriage rates as to make the distinctions necessary.) On a naïve view this would increase the number of categories by a factor of four to 144 (clearly less categories are actually required). So far we have not mentioned regional disaggregation. It is hard to imagine a sensible set of regional projections for England and Wales requiring less than 10 regions; it is not difficult to imagine a need for projections for counties in Britain or the states of the US with 50 or more regions distinguished. This implies disaggregation of the population into a minimum of 360 categories (if marriage is ignored in a ten-region situation), and quite possibly as many as 40,000 ($100 \times 2 \times 4 \times 50$) categories! Most attempts at mathematical formulation of such a projection process would now require the derivation of a full transition matrix of rates for each sex separately, namely two matrices with a minimum of 32,400 ($= 180^2$) cells each and quite possibly 400 million ($= 20,000^2$) cells or more each! (See Rogers, 1968; Rogers, 1975; Feeney, 1970; Feeney, 1973). Use of the accounting procedures suggested by Rees and Wilson (1977) quadruples the number of cells required for the matrix. (If the sexes are combined into a single matrix, as is often the case in mathematical formulations, the matrix sizes are again quadrupled.) Such an approach rapidly becomes computationally impossible, however mathematically elegant. For computational purposes it is both possible and necessary to store the information differently. The great majority of the cells in these giant matrices are zero in all practical applications — where the projection period is of the same length as the age groups (commonly one or five years). Thus in our 32,400 cell example each of the 360 sub-categories can at most contribute to 20 sub-categories (10 for survivors and 10 for births), reducing the number of transition values required to under 3,600 for each sex (or 1,800 for males if fertility is treated as female dominant with a fixed sex ratio at birth); in our 400 million cell example, each of the 40,000 sub-categories can at most contribute to 200 sub-categories (3 × 50 for survivors and 50 for births), reducing the number of transition values required to less than 8 million for each sex! This does not solve all the problems: we have yet to consider whether migration rates require controlling on any further variables. Gleave (1976) produced some evidence that age alone was inadequate to give homogeneity, as was occupational group alone or socio-economic group alone; however, he was unable to use full five-year age groups for the age analyses, and used a rather curious double standardisation procedure. For planning purposes, the population estimates may well require disaggregation into further sub-categories, especially along socio-economic or occupational dimensions and often by single years of age. If further sub-classification is introduced, the number of sub-categories escalates dramatically, as does the number of transition rate estimates required. Not only is the estimation (for several time periods to be useful) of tens of thousands of rates (or more) likely to encounter grave sampling problems, but it will also rapidly require rates which are not available, or not directly derivable from available data. (Rees and Wilson (1977) give a clear account of these estimation problems where disaggregation is solely by age, sex and region. The magnitude of the problems is indicated by the length of their work. In their conclusion they suggest further disaggregation by 'income, social class and other characteristics' (p. 280).)

Projections cannot feasibly be carried out at the individual level, and continual disaggregation cannot take place, however desirable it may seem theoretically. Even the population of Britain is finite! A case has to be made for a different approach. To return to our earlier themes *efficient* sub-classifications have to be found. These may well need to be different for different processes. For example, marriage duration may be an important variable in determining fertility and future births, whereas duration of residence or occupation may be more efficient for obtaining homogeneous groups for migration — whilst this would still require the population disaggregated in great detail, it need not imply such a massive proliferation of rates. In addition, a reasonable case might be made that region of residence is an inefficient classifier for variations in mortality and fertility; again this could achieve a massive reduction in the number of rates to be estimated, although finally the total births (or more correctly survivors from these births) have to be allocated across the regions to obtain the disaggregated base population for the next projection period. This is not an uncommon approach for the practical projector. For example, the regional and county projections for England and Wales adopt an intermediate approach by presuming that regional or county rates are a constant multiple of national rates. More sophistication can be introduced by the use of parametric models, with very few parameters for each region. Such an approach is used for the Greater London Council local projections — see Gilje (1976). Even more attractive is an approach using the relational models suggested by Brass (1974), where regional patterns are fitted using one or two parameters which can more easily be modelled over time. The adoption of a simple relational model here does not necessarily imply that national rates are projected in the same way, and more parameters may be desirable for modelling national rates, or a different approach used.

Much more projection-oriented research has been carried out on this kind of modelling or parameterisation procedure for mortality (Brass (1971 and 1974) has made especially significant contributions), and for fertility (Coale and Trussell, 1974; Page, 1977; Romaniuk, 1973, etc.), and even for marriage (Brass's 1974 adaptation of Coale and McNeil, 1972; also Ewbank, 1974) than for migration. Certainly age patterns of migration have extremely strong similarities and should be parameterisable with few parameters. Again a relational approach might prove most flexible for modelling regional variations around a national average. A simple parameterisation of migration rates with age has been suggested by Cordey-Hayes and Gleave (1973), derived from age-specific migration rates given by Lowry (1966). Further work is required to derive age (and other characteristic?) parameterisations suitable for projection work.

Some authors suggest that adequate projections can be made by treating the decision to move separately from the decision on destination (Gilje (1976), implicit in the Cornell Mobility or Retention Model approach — see Myers *et al.*, 1967; McGinnis, 1968; Henry *et al.*, 1971; Henry, 1971; Morrison, 1967; Land, 1969). There seems to be little evidence as to whether such an assumption is justified. The projections of the Greater London Council appear to go further by assuming destination to be independent of age (Gilje, 1976). Often such decisions are based on expediency rather than sound theoretical reasons. However, it is important to find evidence on such assumptions, as the saving in the number of rates required is substantial if such independence holds, and may yield a worthwhile return even if it holds only approximately by allowing some other variable to be introduced to give a net gain in homogeneity.

10.3 Duration of Residence and Repeated Movement

One aspect of migration which is continually stressed in the literature, especially the technical or stochastic processes related migration literature, is that of the importance of duration of residence and/or repeated migration (see, for example, Willis, 1974, Chapters 5 and 9). Projections which take account of mobility commonly overestimate numbers of movers and concomitantly underestimate numbers of stayers. The earliest technical development to try to overcome this was the mover-stayer model (Blumen *et al.*, 1955; Goodman, 1961; Bartholomew, 1973). This splits the population into a group of stayers who never move, and a group of movers who follow a Markov process. Such a split is unrealistic, and it is extremely difficult to find applications to migration data. Recently Spilerman (1972a) has produced an interesting extension of the mover-stayer model, which substitutes a continuous distribution of movement probabilities underlying each cell for the cruder dichotomy. Essentially he introduces the idea of heterogeneity within groups in the propensity to move, but all movements are assumed to occur according to a constant transition matrix. His paper concludes with an application to some of the migration data presented by Taeuber *et al.* (1968). Spilerman's model provides a noticeable improvement over a traditional Markov chain approach, even though he is working with a cohort which has changing rates over time and age, a violation of the time-homogeneity assumption of both models.

Another approach to dealing with the underestimation of numbers of stayers is contained in the work of the group at Cornell (Myers *et al.*, 1967; McGinnis, 1968; Henry, 1971; Henry *et al.*, 1971). Their model simply introduces duration of residence as an extra sub-classification to make the population sub-groups more homogeneous. As yet, this model does not appear to have been operationalised using migration data. More recently, other authors have argued a case for inclusion of duration of residence in the formulation of stochastic processes to represent migration. Ginsberg (1971, 1972a and 1972b) argues for the application of Semi-Markov processes (he also presents a well reasoned argument in favour of probabilistic models as against regression models, but goes on to suggest incorporation of regression elements). Spilerman (1972b) suggests a somewhat similar extension to include regression estimates. Both these approaches have the attraction of reducing the number of parameter estimates required for a detailed population structure. Spilerman even formulates his model as an individual level model, but it can be extended to groups of homogeneous individuals. Again Spilerman tests his ideas on data from Taeuber *et al.*, 1968. His transition matrix is superficially of 16 cells – he uses four regions of the United States. His coefficients differ with the characteristics of the individuals and are based on a regression analysis. This regression analysis uses dummy variables with five occupational groups, three employment categories, two racial groups, three residence-size categories, four regions of birthplace and additionally uses as variables number of previous residences, age and the square of age, and years at current residence and its square. His best regression only accounts for 5 per cent of the variance, which is unimpressive (he used a stepwise procedure so that only significant variables are included). He correctly recognises some of the problems about fixity of variables for projection purposes and compares his model with and without those variables which are not fixed, or at least effectively fixed (e.g. age). As would be expected, given the inadequacy of the regression analysis, the improvement obtained is very small. Further applications do seem warranted, although individual level (or detailed sub-categorised) data are required, so that such analysis will not be easy.

The other notion which occurs regularly in the literature is that repeated movement is in some sense important (especially Goldstein, 1954 and 1964; Rowntree, 1957). Morrison (1971) states that his 'findings reveal a substantial degree of chronicity, defined as a tendency for observed mobility rates to be the product of repeated and frequent movement by the same individuals rather than single moves by the observed population at risk'. This is an over-strong conclusion to base on the analysis of *place of work* data. He presents no evidence on the proportion of moves, or of movers attributable to chronic movers even for changes of place of work. Goldstein (1954) presents even less evidence; he only presents data on residence at two points in time, and his groups clearly need to be controlled for age (this is obvious from the differing proportions of deaths). Goldstein's (1964) analysis only takes account of moves into and out of 'Greater Copenhagen'; his analysis does control for broad age groups; however, the movers with more than one return move in his Table 2 (p. 1127) never constitute as much as one-third of total movers, and never make more than half of the moves. He restricted his analysis to return moves. Perhaps the most convincing evidence on frequency of move presented to date has been by Rowntree (1957) in his all too brief study based on the National Register. Non-local migrants in the 15-29 age group averaged around 1.7 moves each in a three-year period 1948-50.

The evidence on a duration of residence effect is somewhat stronger, though again patchy. Although often cited (e.g. by Ginsberg, 1972a; Morrison, 1967, etc.), Taeuber (1961) contains no direct information on migration probabilities by duration of residence status. Myers *et al.* (1967) produce evidence for a sample of high-school children of a decline in migration rates with duration of residence for the first two years at least. Rowntree (1957) gives some information on time-lags between moves — but only for up to three years' duration and there is some possibility of a truncation effect for the third year. Morrison (1967) and Land (1969) have both produced quite convincing evidence of declining migration rates with duration of residence, except for the first year. Both these authors were trying to validate the 'axiom of cumulative inertia' inherent in the Cornell thinking. The papers by Eldridge (1965) and Shryock and Larmon (1965) really do not add anything on this topic.

10.4 Some Further Evidence on Repeated Movement and Duration of Residence

10.4.1 Data Used

Kiernan (1979, this volume) gives some preliminary results from her analysis of residential histories for the young people in the National Survey of Health and Development. These data contain a wealth of information on movement of these young people, with the addresses being coded for each time of interview. The analysis presented here will take any change of address as a definition of movement — this is done deliberately to maximise the number of moves available for analysis. All analyses presented will be for the sub-group for whom complete information on all addresses is available, and for whom level of educational attainment is also available — a total of 2,952 cases. It is important to note that these 2,952 young people are all of the same age (within 1 week) — this constitutes a relatively large sample for an age group. The segment of residential history which will be examined is that from the interview in 1962, when they were aged 16, to the interview in 1972, when they were aged 26. The reasons for choice of this interval are that it represents the most mobile set of ages available and the period when these young people were beginning to move independently of their parents. Information is available for eight inter-interview intervals, interviews having been carried out in 1962, 1963, 1964, 1965, 1966, 1968, 1970, 1971 and 1972. These segments will usually be referred to as segments or periods 1, 2, 3, 4, 5, 6, 7 and 8 respectively. The intervals are not of equal length, and as a result migration rates presented are strictly comparable only within each segment.

It is important to be aware of some of the possible problems with these data. There is every reason to suppose that the untraced members of the cohort might be relatively more mobile than those who have been successfully traced at every interview. Some difficulties may arise through interviews (or postal responses) not all taking place at the same instant. A three-month delay in responding to a single questionnaire would lengthen the previous interval and shorten the following one: this could introduce spurious negative inter-period relationships. However, it is likely that this highly selected group of respondents, for whom responses are available at each interview carried out, will be dominated by those who respond very quickly at each interview. Not all moves are covered, as information is only available for the net effect of address changes over each segment as a whole.

The results presented here are a partial analysis of these data. The only explanatory variables considered are social class of origin, which has a simple manual/non-manual split, and level of educational qualifications, divided into those with no qualifications, GCE 'O' level or equivalent, GCE 'A' level or equivalent, and degree. The introduction of social class of origin partly reflects a belief that such origins may be important in their own right, also noting that this is a relatively fixed attribute, and is required for some of the statistical analyses carried out, as the sample was effectively stratified across this dimension with different selection probabilities. The use of educational qualification level again reflects a belief that this is an important variable (see Kiernan (1979, this volume) for some convincing evidence), and also reflects a deliberate choice of a variable which is relatively fixed after age 21 or thereabouts – much more so than occupation, social class, socio-economic group or income, for example. Thus both background variables used might well be suitable controls for projection purposes.

10.4.2 Results

Table 10.1 presents proportions moving in each inter-interview segment by qualification level and social class of origin. Several interesting points emerge. For the period 1962-3 (segment 1) no clear patterning of the proportions can be discerned. This can be taken as evidence that these young people are dependent on their parents for movement when aged 16 or 17. For parents aged about forty to fifty in 1962-3 a crude social class split in 1946 was not a good discriminator for migration rates some seventeen years later (note also that there would be a strong disincentive for parents of the educationally successful to migrate with children of this age). Segment 2 (1963-4, ages 17 to 18) shows very clearly the impact of moves to university and to other institutions such as teacher training colleges. In every subsequent period those who obtained a degree by age 26 exhibit very high mobility, always at least 60 per cent above the overall level. It is also worth noting that this proportionate excess shows a clear inverse relationship with the size of the overall proportion moving: this is probably related to the omission of multiple moves in a period. There is some evidence that the group with 'A' levels are more mobile than their less qualified peers, although this differential may be disappearing with increasing age. There is virtually no evidence of differentials in mobility depending on parents' social class of origin, once level of qualifications has been controlled. It is important to note that the effect of obtaining a degree persists well after age 21 or 22. If this finding holds beyond age 26, this has implications for the study of migration and for population projections. We may have identified a set of 'chronic movers' who have different underlying probabilities of migration over a long period. This suggests that disaggregation by this relatively fixed characteristic may be an efficient sub-classifier. It also suggests that the definitions used for census purposes are inadequate — students away from home are attributed to their parents' homes, yet we have clear evidence that this group is subsequently highly mobile — they should be isolated as migrants as soon as possible. No claim can be made on these data that degree-holders constitute a majority of movers (Goldstein, 1954 and 1964; Morrison, 1971); a claim can be made that they are making a substantial contribution to population heterogeneity.

We turn now to some evidence on the impact of repeated migration and duration of residence. Tables 10.2 and 10.3 present results for segment 8 (1971-2, ages 25 to 26) on proportions moving by number of previous moves and by segment of most recent previous move, which is

	All	1,236	.061	.196	.235	.265	.521	.410	.392	.231
All	None	1,734	.055	.026	.186	.211	.440	.298	.284	.182
	'O' level	704	.072	.089	.168	.241	.426	.382	.361	.196
	'A' level	290	.031	.379	.200	.269	.583	.490	.393	.203
	Degree	224	.054	.509	.442	.424	.759	.594	.549	.402
	All	2,952	.057	.112	.202	.240	.475	.359	.333	.204

Table 10.2: Proportions Moving in Segment 8 (1971-2) by Qualification Level, Social Class of Origin and Number of Moves in Segments 1 to 7 (1962-71)

Social class of origin	Number of moves in segments 1 to 7	Qualification Level				All levels
		None	'O' level	'A' level	Degree	
Manual	0	.243 (230)	.214 (42)	.250 (8)	.000 (1)	.238 (281)
	1	.192 (506)	.161 (93)	.353 (17)	.250 (4)	.192 (620)
	2	.143 (406)	.184 (76)	.400 (20)	.500 (8)	.165 (510)
	3	.139 (151)	.081 (37)	.133 (15)	.375 (8)	.137 (211)
	4	.179 (39)	.286 (14)	.154 (13)	.200 (5)	.197 (71)
	5+	.167 (6)	.000 (3)	.000 (4)	.150 (10)	.174 (23)
Non-manual	0	.280 (50)	.318 (66)	.053 (19)	.250 (4)	.266 (139)
	1	.167 (144)	.148 (149)	.162 (37)	.250 (8)	.160 (338)
	2	.215 (130)	.190 (100)	.216 (51)	.424 (33)	.229 (314)
	3	.167 (54)	.203 (64)	.210 (62)	.389 (54)	.239 (234)
	4	.071 (14)	.289 (45)	.171 (41)	.554 (56)	.333 (156)
	5+	.000 (4)	.333 (15)	.333 (3)	.273 (33)	.273 (55)
All	0	.250 (280)	.278 (108)	.111 (27)	.200 (5)	.248 (420)
	1	.186 (650)	.153 (242)	.222 (54)	.250 (12)	.181 (958)
	2	.160 (536)	.188 (176)	.268 (71)	.439 (41)	.189 (824)
	3	.146 (205)	.158 (101)	.195 (77)	.387 (62)	.191 (445)
	4	.151 (53)	.288 (59)	.167 (54)	.525 (61)	.291 (227)
	5+	.100 (10)	.278 (18)	.143 (7)	.279 (43)	.244 (78)

Number of cases on which rates are based are shown in brackets.

		.000 (?)	.000 (?)	.000 (?)	.218 (37)
1 to 3	.312 (16)	.067 (15)	.000 (5)	.000 (1)	.162 (37)
Stayer	.280 (50)	.318 (66)	.053 (19)	.250 (4)	.266 (139)
7	.138 (492)	.161 (254)	.167 (114)	.350 (123)	.174 (983)
6	.153 (419)	.218 (179)	.245 (98)	.500 (66)	.207 (762)
5	.197 (385)	.188 (112)	.333 (39)	.444 (27)	.213 (563)
4	.212 (85)	.156 (32)	.333 (6)	.000 (1)	.202 (124)
1 to 3	.301 (73)	.105 (19)	.000 (6)	.500 (2)	.250 (100)
Stayer	.250 (280)	.278 (108)	.111 (27)	.200 (5)	.248 (420)

Numbers of cases on which rates are based are shown in brackets.

a close surrogate for duration of residence except for the unequal segment lengths. Many of the rates presented here are unreliable, being based on very few cases. The 'A' level, non-manual stayers have a curiously low mobility rate, although this is based on only 19 cases. Despite this and few other mildly aberrant values, a clear picture emerges. Examining mobility in segment 8 for those with no qualifications or 'O' levels (the rates are generally unreliable for the more highly qualified) related to number of previous moves since age 16, we find the highest mobility rates consistently occur for those who have never moved since age 16 – this is a surprising finding. Presumably further analysis will reveal that many of these young people had married during or just before segment 8 (Speare (1970) in his interesting paper relating mobility rates to life-cycle stage found that 80 per cent of newly-weds moved in the year of marriage for his sample of residence histories in Rhode Island). There is little or no evidence of increasing propensities to move in this period with increasing frequency of move. There is some slight evidence that those who had hitherto moved only once since 1962 had lower mobility rates. For those with no qualifications an efficient sub-classification may be 'stayers' and the rest; for those with 'O' levels it may be stayers, those with 4 or more moves and the rest. Of course such tentative conclusions would require further verification before being adopted for projection purposes. It is worth noting that the degree of heterogeneity exhibited along this dimension of repeated movements is not as substantial as the differences consistently exhibited between degree-holders and the rest.

Turning now to the mobility rates by duration of residence shown at Table 10.3, we find, perhaps not unexpectedly, a somewhat similar pattern emerging. Again for the groups with 'O' level and below (which have adequate numbers of cases) we find the young people who have not previously moved since 16 are the most mobile. There is a noticeable tendency for those who had moved in the previous segment to be relatively immobile. Otherwise there is no clear duration of residence effect. Again no discrimination along this duration of residence dimension exhibits such large differences as does that between degree holders and the rest.

These results on repeated movement and duration of residence are for a single segment. They seem to be at variance with much of the literature; although the repeated movement case is not strongly made in the literature, the evidence on duration of residence is stronger. The sample we are considering is much more concentrated in age than is any subgroup considered in previous studies; we are considering the most mobile period for this cohort, a substantial majority having moved at least once in the three observation segments prior to the last. As this cohort enters a period of less frequent movement, duration of residence may improve as a discriminator. The relatively rapid movement for the previously immobile will probably reduce once the peak marriage ages are passed. These results do indicate the importance of very close control on age for migration studies. Findings based on age groups as broad as ten or fifteen years are not satisfactory within this highly mobile period, as the reasons for and patterns of movement are changing so rapidly, as are the propensities to migrate, leading to substantial lack of population homogeneity (this point is often ignored, see Clark and Huff (1977), an otherwise useful contribution; Morrison (1967) and many others).

10.4.3 Contingency Table Analysis

Whilst the analysis presented so far gives some interesting insights into the problems of repeated movement, a detailed examination of the impact of the patterns and timing of repeated movement requires a different approach. The approach adopted here is to use log-linear models for cross-tabulations of movement within several segments controlled for qualification level and social class of origin. (It is essential to control for social origin in these analyses because of the different sampling fractions used for the two groups.) Our aim is to explore the structure of the tables for insights into the migration process, and to discover whether it is necessary to take account of repeated movement. The results have been obtained using Goodman's (1971) ECTA (Everyman's Contingency Table Analysis) programme. The interested reader should refer to one of the standard texts on the subject (Fienberg (1977) gives the best introduction) for a detailed description.

Our analysis uses the data presented in Table 10.4 on movement in the three most recent segments. The simplest model we could usefully fit would be the 'independence' model, which posits that the proportions in each cell can be approximated adequately by the products of the five marginal proportions relevant to the cell position. To test this formally we would calculate a chi-squared statistic. (The test statistic we shall use throughout is the likelihood ratio chi-square, which has theoretical advantages over the more traditional Pearson test (sum of (observed-expected)^2/expected).) In this case, we would denote such a model as C_6, C_7, C_8, C_0, C_q , where the C is used to denote a margin or configuration over which the model is fitted, and

Table 10.4: Numbers by Mobility Status in Segments 6, 7 and 8 by Qualification Level and Social Class of Origin

Segment 6		Non	Mig	Non	Mig	Non	Mig	Non	Mig
7		Non	Non	Mig	Mig	Non	Non	Mig	Mig
8		Non	Non	Non	Non	Mig	Mig	Mig	Mig
Origin	Qualification								
	None	520	275	247	56	140	51	40	9
	'O' level	82	54	51	33	20	14	6	5
Manual	'A' level	17	17	11	12	8	6	4	2
	Degree	3	4	9	8	2	5	2	3
	All	622	350	318	109	170	76	52	19
	None	119	80	93	28	44	13	14	5
	'O' level	131	86	90	39	38	25	17	13
Non-manual	'A' level	43	59	46	26	10	16	9	4
	Degree	18	29	32	31	12	28	13	25
	All	311	254	261	124	104	82	53	47

Mig = Migrant in segment, Non = Non-migrant in segment.

the subscripts signify the particular margin (or margins) used for the model, with 6, 7 and 8 referring to the appropriate segments, o to social class of origin and q to qualification level. In this case the independence model is of no interest as it clearly fails to fit the data. It is of some interest to consider what the implications of a no interaction or independence model would have been. The first major implication would have been that determination of the probabilities of movement in a single segment did not require information on moves in the other segments; secondly, we would have been able to 'collapse' Table 10.4 across all dimensions other than 8 and still obtain the same estimate for propensity to migrate in period 8, even with a different sample population structure.

Interactions between the variables must then exist. In particular there is a strong relationship between qualification level and movement in each segment. There is also a strong relationship between qualification level and social class of origin. Perhaps taking account of these relationships would be sufficient to explain the structure of the table. We denote this model by $\{C_{6q}, C_{7q}, C_{8q}, C_{oq}\}$, where C_{6q} indicates we are fitting our model on the joint marginal distribution of movement in segment 6 and qualification levels; similarly for the other terms. Control on joint margins in this way implies control on the individual margins as well. The independence model has 8 independent parameters, this model has 20. This model is also inadequate. If we wish to retain a model in which there are no interactions between movements in the various time segments, we would next consider the model $\{C_{6oq}, C_{7oq}, C_{8oq}\}$, where C_{6oq} means we fit our model on the joint marginal distribution of all three variables 6, o and q, and thus on all possible pairs of margins as well as the single margins. This model also fails to provide an adequate account of the structure of Table 10.4, being far out in the tail of the chi-squared distribution. We conclude that an adequate model for Table 10.4 must take account of at least some of the interactions between time segments.

Table 10.5 shows the results of fitting four models which take account of these time segment interactions in varying degree. Although we have reason to believe that the models presented in Table 10.5 are the 'best' available (in the sense of being most parsimonious for a particular level of fit), we cannot be certain of this without extensive further computation. The four models shown are nested and it is legitimate to test for the addition of extra terms using the difference between two nested chi-squared values and the difference in degrees of freedom as a chi-square test of improvement of fit for nested models. Model 2 in Table 10.5 represents a significant improvement over model 1 ($X^2 = 6.11$; 1 df, $0.02 > \text{Pr} > 0.01$), whereas models 3 and 4 do not significantly improve on model 2. We shall thus adopt model 2 as being an adequate description of the structure of Table 10.4. (Model 4 would probably represent 'overfitting' Table 10.4.) Table 10.6 gives the values of the parameter estimates for model 2 (see Goodman, 1972 and 1973; Fienberg, 1977; or Bishop *et al.*, 1975, for detailed explanation). Controlling for conjoint variation over all the marginals fitted for model 2, the parameter estimates show that there are negative relationships between movement in successive segments, but that there is no evidence of a relationship between movement in segment 6 and movement in segment 8 (as no C_{68} appears in the model). As mentioned earlier, it is possible that spurious negative relationships between successive segments have arisen through tardy replies to the questionnaire at the end of the first of the two segments in question. An alternative and more likely explanation is that people who have very recently moved are less likely to move again for a while due to the costs incurred in moving, as has been found elsewhere. Movement in segment 7 is apparently related to social class of origin, but not too strongly, with people of non-manual origin being slightly more likely to

Table 10.5: Results of Fitting Several Log-Linear Models to Table 10.4

Model margins fitted	X^2 LR	Degrees of freedom	Probability
1 C_{67}, C_{6q}, C_{78}, C_{7q}, C_{8q}, C_{oq}	52.80	42	0.123
2 C_{67}, C_{6q}, C_{78}, C_{7q}, C_{7o}, C_{8q}, C_{oq}	46.69	41	0.250
3 C_{7oq}, C_{8oq}, C_{67}, C_{78}, C_{6q}	34.87	34	0.427
4 C_{67q}, C_{7oq}, C_{8oq}, C_{78}	27.76	31	0.65 approx.

Table 10.6: Parameter Estimates for Model 2 of Table 10.5

The model is C_{67}, C_{6q}, C_{78}, C_{7q}, C_{7o}, C_{8q}, C_{oq}

or

$$\log (P_{ijklm}) = U + U_6(i) + U_7(j) + U_8(k) + U_q(l) + U_o(m) + U_{67}(ij) + U_{6q}(il)$$
$$+ U_{78}(jk) + U_{7q}(jl) + U_{7o}(jm) + U_{8q}(kl) + U_{qo}(lm)$$

where i, j, k, m = 1, 2 and l = 1, 2, 3, 4.

For variables 6, 7, 8 and o the U-values shown below are for the first category only. The other values follow from the U-values being constrained to sum to zero across each dimension. For variable q all four values are shown. The first category for each variable is non-movement, no qualifications and non-manual.

$U = 3.043$ $U_6 = 0.154$ $U_7 = 0.303$ $U_8 = 0.611$ $U_o = 0.257$

$U_{67} = -0.134$ $U_{78} = -0.105$ $U_{7o} = -0.056$

Levels of q	U_q	U_{6q}	U_{7q}	U_{8q}	U_{qo}
1: No. quals.	0.957	0.338	0.261	0.190	−0.843
2: 'O' Level	0.360	0.127	0.100	0.130	0.012
3: 'A' Level	−0.548	−0.104	0.011	0.100	0.265
4: Degree	−0.769	−0.361	−0.372	−0.420	0.566

move (this does not appear important for segments 6 or 8, which is curious, and both models 1 and 3 or 4 are more symmetrical in this respect — the relationship with movement in segment 7 may just appear stronger due to sampling variation). The structures of the parameter estimates for the interactions between qualification levels and ⋯⋯⋯ movement in each of the time segments are reassuringly consistent, with degree-holders being very much more likely to move. There is some evidence of the differentials between the remaining groups narrowing over time, as was noted earlier. Finally, there is the expected very strong negative relationship between qualification level and social class of origin.

Our analysis so far has concentrated on the structure of relationships within Table 10.4. Through the use of log-linear models we have obtained useful insights into this structure. For many purposes, especially projection work, we are interested in predictive models rather than structural models. When dealing with rates the usual, sensible approach would be to work with logit-linear models. This involves a simple adaptation of our log-linear analysis and there are advantages to using this approach (see Fienberg, 1977, Chapter 6), especially where the explanatory variables are not all design variables. In our case only social class of origin should be regarded as a design variable, as the sample was stratified on this variable. The other variables which we use to estimate movement in period 8, namely qualification level and movement in segments 6 and 7, should just be regarded as response variables. Thus we are in a position to gain information about the necessary control variables to be taken into account in a logit-linear analysis from the log-linear analysis. The reformulation of the log-linear model given in Table 10.6 as a logit-linear model leads to:

$$\log (P_{ij11m}/P_{ij21m}) = [U_8(1) - U_8(2)] + [U_{78}(j1) - U_{78}(j2)]$$
$$+ [U_{8q}(11) - U_{8q}(21)]$$
$$= 2[U_8(1) + U_{78}(j1) + U_{8q}(11)]$$
$$= W + W_7(j) + W_q(l).$$

Thus for predictive purposes our model simplifies a great deal, with movement in the previous period and qualification level being the relevant inputs.

Given the substantial simplification achieved for predictive work and the clarity of the structure emerging from Table 10.4, we are encouraged to study more complex tables. We have chosen to pursue the path of introducing more detailed migration history information, although it is quite possible that more could be gained by introducing other background variables of relative fixity. Table 10.7 shows mobility patterns in segments 7 and 8 by qualification levels, social class of origin and number of moves in segments 1 to 6. (We have also tried some analyses on a yet more complicated table which maintains segment 6 as a separate period, and introduces frequency of movement in segments 1 to 5. Whilst the analysis presents several problems, especially through the large numbers of random zeros, the results which emerged were in general very similar to those described here. Space considerations prevent further discussion of these data.) It is again possible to demonstrate that no adequate model of the structure of Table 10.7 can be found without taking some account of interactions between movements in various segments. The most satisfactory model tried is shown in Table 10.8 (X^2 = 99.50, 91 degrees of freedom, Pr = .254). (Addition of C_{70q} and C_{80q} (and thus C_{70} and C_{80}) gives X^2 of 80.65 on 83 df with Pr > .5 — a gain of 18.85 in X^2 for 8 df, $0.02 > Pr > 0.01$ — although this represents a significant gain we have chosen to use the simpler model in the hope of avoiding overfitting. The interpretations placed on the parameter estimates would not change, although the actual values would change slightly.)

Turning now to the interpretation of the parameter estimates given at Table 10.8, we find several similarities to our earlier analysis. There is again a negative relationship between movement in segments 7 and 8, with very similar estimates. There is the strong positive relationship between qualification level and non-manual origin, again with extremely similar estimates. The interactions between qualification levels and movement in segments 7 and 8 are not quite so well behaved: degree-holders are still consistently much more mobile, those without qualifications least so, but the intermediate categories of 'O' and 'A' level are reversed. (This reversal is remarkably consistent, as will be seen below and may well be related to the kinds of occupations these two groups enter; there may also be considerable remaining heterogeneity within these groups, for example in terms of vocational qualifications.) By far the strongest interaction involving frequency of movement in periods 1 to 6 is that with qualification level, with degree-holders being consistently more mobile and those without qualifications very much less so, although there is a reversal for the 'O' level holders who had moved twice or more, and the 'A' level holders were less likely to have moved four or more times. The third order interactions, 7fq and 8fq, are more complex, but do present a coherent interpretation. Amongst non-movers in segments 1 to 6 those with no qualifications are relatively more likely to move in segment 7 and segment 8, those with degrees much less so (although it should be noted that only 8 degree-holders had not moved by the end of segment 6; note also that all these statements are conditional upon all the other factors which enter into the overall model). Amongst those who moved four or more times in segments 1 to 6, those with 'O' levels are relatively more likely to move in segments 7 and 8, those with 'A' levels less so. Finally, there are small, generally positive relationships between frequency of movement in segments 1 to 6 and movement in segments 7 and 8; those of non-manual origin are more likely to be frequent movers in segments 1 to 6;

Table 10.7: Numbers by Mobility Status in Segments 7 and 8, by
Qualification Level, Social Class of Origin and Number of Moves in
Segments 1 to 6

Origin		Non-manual				Manual			
Segment 7		Non	Mig	Non	Mig	Non	Mig	Non	Mig
Segment 8		Non	Non	Mig	Mig	Non	Non	Mig	Mig
Qualification level	Number of moves segments 1-6								
	0	36	37	14	6	174	77	56	18
	1	83	45	18	8	332	144	79	17
None	2	57	26	20	4	204	57	41	10
	3	19	10	5	1	73	23	11	3
	4+	4	3	0	0	12	2	4	1
	0	45	26	21	5	33	19	9	0
	1	101	37	17	6	59	35	15	8
'O' level	2	44	30	13	5	27	19	6	1
	3	21	26	8	9	15	8	2	2
	4+	6	10	4	5	2	3	2	0
	0	18	7	1	1	6	3	2	1
	1	24	16	5	2	8	5	5	2
'A' level	2	24	24	9	5	7	4	6	1
	3	25	23	8	5	9	7	1	2
	4+	11	2	3	0	4	4	0	0
	0	3	1	1	0	1	2	0	0
	1	5	8	2	3	1	1	1	1
Degree	2	11	16	11	9	3	3	3	2
	3	17	17	12	18	2	4	1	0
	4+	11	21	14	8	0	7	2	2

Mig = migrant in segment, Non = non-migrant in segment.

all of these patterns contain small anomalies, for example the 4+ movers are less mobile in period 7 than those who had moved three times (exhaustion?), but nevertheless are broadly interpretable.

Again if we are interested in predictive work this model can be reformulated as a logit-linear model giving:

Table 10.8: Parameter Values of the Model Chosen for Table 10.7

Model is C_{7fq}, C_{8fq}, C_{78}, C_{of}, C_{oq}

The model terms are not written out in full, the extension of the U-formulation given in Table 10.6 being straightforward; variables 7, 8 and o are dichotomous and the U-values are shown only for the first category; for variables q and f all values are shown, but are constrained to sum to zero; category 1 for each variable is as follows — non-migrant, non-manual, no qualification, and no moves in segments 1 to 6.

$U = 1.873$	$U_7 = 0.296$	$U_8 = 0.661$	$U_o = 0.257$	$U_{78} = -0.116$
Levels of q	U_q	U_{7q}	U_{8q}	U_{oq}
1: None	0.835	0.287	0.162	−0.820
2: 'O' level	0.474	−0.048	−0.004	0.035
3: 'A' level	−0.477	0.067	0.140	0.253
4: Degree	−0.832	−0.307	−0.298	0.532

		Levels of f				
U-value	Levels of q	1 (0)	2 (1)	3 (2)	4 (3)	5 (4+)
f	—	−0.270	0.496	0.508	0.159	−0.893
7f	—	0.132	0.000	0.002	−0.107	−0.027
8f	—	0.180	0.035	−0.079	−0.056	−0.080
of	—	−0.071	−0.104	0.020	0.085	0.070
	1	1.057	0.673	0.118	−0.638	−1.209
	2	0.591	0.273	−0.344	−0.325	−0.194
fq	3	−0.161	−0.114	0.108	0.340	−0.174
	4	−1.487	−0.832	0.118	0.623	1.578
	1	−0.294	−0.067	0.093	0.146	0.121
	2	0.073	0.234	0.074	−0.068	−0.312
7fq	3	−0.001	−0.034	−0.157	−0.111	0.303
	4	0.223	−0.133	−0.010	0.032	−0.112
	1	−0.339	−0.003	0.086	0.213	0.043
	2	−0.159	0.170	0.243	0.010	−0.263
8fq	3	0.031	−0.133	−0.181	−0.034	0.318
	4	0.468	−0.033	−0.148	−0.189	−0.097

$$\log (P_{i1klm}/P_{i2klm}) = 2[U_8(1) + U_{78}(i1) + U_8 f(1l) + U_8 q(1m) + U_8 fq(1lm)]$$
$$= w + w_7(i) + w_f(l) + w_q(m) + w_{fq}(lm)$$

Thus to predict movement in period 8 we should need information on movement in segment 7 and a cross-classification of movement in segments 1 to 6 and qualification levels. This is still an important simplification. Although information on social class of origin is not used, it was used in obtaining the particular parameter estimates given here. The parameter estimates do depend on the particular log-linear model fitted, but should not be very different from those which would be obtained taking account of the full cross-classification of all the dependent variables, as is often suggested. The advantage of our approach is that we obtain useful information on the interrelationships present and have the potential of simplifying the cross-tabulation needed as input to logit-linear modelling.

The analysis of these quite complex cross-tabulations raises several interesting points which require further study and could only come from a model-based approach to the data, owing to the complexity of the interrelationships. We have found some evidence that frequency of past movement helps explain variability in more recent movement: this seems to be so both for the most recent previous period and for a summary of earlier moves. The relationship is negative for the last previous period, but positive before. We still may not assert this to be a repeated movement effect without considerable further examination of other variables. We have demonstrated that level of qualifications is of very great importance in determining migration frequencies in all periods, much more so than any of our frequency indicators. We find from our analysis of Table 10.7 that the effect of frequency of movement on moves in segments 7 and 8 is not a 'pure' effect, but is strongly interacting with qualification levels, which is a probable indication that other background variables not included in our analysis here are causing heterogeneity. We need to answer questions about the identity and characteristics of the groups identified by the third-order interactions: who are the highly mobile 'O' level group, why does mobility slow down for the 'A' level group, etc.? Another interesting finding to emerge from our analysis of Table 10.7 is that the apparent very strong tendency for non-movers to move in segment 8 identified in Tables 10.2 and 10.3 is not so apparent in a fuller analysis. Only the group who have no qualifications and had not moved in segments 1 to 6 were identified as more likely to move in segments 7 and 8 — presumably this corresponds to the leaving-home stage of the life-cycle. However, introduction of further variables whilst retaining frequency of movement is virtually impossible, the numbers per cell getting too small for useful analysis. We choose to stop our analysis at this point, emphasising that the effects of frequency of past movement are identifiable, but not the most important control variable for migration analysis. Qualification level and age are almost certainly more useful and easier to introduce for projection work. After these, frequency of movement is a possible competitor, but has been established as no more. We must restress the need for careful study of sources of heterogeneity before insisting on duration of residence or repeated migration effects. More work needs to be done in this field.

It remains a possibility that some of our results have been distorted by the nature of the data used or by sampling errors. The problems with the data base were outlined earlier, but non-fixity of interview date, likely selective omissions of the most mobile and non-identification of all changes of address are the most likely to have caused difficulties. The analysis seems too consistent for these to have caused major problems. Although there are such problems, it must be stressed that the data set used here is of very high quality, and as good as or probably better than any other in the world, having the advantage of being prospective, giving a wealth of information never normally available, of which we have used just a fragment.

10.5 Conclusion

In this chapter we have raised many issues which are of vital importance to projection work. One of the key ideas is that of 'efficient sub-classification' (following Brass's 1974 terminology). The importance of models to simplify the number of items requiring projection has been stressed, as has the relationship of recent work in stochastic models of mobility to population projections, especially in the area of migration. The particular difficulties of regional projections mainly arise through the high levels of disaggregation required and it is argued that efficient sub-classification and modelling offer hope of solution.

The chapter then turns to one particular aspect of projections, namely migration, and considers further the need for introduction of duration of residence or frequency of past movement as efficient sub-classifiers for projecting migration. After a brief review of the literature, we examine some data from a longitudinal study (see also Kiernan, Chapter 9). Whilst these data support in part the need for information on past migration frequency for predictive purposes, qualification level is shown to be a more efficient sub-classifier. In addition, it is argued that much of the remaining frequency of past movement effects is probably due to population heterogeneity, as the frequency effects were interacting in a regular but complex way with qualification level. Our suggestions for control variables to give efficient sub-classification for migration projection work would be as follows — age (in considerable detail, preferably single years for the most mobile ages); educational qualification level (almost certainly substituting students on a degree course for degree-holders so as to identify the most mobile group at as early an age as possible); subsequently we would regard information on movement in a short recent period (perhaps one year as in some census questions) and on frequency of movement in a period before that as candidates, competing with other socio-economic variables. It should be noted that frequency of movement in a period is a difficult variable to handle for projection work as it requires complex disaggregation. There is, of course, a danger that even this would require too much detail when sub-classified by region. More work also needs to be done to investigate the efficient classification of regions.

These conclusions must remain tentative: owing to sample size constraints we were unable to examine regional variability and we needed to work with all moves rather than inter-regional or inter-county migration. However, up to the level of disaggregation permitted by the sample, Kiernan (Chapter 9) finds many similar results for inter-regional migrants, with qualification level perhaps being an even better sub-classifier at this level. One additional reservation must also be made, namely that the members of the sample were aged 26 at the most recent interview considered here: it remains to be seen whether all the relationships found here persist as strongly later in life.

Our findings and discussion do have important consequences for census definitions and tabulations. First, the attribution of higher education students to their parents' homes does not make sense (only Oxbridge has terms totalling less than half a year) and does positive harm for migration study by delaying the identification of a mobile subgroup. The implications for migration tabulations should be more far-reaching. There is a strong need for tabulation of at least in- and out-migrants to each region by single years of age. There is almost certainly a need for several tabulations of migration by qualification level. Up to now the overwhelming emphasis of the migration tables has been on economic variables such as occupation and industry. These economic or occupational variables are of doubtful utility for projection as they lack the fixity of education or other qualification measures. There has often been too much detail on the origin of migrants: with the possible exception of immigrant groups, the origin of in-migrants makes little difference to a region or city. The main reason for wishing to maintain some detail on origin is of course for projection purposes, but we need to ask carefully how much detail is necessary for such purposes. Is it adequate to identify origins within county, then region and perhaps one or two neighbouring regions and then the rest of the country? Undoubtedly such a policy would save much on printing and tabulation costs. Some difficulties would be raised by complete inter-county matrices of flows not being available. It is likely that the extra tabulations permitted for other variables would more than offset these difficulties in terms of efficient projections. As the migration volumes constituted a substantial proportion of the total printed output of the 1971 census and a very high proportion among the special topic volumes, these issues are of considerable importance.

Note

1. The author wishes to thank Miss Kathleen Kiernan, of the Medical Research Council Unit of Environmental Factors in Mental and Physical Illness, for her kindness in making available the data analysed in the second half of this paper. He also thanks Dr J.W.B. Douglas, Director of the Unit, for granting formal permission for these data to be used here.

References

Bartlett, M.S. 1973. A note on Das Gupta's two-sex population model. *Theoretical Population Biology*, 4, 418-24
Bishop, Y.M., Fienberg, S.E. and Holland, P.W. 1975. *Discrete Multivariate Analysis*. Cambridge, Mass.: MIT Press
Blumen, I., Kogan, M. and McCarthy, P.J. 1955. The industrial mobility of labor as a probability process. *Cornell Studies of Industrial and Labor Relations*, 6. Ithaca, New York: Cornell University
Brass, W. 1971. On the scale of mortality. In *Biological Aspects of Demography*, ed. W. Brass. London: Taylor and Francis
Brass, W. 1974. Perspectives in population prediction: illustrated by the statistics of England and Wales. *Journal of the Royal Statistical Society*, series A, 137, 532-83
Clark, W.A.V. and Huff, J.O. 1977. Some empirical tests of duration-of-stay effects in intraurban migration. *Environment and Planning*, A, 9, 1357-74
Coale, A.J. and McNeil, D.R. 1972. The distribution by age of the frequency of first marriage in a female cohort. *Journal of the American Statistical Association*, 67, 743-9
Cordey-Hayes, M. and Gleave, D. 1973. *Migration Movement and Differential*

Growth of City Region in East and West. Centre for Environmental Studies,
    Research Paper No.1
Das-Gupta, P. 1972. On two-sex models leading to stable populations. *Theoretical
    Population Biology*, 3, 358-75
Duchêne J. and Gillet-de-Stefano, S. 1974. Ajustement Analytique des Courbes
    de Fécondité Générale. *Population et Famille*, 32, 53-93
Eldridge, H.T. 1965. Primary, secondary and return migration in the United
    States, 1955-60. *Demography*, 2, 444-55
Ewbank, D. 1974. An examination of several applications of the standard pattern
    of age at first marriage. PhD thesis, Princeton University, New Jersey
Feeney, G.M. 1970. Stable age by region distributions. *Demography*, 7, 341-8
Feeney, G.M. 1973. Two models for multiregional population dynamics.
    Environment and Planning, 5, 31-43
Fienberg, S.E. 1977. *The Analysis of Cross-Classified Categorical Data.*
    Cambridge, Mass.: MIT Press
Gilje, E.K. 1976. Population and household projections for the London boroughs.
    Paper presented at a Conference of the Population Geography and
    Quantitative Methods Study Groups of the Institute of British Geographers,
    Sheffield (mimeographed)
Ginsberg, R.B. 1971. Semi-Markov processes and mobility. *Journal of
    Mathematical Sociology*, 1, 233-62
Ginsberg. R.B. 1972a. Critique of probabilistic models: application of the
    Semi-Markov model to migration. *Journal of Mathematical Sociology*, 2, 63-82
Ginsberg. R.B. 1972b. Incorporating causal structure and exogenous information
    with probabilistic models: with special reference to choice, gravity, migration
    and Markov chains. *Journal of Mathematical Sociology*, 2, 83-103
Gleave, D. 1976. Macroscopic representations of causal factors in long-range
    migration. Paper presented at a Conference of the Population Geography and
    Quantitative Methods Study Groups of the Institute of British Geographers,
    Sheffield (mimeographed)
Goldstein, S. 1954. Repeated migration as a factor in high mobility rates.
    American Sociological Review, 19, 536-541
Goldstein, S. 1964. The extent of repeated migration: an analysis based on the
    Danish population register. *Journal of the American Statistical Association*,
    59, 1121-32
Goodman, L.A. 1961. Statistical methods for the mover-stayer model. *Journal of
    the American Statistical Association*, 56, 841-68
Goodman, L.A. 1971. The analysis of multidimensional contingency tables:
    stepwise procedures and direct estimation methods for building models for
    multiple classifications. *Technometrics*, 13, 33-61
Goodman, L.A. 1972. A general model for the analysis of surveys. *American
    Journal of Sociology*, 77, 1035-86
Goodman, L.A. 1973. Causal analysis of data from panel studies and other kinds
    of surveys. *American Journal of Sociology*, 78, 1135-91
Henry, L. 1972. Nuptiality. *Theoretical Population Biology*, 3, 135-52
Henry, N.W. 1971. The retention model: a Markov chain with variable transition
    probabilities. *Journal of the American Statistical Association*, 66, 264-7
Henry, N.W., McGinnis, R. and Tegtmeyer, H.W. 1971. A finite model of
    mobility. *Journal of Mathematical Sociology*, 1, 107-18
Keyfitz, N. 1968. *Introduction to the Mathematics of Population*. Reading,
    Mass.: Addison-Wesley
Keyfitz, N. 1972. On future population. *Journal of the American Statistical
    Association*, 67, 347-63
Kiernan, K.E. Chapter 9, this volume

Land, K.C. 1969. Duration of residence and prospective migration: further evidence. *Demography*, 6, 133-40

Lowry, I.S. 1966. Migration and metropolitan growth: two analytical models. San Francisco: Chandler

McFarland, D.D. 1975. Models of marriage formation and fertility. *Social Forces*, 54, 66-83

McGinnis, R. 1968. A stochastic model of social mobility. *American Sociological Review*, 33, 712-22

Morrison, P.A. 1967. Duration of residence and prospective migration: the evaluation of a stochastic model. *Demography*, 4, 553-61

Morrison, P.A. 1971. Chronic movers and the future redistribution of population: a longitudinal analysis. *Demography*, 8, 171-84

Myers, G.C., McGinnis, R. and Masnick, G. 1967. The duration of residence approach to a dynamic stochastic model of internal migration: a test of the axiom of cumulative inertia. *Eugenics Quarterly*, 14, 121-6

Page, H. 1977. Patterns underlying fertility schedules: a decomposition by both age and marriage duration. *Population Studies*, 31, 85-106

Rees, P.H. and Wilson, A.G. 1977. *Spatial Population Analysis*. London: Arnold

Rogers, A. 1968. *Matrix Analysis of Inter-regional Population Growth and Distribution*. Los Angeles: University of California Press

Rogers, A. 1975. *Introduction to Multiregional Mathematical Demography*. New York: John Wiley

Romaniuk, A. 1973. A three parameter model of birth projections. *Population Studies*, 27, 469-78

Rowntree, J. 1957. *Internal Migration: A Study of the Frequency of Movement Migrants*. G.R.O. Studies on Medical and Population Subjects, no. 11. London: HMSO

Ryder, N.B. 1965. The measurement of fertility patterns. In *Public Health and Population Change*, eds. M.C. Sheps and J.C. Ridley. Chicago: University of Chicago Press

Shryock, H.S. and Larmon, E.A. 1965. Some longitudinal data on internal migration. *Demography*, 2, 579-92

Speare, A.J. 1970. Home ownership, life cycle stage and residential mobility. *Demography*, 7, 449-58

Spilerman, S. 1972a. Extensions of the mover-stayer model. *American Journal of Sociology*, 78, 599-626

Spilerman, S. 1972b. The analysis of mobility processes by the introduction of independent variables into a Markov chain. *American Sociological Review*, 37, 277-94

Sykes, Z.M. 1969. Population projections and Markov chains. *International Union for the Scientific Study of Population, Conference*, London, 1, 170-4

Taeuber, K.E. 1961. Duration of residence analysis of internal migration in the United States. *The Milbank Memorial Fund Quarterly*, 39, 116-31

Taeuber, K.E., Chiazze, L. and Haenszel, W. 1968. Migration in the United States: an analysis of residence histories. *United States Public Health Monograph*, no. 77. Washington, D.C.: US Department of Health, Education and Welfare, Health Services and Mental Health Administration

Willis, K.G. 1974. *Problems in Migration Analysis*. Farnborough: Saxon House

11 POPULATION FORECASTS FOR BRITISH REGIONS: A COMPARISON

Philip Rees

11.1 Introduction

The purpose of this chapter is twofold. It is intended, first, to review the results of a series of regional projection exercises carried out for British regions in the past two decades, and, secondly, to describe a set of further projections carried out using some recently developed multi-regional models of population change. Comparison among the various projections will be made in order to expose the differences and similarities in underlying models, and in the nature of the assumptions input to those models. The comparisons will be rather general in nature, and for the specific mathematics of each model the reader is referred to the original sources given below.

The first set of projections to be reviewed is that of the National Institute of Economic and Social Research (hereafter referred to as NIESR) carried out in 1963-4 and reported in published form in Stone (1970). The first step in the study of 'Urban Development in Britain' was the preparation of a set of alternative national and regional projections to form the basis of an assessment of future housing demand. The national projections are reported in Chapter 2 of Stone (1970), the regional projections are outlined in Chapter 3, the detailed projection results for regions are given in Appendix 3, and the methodology used is described in Appendix 4.

The second set of projections is that prepared by the Office of Population Censuses and Surveys (hereafter referred to as OPCS) and its predecessor the General Register Office. These were initially prepared for the National Plan using a mid-1965 starting-point, and revised subsequently with mid-1968, mid-1969, mid-1971, mid-1973 and mid-1974 starting-points (Campbell, 1976). Those with starting-points at mid-year 1965 (Central Statistical Office 1966), mid-year 1971 (OPCS, 1973), mid-year 1973 (OPCS, 1975) and mid-year 1974 (Campbell, 1976) are examined here.

The third, fourth and fifth set of projections to be described are those developed by the author in a study of 'Spatial Demographic Growth in British Regions' (Rees, 1975, 1976a) and in a report on 'The Future Population of East Anglia and its Constituent Counties'

(Rees, 1977). The third set involves use of the growth rates matrix model developed by Rogers (1968); the fourth set makes use of the accounts based model developed by Rees and Wilson (1973, 1977); and the fifth set uses a multi-regional cohort survival model that combines features of the growth matrix and accounts-based models.

One of the problems in comparing the results of these different sets of projections is the non-comparability of the regional definitions involved. The NIESR study team developed their own set of regions which differs from the Standard Regions at that date (mid-1963), or subsequently. The regions used in the mid-1965 and mid-1971 OPCS projections differ from those based on mid-1973 or mid-1974 which use the new Standard Regions revised subsequent to local government reorganisation on 1 April 1974. Matrices were developed that showed how the populations of the regions of each study were spread (in proportions) among the post-1974 Standard Regions, and the projected populations were converted to a new region basis using this information (see Stillwell, 1976, for a description of this process).

A decision was also taken to focus attention, for present purposes, on a three-region aggregation of the standard region set: namely, East Anglia, the South-East and the Rest of Britain, the regional set used in Rees (1977). The results for three regions can be conveniently graphed and analysed within the constraints of the present chapter.

In the next section of the chapter, we review the general characteristics of the models and assumptions used in each set of projections. Subsequently, in the following five sections the results of each projection set are considered in detail.

11.2 General Characteristics of the Projections

In Table 11.1 an attempt is made to set out the principal attributes of each set of projections. The projections can be distinguished first as either single-region or multi-region. In a single-region projection model each region is treated separately. The growth path of the population of a region is unaffected by what happens elsewhere and does not influence the populations of other regions. In a multi-regional model, all regions of interest are considered together and connected by some kind of interaction matrix of rates or flows or both. Since outflows from one region are inflows to another in a multi-region model, the growth paths of the regional populations can be intimately linked. All the projections described here attempt to close the population system considered either by including a net inflow from all other regions as in the single-region case, or by including an additional rest-of-the-world region in the

Table 11.1: General Characteristics of the Projections

Characteristics	Population projection sets		
	NIESR Set	OPCS Set	GRM Set
1. Treatment of regions	Single	Single	Multi
2. Projection period length	5-year	5-year	5, 1-year
3. Treatment of age and sex	Disaggregated	Disaggregated	Aggregate
4. Treatment of mortality: type of rates used	Survival rates from RG's projection	Life table derived survival rates	Survival rates incorporated in growth rates
temporal variation	Variable	Variable	Constant
spatial variation	Constant	Variable	Variable
5. Treatment of fertility: type of rates used	Age-specific fertility rates derived from marriage analysis	Age-specific fertility rates	Birth rates incorporated in growth rates
temporal variation	Variable	Variable	Constant
spatial variation	Constant	Variable	Variable
6. Treatment of migration: method used	Net migrants added	Net migrants added	Migration rates incorporated in growth rates. Immigrants added
temporal variation	Variable	Variable	Constant
spatial variation	Variable	Variable	Variable

Notes: NIESR = National Institute of Economic and Social Research; OPCS = Office of Population Censuses and Surveys; GRM = Growth rates model.

analysis as in the multi-region case.

The time interval over which the projection moves forward is, in each case, five years used in conjunction with five-year age groups with the exception of one of the growth rate model projections with a one-year time interval. By way of contrast, most national level projections use a one-year time interval together with single years of age (e.g. OPCS, 1976). It would be advantageous to use a one-year time interval and one-year age groups in regional projections, but the relevant data are rarely available, particularly for migrants. Even if they were available, the numbers in each model category would be too small to be regarded

Table 11.1 *(contd.)*

Characteristics	Population projection sets	
	ABM set	MRCS set
1. Treatment of regions	Multi	Multi
2. Projection period length	5-year	5-year
3. Treatment of age and sex	Aggregate	Disaggregated
4. Treatment of mortality: type of rates used	Accounts derived crude death rates	Accounts derived survival rates
temporal variation	Constant	Variable
spatial variation	Variable	Variable
5. Treatment of fertility: type of rates used	Accounts derived crude death rates	Cohort-specific fertility rates
temporal variation	Constant	Variable
spatial variation	Variable	Variable
6. Treatment of migration: method used	Migration rates. Immigrants added	Migration and stayers rates. Immigrants added
temporal variation	Constant	Constant
spatial variation	Variable	Variable

Notes: ABM = Accounts-based model; MRCS = Multi-regional cohort survival model.

as statistically reliable. It is possible to combine one-year time intervals with five-year age groups in the construction of population accounts (Rees and King, 1974; Rees and Wilson, 1977) but models based on such accounts have properties which make them unusable for projection purposes.

Items 4 to 6 in Table 11.1 describe how the projection series treat the three major components of population change. The age-sex disaggregated projections treat mortality and fertility in comparable ways through the use of age-group-specific survival and fertility rates.

The ways in which these rates are calculated differ somewhat, however. The NIESR survival rates are derived directly from the population figures in the Registrar-General's (RG) projections with 1963 and 1964 starting dates. The OPCS survival rates are, as far as one can gather, derived from selecting appropriate single-year survival rates from national life tables. The MRCS survival rates are initially derived for each region from a set of population accounts. This latter procedure has the advantage that, although the construction of such accounts is an involved process (Rees and Wilson, 1977, Part 3; Plessis-Fraissard and Rees, 1977), survival rates are easily, directly and unambiguously calculated from those accounts. The survival component in the growth matrix model (GRM) is derived also from the accounts but is submerged in the general calculation of the growth rates. The accounts-based model set of projections is, interestingly enough, the only one that uses death rates directly, derived from the sets of accounts.

It is in the treatment of migration that the crucial differences between the projection sets occur. The NIESR and OPCS projections add to the population that has been survived or has been born and survived, vectors of net migrants. Scenarios of net migration are developed and applied to the 'naturally projected' populations. In the NIESR projections this appears to be done after the natural change projections have been carried out, a most extraordinary procedure! This means that net migrants in one period have no influence on births in the region in the next period. A more sensible procedure of adding in the net migrants in each time interval is adopted in the OPCS projections.

In the multi-regional models migration is dealt with by applying rates of survival and relocation to the initial population; the stayers or non-migrants are calculated in a similar fashion in the GRM and MRCS projections, but emerge as a residual in the ABM projections. Some recent research (Rogers, 1976) has indicated such treatment of migration in a multi-regional fashion via rates is clearly superior to employing the net migration concept. One problem with using multi-regional models' migration rates is that they are difficult to forecast themselves. It is much easier to vary the profile of net migration flows. The row in Table 11.1 that indicates how migration is treated temporally shows that variable assumptions have been used in the net migration projections, whereas constant assumptions characterise the multi-regional projections. There is no conceptual or programming difficulty involved: it is simply that there is relatively little in the way of good time series on which to base the forecasting of rates. The alternative strategy of modelling migration flows using a variety of spatial interaction (gravity) models has yet to be tried out in a projection context.

Let us now turn from the general to the particular and look at the sets of projections in detail, starting with those of the NIESR.

11.3 The NIESR Projection

Figure 11.1 displays the results of the NIESR projections. The key to Figure 11.1 and subsequent figures is contained in Table 11.2. Some nine possible scenarios were drawn up, resulting from the combination of three levels of fertility rates with three patterns of net migration. The middle set of fertility rates are approximately those of the Registrar-General, and higher and lower sets were proposed. The total fertility rates associated with the sets of age-specific fertility rates were approximately as shown in Table 11.3 (as best can be ascertained from the text).

Rates for intermediate years fell between the current levels for 1962 and the levels assumed for 2004. Thus, although the ultimate level of 1.99 children per woman is forecast for the lower birth-rate scenarios, the total fertility rate level only falls below 2.1 (approximate replacement level) after 2000.

The first pattern of migration assumed involves a continuation of population losses from the Northern regions (Scotland, North, North-West, Yorkshire and Humberside) and gains by all the Southern. The second pattern of migration involves continuing losses from the Northern regions but a shift of gains in the South away from the West Midlands and the South-East towards the more 'rural' regions (East Anglia, South-West, East Midlands, Wales). The third pattern sees a revival in the Northern regions at the expense of the Southern regions.

Given an elapse of 14 years from the starting-point of the NIESR projections, we are able, in part, to evaluate the success or failure of this wide range of possible scenarios against actual outcomes. The high

Table 11.3: Total Fertility Rates Associated with the NIESR projections

	1962 rates	2004 rates
High assumptions	2.84	3.07
Registrar-General's assumptions	2.84	2.75
Low assumptions	2.84	1.99

Figure 11.1: The 1963-based NIESR Projections

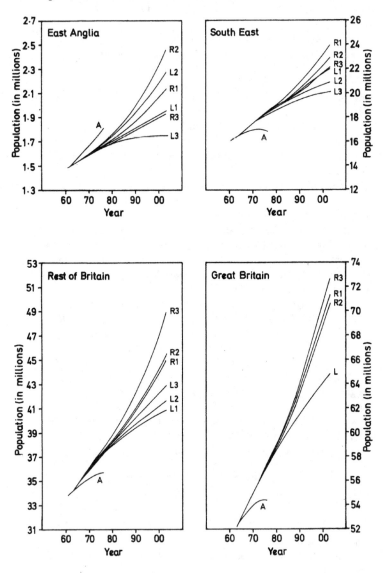

See Table 11.2 for key

birth-rate scenarios can with hindsight be regarded as 'pie in the sky' and are not plotted on Figure 11.1. In fact, the Great Britain graph reveals that even the lower birth-rate scenarios drastically overestimate the projected population – the overestimate is 2.9 millions by mid-year 1976. This is a consequence of the drastic fall in fertility since 1964. When we look at the goodness of fit of the various migration patterns we see that a different pattern gives the best fit in each case. The East Anglia projection is closest to the mark when migration pattern two is employed. By 2003 the R2 projection for East Anglia is approximately on the trend line extrapolated forward from the experience of 1961-76. The age composition of the populations would be quite different, however. Migration pattern three is most successful for the South-East, and migration pattern one for the Rest of Britain.

If the NIESR projections hold a lesson for us, it is that projections can be drastically wrong, and that it is essential to revise them in the light of the latest information, particularly in view of the delay between analysis and publication, which was six years in NIESR's case.

11.4 The OPCS Projections

This lesson is well understood by the bodies charged with producing official projections of the British national and regional populations – the Government Actuary's department and the Office of Population Censuses and Surveys (OPCS). National projections have been revised each year for some time now, and regional and local projections are now on an annual basis.

In Figure 11.2 are plotted a selection of OPCS regional and national projections. Drastic downward revision of the projected populations of Great Britain, the South-East and the Rest of Britain occurs between the mid-1965-based projection and that based on 1974. In fact, the 1973- and 1974-based projections for the South-East show a forecast decline in that region's population between 1976 and 1981, and only a small recovery subsequently. Great Britain's population and the Rest of Britain's population show similar patterns of very little growth to 1981, and resumed moderate growth thereafter.

A glance forward at Figure 11.7 shows that this picture is heavily dependent on the assumption that fertility levels will recover to a level of 2.2 children per woman in the early 1980s (the OPCS, A projection line). If this recovery is delayed or does not come to pass, slower or negative growth is in prospect (OPCS, B; OPCS, C; OPCS, D Projections).

The projection for East Anglia (Figure 11.2) shows a rather different

Table 11.2: Key to the Figures Showing the Projected Population of East Anglia, the South-East, the Rest of Britain and Great Britain

---

1. Figure 11.1 The 1963-based NIESR projections

    L1 = lower birth rate, migration pattern one
    L2 = lower birth rate, migration pattern two
    L3 = lower birth rate, migration pattern three
    R1 = Registrar-General's birth rate, migration pattern one
    R2 = Registrar-General's birth rate, migration pattern two
    R3 = Registrar-General's birth rate, migration pattern three
    L = lower birth rate, all migration patterns
    A = actual population trends, mid-year 1961 to mid-year 1976

2. Figure 11.2 Various OPCS projections

    65 = projections with a mid-year 1965 starting date
    71 = projections with a mid-year 1971 starting date
    73 = projections with a mid-year 1973 starting date
    74 = projections with a mid-year 1974 starting date

3. Figure 11.3 Growth rate model projections

    GRM = growth rates model with growth rates of 1966-71 period
           ('M' set) and immigrant flows for 1966-71
    GRN = growth rates model with growth rates of 1971-6 period
           ('N' set) and immigrant flows for 1971-6
    GRC = growth rates model with growth rates of 1970-1 period
           with closed system

4. Figure 11.4 Accounts-based model projections

    AFN = accounts based model with migration flows of 1971-6 period
           ('N' set)
    ARM = accounts-based model with migration rates of 1966-71 period
           ('M' set) and immigrant flows for 1966-71
    ARN = accounts-based model with migration rates of 1971-6 period
           ('N' set) and immigrant flows for 1971-6

5. Figure 11.5 Multi-regional cohort survival model projections, 1966-71 period based ('M' scenario) with a census date 1971 starting-point

    A = high fertility scenario, total fertility rate of 2.2
    B = replacement fertility scenario, total fertility rate of 2.1
    C = current fertility scenario, total fertility rate of 1.8
    D = lower fertility scenario, total fertility rate of 1.5

6. Figure 11.6 Multi-regional cohort survival model projections, 1971-6 period based ('N' scenarios) with a mid-year 1976 starting-point

    A = high fertility scenario, total fertility rate of 2.2
    B = replacement fertility scenario, total fertility rate of 2.1
    C = current fertility scenario, total fertility rate of 1.8
    D = lower fertility scenario, total fertility rate of 1.5

7. Figure 11.7 A comparison of population projections for Great Britain

    NIESR R3 = Figure 1's R3 projection
    NIESR L = Figure 1's L projection

Table 11.2. *(contd.)*

OPCS 71	=	Figure 2's 71 based projection
OPCS H	=	OPCS high variant projection, total fertility rate of 2.3
OPCS A	=	OPCS central variant projection, total fertility rate of 2.2
OPCS B	=	OPCS low variant projection, total fertility rate of 2.1
OPCS C	=	OPCS continuing low variant projection, total fertility rate of 1.8
N76 A	=	Figure 6's A projection
N76 D	=	Figure 6's D projection

story: the fall in fertility has been counterbalanced in part by the increasing strength of migration flows to East Anglia, particularly in the 1973- and 1974-based projections. Since East Anglia's gain in population is the South-East's loss (over 50 per cent of the in-migrants to East Anglia come from the South-East), the projected populations of East Anglia and the South-East are inextricably linked. A strong case can therefore be made for designing a projection model that reflects this dependency. We now turn to a discussion of the results of a set of such models.

11.5 The Growth Rate Model Projections

A model that does explicitly represent inter-regional dependency is the growth rate model of Rogers (1968, 1971). Age and sex are ignored in this model in order to focus on inter-regional interaction. Two recent papers (Rees, 1976b and 1977) employ a form of this model in which the growth rates are calculated from sets of multi-regional population accounts. The growth rate that connects region i and region j, by which region i's population is multiplied in the model, is defined as the number of surviving migrants between region i and region j plus the number of surviving infant migrants divided by the total number in the region at the start of the period. If region i and j are the same, the numerator contains the number of surviving stayers and surviving infant stayers. A matrix of such growth rates pre-multiplies a vector of start-of-period regional populations to yield a vector of end-of-period regional populations. To this vector is added, in the Rees (1977) version of the model, a vector of surviving immigrants from outside the system of regions of interest. In Rees (1976b) the system is closed by the inclusion of the Rest of the World as a region of interest.

The results of using this model are displayed in Figure 11.3. The designation GRC refers to the growth rates model closed system version of Rees (1976) which uses a set of one-year population accounts for 1970-1 (April 24/25 to April 24/25) for the derivation of the growth

Figure 11.2: Various OPCS Projections

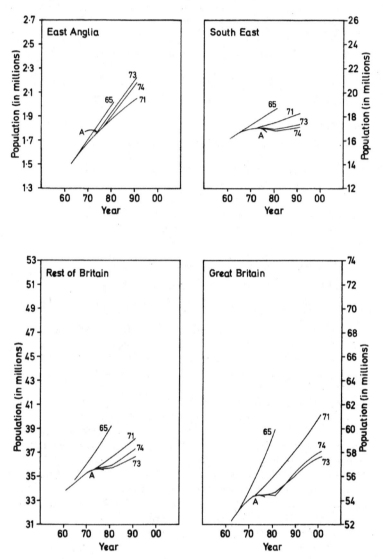

See Table 11.2 for key

Figure 11.3: Growth Model Projections

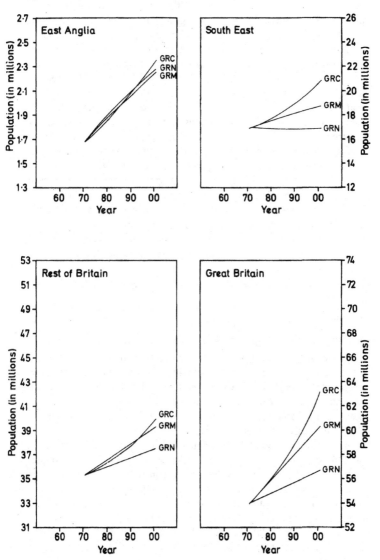

See Table 11.2 for key

rates matrix. The labels GRM and GRN refer to growth rate models based on 1971-6 population accounts, the 'M' set, and based on 1971-6 population accounts, the 'N' set. The growth rates matrices for 1970-1, 1966-71 and 1971-6 are used as constant multipliers in their respective projections to 2001. The GRM and GRN projections show approximately the behaviour one would expect having already looked at the OPCS projections of 1971, 1973 and 1974. The GRM projection is very close to that of 1971, and the GRN projection is slightly below that for 1973. The GRC projection, however, differs markedly from the mid-1971-based OPCS projections, with substantially more growth towards the end of the projection period. The reason is that Britain in this projection is 'open' to flows from the Rest of the World. These flows increase over the projection period as a result of the multiplication of a constant rate of out-migration from the Rest of the World to the regions of Britain by an increasing Rest of the World population. Since these flows are, in reality, governed by a legislation and restrictive quotas, it would seem more appropriate to introduce them into the projection as constant exogenous flows (as in the GRM and GRN projections) or constant net flow terms (the OPCS projections) rather than include them as rate terms in the model. The level of immigration to Great Britain in 1971-6 was, in fact, very similar to that in 1966-71.

11.6 The Accounts-based Model Projections

A similar set of aggregate (all age, all sex) projections was carried out, using the same input information as was used for the GRM and GRN growth model projections, but employing a different projection model — the accounts-based model. The projection results of Figure 11.4 reveal very little difference between the growth rates model forecasts and the accounts-based model forecasts. Compare GRM with ABM, and GRN with ABN in Figures 11.3 and 11.4.

If a constant flows (AFN) version of the accounts-based model is used, there appears to be relatively little effect, except for East Anglia. The AFN projection involves the use of a constant migration flows matrix rather than a constant rates matrix, and the results parallel, for East Anglia, those of the OPCS (1973, 1974) constant net flows projections. In the constant rates projection (ARN), the forecast increases in the population of East Anglia are affected by the forecast decreases in the population of the South-East (see Figure 11.4).

Figure 11.4: Accounts-based Model Projections

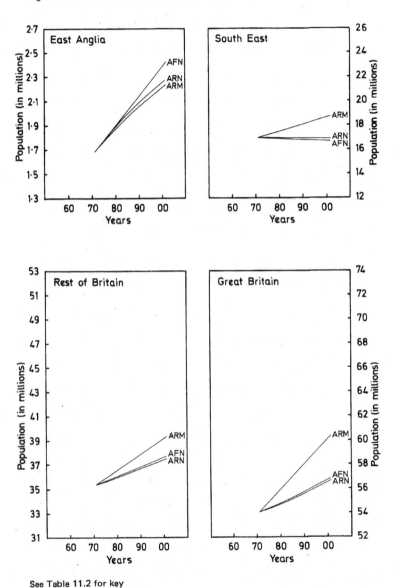

See Table 11.2 for key

Figure 11.5 Multi-regional Cohort Survival Model Projections 1966-71 Period Based ('M' Scenarios) with a Census Date 1971 Starting-point

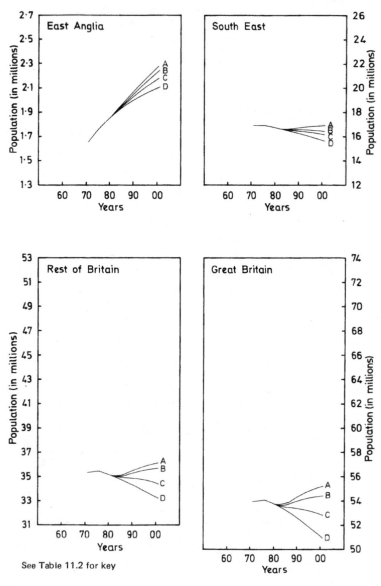

See Table 11.2 for key

Figure 11.6: Multi-regional Cohort Survival Model Projections 1971-6 Period Based ('N' Scenarios) with a Mid-year 1976 Starting-point

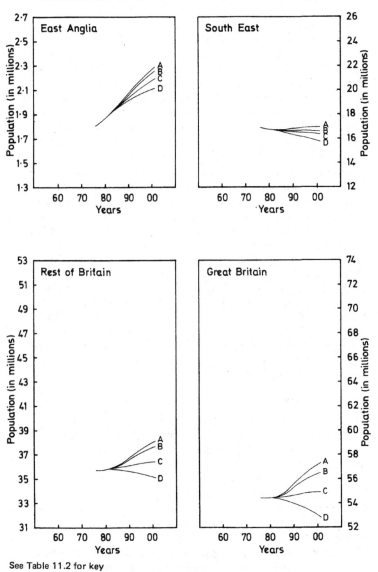

See Table 11.2 for key

11.7 The Multi-regional Cohort Survival Model Projections

To be truly effective, of course, a multi-regional projection model must be disaggregated by age group and by sex, and must allow the incorporation of flexible schedules of survival rates, fertility rates and migration rates. The model underpinning the projections shown in Figures 11.5 and 11.6, described in detail in Rees (1977), does this. Figure 11.5 shows the results of a series of projections incorporating the migration pattern of 1966-71, a forecast increase in regional survival rates and four sets of possible fertility rates. The projections of Figure 11.6 incorporate the same assumptions about survival rates and fertility rates with the estimated migration pattern for 1971-6, and a mid-1976 starting population.

The shift in migration pattern from that of 1966-71 (Figure 11.5) to that of 1971-6 makes relatively little difference to East Anglia and the South-East, but quite a substantial difference to the Rest of Britain and Great Britain as a whole. The reason for this is that the population loss to the Rest of the World is substantially reduced over the decade (1966-76), principally as a result of reduced emigration. Variation in fertility makes relatively more difference in the bigger regions (Rest of Britain, Great Britain) in the forecast populations. The migration currents leading to substantial growth (East Anglia) or steady decline (South-East) tend to overwhelm the natural increase effects. Even if the total fertility rate in East Anglia were to fall to a level of 1.5 by 1986-91 (scenario D), the population of the region would still increase from 1.8 in 1976 to 2.1 millions in 2001. Only under scenario A (total fertility back to 2.2 by 1986-91) will the South-East's population recover to 1976 levels by 2001.

11.8 Conclusions

Figure 11.7 puts together, for Great Britain, a selection of the projections discussed in the paper. The range is clearly enormous: between the lowest and highest figures for 2001 stretches a gap of nearly 18 millions. To what can we attribute this range?

The first candidate we might put forward, on the basis of Table 11.1, is that of model structure. Evidence for this in the aggregate case has been clear, but elsewhere straightforward comparisons are difficult. A second candidate for consideration is the nature of the rate and flow assumptions input to the projection. Figure 11.7 reveals that these are clearly crucial. On balance, my guess would be that about 75 per cent of the variance between forecasts could be attributed to variance in

Figure 11.7: A Comparison of Population Projections for Great Britain

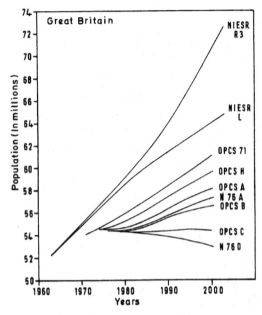

See Table 11.2 for key

input assumptions and about 25 per cent to variance in model form.

What is still needed, therefore, is an integration of the comparative evaluation of different models under the same set of assumptions carried out by Rogers (1976) and the comparative evaluation of different assumptions for the same set of models begun here in Figures 11.5, 11.6 and 11.7, with the proviso that all the models evaluated should be closed, and allow inputs flexible simultaneously over space and time.

References

Campbell, R.A. 1976. Local population projections. *Population Trends*, 5 (September), 9-12

Central Statistical Office. 1966. *Abstract of Regional Statistics*, no. 2. London: HMSO

OPCS. 1973. *The Registrar-General's Statistical Review of England and Wales for the Year 1971*, Part II. Tables, Population. London: HMSO

OPCS. 1975. *Regional Population Projections. Mid-1973 Based. New Standard*

Regions of England and Wales. London: HMSO

OPCS. 1976. *Population Projections, 1974-2014,* Series PP2, no. 5. London: HMSO

Plessis-Fraissard, M. and Rees, P.H. 1977. A computer program for constructing age-sex disaggregated multi-regional population accounts (DAME): a full description. Working Paper 170, School of Geography, University of Leeds

Rees, P.H. 1975. First progress report on SSRC grant HR2914

Rees, P.H. 1976a. Second progress report on SSRC grant HR2914

Rees, P.H. 1976b. Modelling the regional system: the population component. Working Paper 148, School of Geography, University of Leeds

Rees, P.H. 1977. The future population of East Anglia and its constituent counties (Cambridge, Norfolk and Suffolk). A report prepared for the East Anglian Economic Planning Council by the University of Leeds Industrial Services Ltd. under Department of Environment Contract number DGR/461/23, 'East Anglia: research into population'

Rees, P.H. and King, J.R. 1974. A simple model for population projections applied to ethnic group and small area populations. Working Paper 76, School of Geography, University of Leeds

Rees, P.H. and Wilson, A.G. 1973. Accounts and models for spatial demographic analysis 1: aggregate population. *Environment and Planning,* 5, 61-90

Rees, P.H. and Wilson, A.G. 1977. *Spatial Population Analysis.* London: Edward Arnold

Rogers, A. 1968. *Matrix Analysis of Inter-regional Growth and Distribution.* Berkeley and Los Angeles: University of California Press

Rogers, A. 1971. *Matrix Methods in Urban and Regional Analysis.* San Francisco: Holden-Day

Rogers, A. 1976. Shrinking large-scale population-projection models by aggregation and decomposition. *Environment and Planning A,* 8, 515-41

Stillwell, J.C.H. 1976. User's guide to a simple matrix aggregation program. Working Paper 141, School of Geography, University of Leeds

Stone, P.A. 1970. *Urban Development in Britain: Standards, Costs and Resources 1964-2004,* Volume 1, Population Trends and Housing. National Institute of Economic and Social Research, Economic and Social Studies XXVI. Cambridge: Cambridge University Press

NOTES ON CONTRIBUTORS

William Brass, Centre for Population Studies, London School of
Hygiene and Tropical Medicine, Keppel Street, London WC1E 7HT.

John Ermisch, Policy Studies Institute, 1/2 Castle Lane, London
SW1E 6DR.

David Eversley, Policy Studies Institute, 1/2 Castle Lane, London
SW1E 6DR.

David Gleave, Centre for Environmental Studies, 62 Chandos Place,
London WC2N 4HH.

John Hobcraft, Department of Social Statistics, University of
Southampton, Southampton SO9 5NH.

Mohammad Kabir, Centre for Population Studies, London School of
Hygiene and Tropical Medicine, Keppel Street, London WC1E 7HT.

Stephen Kennett, Department of the Environment, Inner Cities
Directorate 3, 2 Marsham Street, London SW1.

Kathleen Kiernan, Centre for Population Studies, London School of
Hygiene and Tropical Medicine, Keppel Street, London WC1E 7HT.

Richard Lawton, Department of Geography, University of Liverpool,
Roxby Building, PO Box 147, Liverpool L69 3BX.

Elizabeth Overton, Policy Studies Institute, 1/2 Castle Lane, London
SW1E 6DR.

Derek Palmer, Centre for Environmental Studies, 62 Chandos Place,
London WC2N 4HH.

Philip Rees, School of Geography, University of Leeds, Leeds LS2 9JT.

John Simons, Centre for Population Studies, London School of
Hygiene and Tropical Medicine, Keppel Street, London WC1E 7HT.

Richard Wall, Cambridge Group for the History of Population and
Social Structure, University of Cambridge, 27 Trumpington Street,
Cambridge CB2 1QA.

INDEX

Printed in the United States
by Baker & Taylor Publisher Services